CAMBRIDGE STUDIES IN
MEDIEVAL LIFE AND THOUGHT

NEW SERIES, VOL. 3

CRUSADING WARFARE
(1097–1193)

SAHYUN

CRUSADING WARFARE
(1097–1193)

BY

R. C. SMAIL

Emeritus Fellow of Sidney
Sussex College, Cambridge

The right of the
University of Cambridge
to print and sell
all manner of books
was granted by
Henry VIII in 1534.
The University has printed
and published continuously
since 1584.

CAMBRIDGE UNIVERSITY PRESS

Cambridge
London   New York   New Rochelle
Melbourne   Sydney

Published by the Press Syndicate of the University of Cambridge
The Pitt Building, Trumpington Street, Cambridge CB2 1RP
32 East 57th Street, New York, NY 10022, USA
10 Stamford Road, Oakleigh, Melbourne 3166, Australia

First published 1956
Reprinted in Cambridge University Press Library Editions 1967
First paperback edition 1972
Reprinted 1976, 1978, 1987

First printed in Great Britain by the Broadwater Press Ltd.
Welwyn Garden City, Hertfordshire
Reprinted in Great Britain by
Redwood Burn Limited, Trowbridge, Wiltshire

Library of Congress catalogue card number: 56–58455

ISBN 0 521 21315 6 (hard covers)
ISBN 0 521 09730 4 (paperback)

PREFACE

EUROPEAN feudal society during the eleventh and twelfth centuries was organized for war, yet little is known of the ability displayed by the knights and their leaders in military operations. The most accessible sources of information, for students and general readers alike, are histories of the art of war which survey the whole medieval period. Since no one scholar can hope to master the sources for the history of so great a subject through a millennium, such works need to be rooted in the more limited researches of specialists. Attempts at synthesis have been only partially successful because such special studies are comparatively few in number. More are needed for the better understanding of medieval warfare, and therefore of an important aspect of medieval life, and that need is the justification for this book. Many historians of the art of war have recognized the interest of its subject, and have written on it with distinction; but their treatment has been brief, and none has been able to undertake a study in the detail now attempted.

There is a further difference. Most of these scholars have confined their interest in war to events on the battlefield, and have looked no further. As a result military history too often stands unnaturally isolated from other fields of historical study. In this book an attempt is made to give due importance to the fact that warfare was an integral part of the whole life of Latin Syria, and that it affected, and was affected by, other aspects of that life. Political and social institutions in the crusaders' states are therefore considered in connexion with their warfare, and a little is thereby added to our knowledge of Frankish society. In particular it further reveals the high abilities of the early Latin kings of Jerusalem in the military sphere of government. So far from being rulers, as they are sometimes represented, with no more than theoretical powers, the history of warfare shows that they could organize campaigns and command in the field with impressive authority.

The authors of the main sources on which this book is based

were Franks of Europe or of Syria. Their work has been used because they either took part in the military events which they described, or else witnessed them, or because they had unusually good knowledge of Syrian affairs. The Muslim, Syriac, Armenian, and Greek sources normally used by historians of the Crusades have been laid under contribution, but only those which are available in translation. Scholars better equipped for research into Byzantine and Arabic sources might well take this subject further, and it is to be hoped that one of them will do so.

The sources used have all been in print for many years, most of them for at least a generation, many for a century. The only exceptions are the monuments of the Franks in Syria, of which a large number remain virtually unexplored by students of the Crusades. I should like therefore to record my gratitude to those whose generosity made it possible for me to undertake research in Syria as well as in this country: the Governing Body of my College, the Governors of Christ's Hospital, and the Worshipful Company of Goldsmiths. I am deeply indebted to Sir Ernest Barker, whose interest in my work has enabled it to survive all interruptions, and who during many years has given me so much of his time and learning; to the President of Magdalen College, Oxford, and to Mr C. N. Johns, who have so generously placed at my disposal their great knowledge of the medieval monuments of Syria; to Dr J. Prawer, of the Hebrew University of Jerusalem, foremost among those scholars whose researches are now deepening our knowledge of the Latin settlement in Syria; to the Editor of this series for indispensable help and unexampled patience.

R. C. S.

CAMBRIDGE
January 1954

CONTENTS

LIST OF PLATES

Plates I–VIII are collated between pp. 244 and 245

Frontispiece Sahyun

VIII (*a*) Sahyun: lintel and relieving arch

(The central voussoir and that on the left both bear
masons' marks, left in relief, in the form of the kite-
shaped shield employed by western knights of the
eleventh and twelfth centuries)

(*b*) Sahyun: archère

LIST OF MAPS

LIST OF PLANS

LIST OF ABBREVIATIONS

RHC	*Recueil des historiens des croisades.*
Doc. arm.	*Documents arméniens.*
Hist. occ.	*Historiens occidentaux.*
Hist. or.	*Historiens orientaux.*
AA	Albertus Aquensis in *RHC, Hist. occ.* IV.
AHR	*American Historical Review.*
AM	Ibn al-Athir, *Atabecs de Mosul,* in *RHC, Hist. or.* II.
Anna	Anna Comnena, *Alexiad,* trans. Dawes.
Anon.	*Anonymi gesta Francorum,* ed. Bréhier.
AS	Abu Shamah, *Livre des deux jardins,* in *RHC Hist. or.* IV.
AS, v	*Idem,* in *RHC, Hist. or.* v.
BD	Beha ed-Din, *Anecdotes et beaux traits de la vie du Sultan Youssof* in *RHC, Hist. or.* III.
BEC	*Bibliothèque de l'École des chartes.*
Cart. Hosp.	*Cartulaire des Hospitaliers,* ed. Delaville le Roulx.
Delbrück	Delbrück, *Geschichte der Kriegskunst im Rahmen der politischen Geschichte.*
Delpech	Delpech, *La Tactique au XIIIème siècle.*
EHR	*English Historical Review.*
Ep. mor.	*Epistola de morte Friderici,* ed. Chroust.
Eracles	*L'Estoire de Eracles empereur et la conqueste de la terre d'outremer; la continuation de l'estoire de Guillaume arcevesque de Sur* in *RHC, Hist. occ.* II.
Ernoul	*Chronique d'Ernoul,* ed. Mas Latrie.
Est.	*Estoire de la Guerre Sainte,* ed. Paris.
Fulcher	Fulcherius Carnotensis in *RHC, Hist. occ.* III.
Galt.	Galterius Cancellarius, ed. Hagenmeyer.
Grousset	Grousset, *Histoire des croisades.*
Heermann	Heermann, *Gefechtsführung abendländischer Heere im Orient.*
HEF	*Historia de expeditione Friderici imperatoris.*

HEp	*Epistulae et chartae*, ed. Hagenmeyer.
HP	*Historia peregrinorum*, ed. Chroust.
IA	Ibn al-Athir, *Kamel-Altevarykh*, in *RHC, Hist. or.* I.
IA, II	*Idem*, in *RHC, Hist. or.* II.
Ibelin	*Le Livre du Jean d'Ibelin*, in *RHC, Lois*, I.
IQ	Ibn al-Qalanisi, *Damascus Chronicle*, ed. Gibb.
Itin.	*Itinerarium peregrinorum*, ed. Stubbs.
JV	Jacobus de Vitriaco, ed. Bongars.
KD	Kemal ed-Din, *Chronique d'Alep*, in *RHC, Hist. or.* III.
KD in *ROL*	*Idem*, continued in *Revue de l'Orient latin.*
Köhler	Köhler, *Kriegswesen in der Ritterzeit.*
Libellus	*De expugnatione Terrae Sanctae libellus*, ed. J. Stevenson.
ME	Matthew of Edessa,*Chronique*,in *RHC,Doc. arm.*I.
Odo	Odo de Diogilo, *La Croisade de Louis VII, roi de France*, ed. H. Waquet.
Oman	Oman, *History of the Art of War in the Middle Ages.* 2 vols.
RA	Raimundus de Aguilers in *RHC, Hist. occ.* III.
RC	Radulfus Cadomensis, in *RHC, Hist. occ.* III.
Reg.	*Regesta regni hierosolymitani*, ed. Röhricht.
Règle	*La Règle du Temple*, ed. Curzon.
RGKJ	Röhricht, *Geschichte des Königreichs Jerusalem.*
ROL	*Revue de l'Orient latin.*
Runciman	Runciman, *History of the Crusades.*
Survey	Conder and Kitchener, Survey of western Palestine.
Usamah	Usamah ibn Munqidh, *Memoirs*, ed. Hitti.
WT	Willermus Tyrensis in *RHC, Hist. occ.* I.
ZDPV	*Zeitschrift des deutschen Palästina-Vereins.*

CHAPTER I

THE HISTORIANS OF CRUSADING WARFARE

I. SCOPE OF THE SUBJECT

THE military achievements of the Crusaders during the twelfth century form a complete chapter in the history of medieval warfare. Its beginning is the foundation of the Latin states in Syria as a result of the First Crusade; its middle is the story of their expansion and then of their defence against Muslim states based on Aleppo, Damascus, and Egypt; the end lies in the events of the Third Crusade, when the joint strength of the Latin kingdom and the reinforcements from western Europe could recover only a few of the towns and territories lost to Saladin in 1187 and 1188. Throughout the period there is reasonable though not complete continuity both in the succession of military events and in the recording of them by contemporaries who travelled or made their home in Latin Syria, and who were sometimes eyewitnesses of the events they described. Generally speaking, the wars were fought around one main issue: the existence of the Latin states. They took place in one theatre: the lands which lie between the eastern end of the Mediterranean and the Syrian desert. Throughout the period the opposing armies preserved the same essential characteristics in organization, arms, and tactics, and these elements of unity and continuity appear to make possible a single and connected exposition of this warfare by the military historian.

The story of military events in Latin Syria has indeed been told in every detailed history of the Crusades, but analysis has not kept pace with narration. The significance of those events has not been drawn out, and they have been little related to other aspects of medieval history; yet there are two fields of study which demand such relation, and the first is the history of the crusaders' states themselves. Beneath the story of the often-told narrative lies the fact that the Syrian Franks of the twelfth century used warfare as an instrument to establish and to maintain themselves in the Levant. War was a part, and an essential part, of the whole life of Latin Syria. The means of waging war available to the Franks and the uses to which they put them were interconnected with considerations of policy and with legal and economic relationships within a feudalized society. The study of warfare and that of political and social organization illuminate and complete each other.[1] This task has scarcely been attempted in respect of the Latin East. Professor Lot has recently emphasized the interrelation between the military and other aspects of history,[2] but his demonstration of it in that section of his work dealing with the Crusades and the Latin East is disappointing. He is content merely to recount the succession of military, against a background of political, events; the result is indistinguishable from the general histories of Bréhier and Grousset.[3] Historians of institutions have gone deeper and have examined the structure of the military forces organized by the kings of Jerusalem,[4] but no special study has been made of military methods. It is the purpose of the present work to discuss these methods as part of, and in relation to, the general history of Latin Syria.

There is a second field of which crusading warfare forms an essential part. Latin Syria was created by conquest and settlement, and each process was dominated by knights from western Europe. Their campaigns in the east were part of the whole military experience of Western feudal society, and all historians of the art of war in the Middle Ages have laid them under contribution. A survey of this literature is a convenient and logical starting-point for this present study, and will serve to clarify the viewpoint from which it is written.

[1] The point has not so far impressed itself on historians of the Crusades. It is significant that in two recent surveys of crusading historiography, in which many aspects of the subject are considered and suitable topics for future research indicated, no mention is made of the Syrian Franks as soldiers. See T.S.R. Boase, 'Recent Developments in Crusading Historiography' in *History*, n.s. XXII (1937), p. 110; J. L. La Monte, 'Some Problems in Crusading Historiography' in *Speculum*, XV (1940), p. 57.

[2] F. Lot, *L'Art militaire et les armées au moyen âge*, I, p. 17.

[3] Lot, I, pp. 124–30, 137–53. See review in *EHR*, LXIV, pp. 92–5.

[4] G. Dodu, *Histoire des institutions monarchiques dans le royaume latin de Jérusalem (1099–1291)*, pp. 173–234; F. Chalandon, *Histoire de la Première Croisade*, pp. 315–29; J. L. La Monte, *Feudal Monarchy in the Latin Kingdom of Jerusalem, 1100 to 1291*, pp. 138–65.

II. MILITARY HISTORIES OF THE CRUSADES

The difficulties of writing the history of medieval warfare have been remarked by acknowledged authorities on the subject. The wars of classical antiquity can be subdivided into certain great themes, such as the age-long struggle between Greek and Persian, or that between the armies of the Roman Empire and the peoples beyond her borders. Similarly in modern times conflicts between the nation-states form separate chapters in the whole history of warfare. Compared with this the medieval historian is at a disadvantage.[1] Between the sixth and sixteenth centuries many peoples appeared on the European scene. The history of the period was dominated neither by a great empire nor by a small number of solidly founded states. During most of the period the authority of state government, and the efficiency of political institutions were alike limited. Rulers were often unable to control their great subjects, and as a result much medieval warfare was semi-private and on a small scale. There were no standing professional armies moulded by a system and tradition of drill and discipline, so that such armed forces as there were had too little training or power of controlled manœuvre to put into practice any but the simplest tactical plans. Furthermore, campaigns and battles were not usually recorded, as in the ancient world, by writers with experience or an intelligent interest in war; nor, with few exceptions, has the age left anything comparable to the official records of military operations and administration of modern times. As a result of these conditions, reconstruction of the subject is difficult and so is its subdivision;[2] and although there are histories of outstanding excellence of single episodes of medieval warfare,[3] the most authoritative works in this field are still general surveys of western European military history which cover the whole or some considerable part of the Middle Ages. It is as part of such surveys that the military history of the Latin states has hitherto been considered.

One of the earliest examples of such a treatment of the subject was provided by Max Jähns.[4] That part of his work which deals

---

[1] W. Erben, *Kriegsgeschichte des Mittelalters*, Beiheft 16 *der Historischen Zeitschrift*, p. 1.   [2] Delbrück, III, p. 277.

[3] Pre-eminent among them, J. E. Morris, *The Welsh Wars of Edward I*.

[4] M. Jähns, *Handbuch einer Geschichte des Kriegswesens von der Urzeit bis zur Renaissance*.

with the Middle Ages shows that, for his method as well as for much of his matter, he owes much to an earlier and altogether slighter study by Martin Baltzer.[1] This scholar was interested primarily in the organization of military forces and the methods of warfare employed in Germany between the ninth century and the end of the twelfth. His work is essentially a collection of the most important references to these matters contained in the contemporary sources of German history, and as such it is still valuable.[2] In the subdivisions of his work he considers, besides tactical methods, such subjects as the strength of military forces, the provisioning of men and horses, their weapons and armour, the ordering of camps and the baggage train. Jähns exceeds him not only in the types of evidence which he uses,[3] but in the number of military activities he considers, and in the geographical area of which he takes account. Thus Jähns gathers his material from the history of peoples other than the German, and among these he includes the Franks of Latin Syria.

In accordance with Baltzer's methods, Jähns's work is subdivided into sections, each of which deals with some aspect of medieval military activity, and to each of which the history of various European peoples contributes its quota of evidence. The *Handbuch* therefore contains scattered references to the Latin states, and three short surveys of some particular aspects of their warfare.[4] But there is no chapter or section devoted to the military history of Latin Syria as a whole.

The decade following the publication of the *Handbuch* saw the appearance of other works on medieval military history by scholars whose methods were very different from those of Baltzer and Jähns. General Köhler, whose principal work appeared between 1886 and 1890,[5] was a retired regular officer who had seen forty years' service in the Prussian artillery. He attempted to bring to the study of medieval military history the methods by which the

---

[1] M. Baltzer, *Zur Geschichte des deutschen Kriegswesens in der Zeit von den letzten Karolingern bis auf Kaiser Friedrich II.*

[2] See the use made of Baltzer's work by E. v. Frauenholz, *Das Heerwesen der germanischen Frühzeit, des Frankenreiches und des ritterlichen Zeitalters.*

[3] Jähns makes considerable use of archaeological and pictorial evidence, as well as of the illustrations in the works of Viollet-le-Duc.

[4] E.g. Jähns, *Handbuch*, pp. 586–9, 630–2, 682–4.

[5] G. Köhler, *Die Entwickelung des Kriegswesens und der Kriegführung in der Ritterzeit von Mitte des 11 Jahrhunderts bis zu den Hussitenkriegen.*

staffs of modern national armies use historical examples to assist in the formulation of principles of warfare: thorough and detailed examination of selected actions and campaigns, followed by generalization from the results of such research. Köhler's first two volumes were devoted to the first part of this process. In them he carefully reconstructed a number of battles, campaigns, and sieges drawn from every century from the eleventh to the fifteenth. He selected those of which he considered the records to be sufficiently complete to make research profitable.[1] His third volume contains the consequent generalizations on many aspects of medieval warfare: the classes of soldiers; machines, weapons, and armour; the use of these men and materials in sieges and combats; the strategy behind these events and the leadership by which it was directed.

Köhler's method is beyond reproach so long as the contemporary sources are correctly evaluated, and this condition becomes of prime importance when use is made of medieval narrative histories. The trustworthiness of the available text; the relationship in time and space of the narrator to the events which he describes; his knowledge and experience of warfare; the extent to which he regards the description of military events as an opportunity for displaying his literary powers and his knowledge of classical models, are all factors which should be considered in determining the importance to be attached to any particular source, as is obvious.[2] Köhler was severely attacked in reviews of his work for his uncritical use of the texts, and though he defended himself with energy and a bitter resentment against his opponents, they had exposed his most considerable weakness.[3]

---

[1] Köhler, I, Vorbemerkungen, pp. iii-iv.

[2] The matter is well discussed by Erben in *Kriegesgeschichte*, pp. 31-41.

[3] The breadth of his theme and the great volume of material which he handled led Köhler to make many inconsistent and self-contradictory statements. Many of his errors are mercilessly exposed in Delbrück, III, pp. 321-8 and 677-82.

Köhler's defence and counter-attack against Winkelmann, Ficker, Baltzer, and other critics appear in the prefaces to the various volumes of his *Kriegswesen*. His opponents allowed that he spoke with authority as a soldier, but that he lacked the necessary training as a historian. No verdict could have offended Köhler more deeply, and his infuriated protests have the intensity of a *cri de cœur*. See *Kriegswesen*, I, Vorb. p. xxx: 'Ich bin weit entfernt von dem Standpunkte Fickers, der einem preussischen General die Fähigkeit abspricht, sich die Regeln der historischen Methode anzueignen, etc.' For just reviews

The same criticism could not be brought against Otto Heermann, who in 1888 published the result of what is still the best piece of research ever made into the military history of the Crusades and the Latin states.[1] This work appeared after the publication of Köhler's first two volumes, but before that of his third, in the foreword of which he hails Heermann as a disciple of his method.[2] But there was an important difference, more apparent to the general's critics than to himself: a prominent feature of Heermann's work was his critical assessment of the available sources. As the title implies, Heermann's work covered only a limited aspect of military history. He was concerned only with the disposition and handling of forces on the battlefield. Using the sources with outstanding skill, Heermann reconstructed most of the important battles fought during the First Crusade, as well as of those in which the armies of the Latin states were engaged, down to Baldwin II's attack on Damascus in 1126. After his presentation of these engagements he provided in the last section of his essay a summary of general conclusions based on the earlier part of his work.

The subsequent publication of Köhler's third volume appears to show that he paid his supposed disciple the compliment of imitation. Elsewhere in his work Köhler had used events from crusading history to illustrate many of the subjects he was considering, but there had been no consecutive study of the military history of Latin Syria. The detailed study of medieval battles and campaigns contained in his first two volumes include none from the warfare of the Crusaders, because too many important factors concerning them, and in particular the ground on which they were fought, remained unknown. Köhler considered, however, that the facts which were available illustrated certain aspects of medieval tactics, and in that part of his work on 'die höhere Taktik' he included a section entitled 'Die Taktik der abend-

---

of Köhler's work see Baltzer in *Historische Zeitschrift*, Neue Folge, Band 21 (1887), pp. 458–62 and Band 24 (1888), pp. 296–9.

[1] O. Heermann, *Die Gefechtsführung abendländischer Heere im Orient in der Epoche des ersten Kreuzzugs.*

[2] Köhler, III, pt. 2, Vorb. p. iii. But elsewhere, *ibid.* III, pt. 3, Vorrede, p. v, Köhler criticizes Heermann in his usual 'grobem Ton' for presuming to generalize on medieval military history after the study of so short an episode.

ländischen Heere im Orient während der Kreuzzüge'.[1] Its likeness to Heerman's work is not limited to the title. Heermann gave an account of seventeen battles fought by the Crusaders; he began with Dorylaeum (1097) and ended with Marj es Suffar (1126); to these accounts he added a summary of his conclusions. In the first part of his survey Köhler studied thirteen battles, all of which had been described by Heermann, and after his account of Marj es Suffar Köhler inserted a similar summary. He completed this section of his work by accounts of battles fought in Syria later in the century.

The year 1886 had seen the publication of an important work on medieval warfare by Henri Delpech.[2] As his title implies, Delpech was not primarily interested in Latin Syria. He considered that military tactics in thirteenth-century Europe were exemplified on the battlefields of Muret and Bouvines, and his first volume contains a detailed reconstruction of these two engagements. He then turned to inquire into the development of the tactics employed by the combatants. Among their principal sources he placed the writings of Vegetius and the practice of the crusaders in Syria during the twelfth century. This led him to study their warfare.

His consequent researches were not entirely objective. In his view the tactics employed at Muret and Bouvines had included a mobility in manœuvre by the mounted troops, a skill and precision in the movements of the foot-soldiers and, above all, combined action by these two arms; and in searching through histories of the Crusades, and especially that of William of Tyre, he was looking for these innovations. Thus it will be noted that he limited his outlook by the objects which he set himself, and that, like Heermann and Köhler, he was interested primarily in tactical questions. He was moreover always prone to read too much into the text of the medieval authorities on whom he relied, and on innumerable points of detail he has been corrected by German scholars. Indeed so many of his generalizations on crusading warfare are plainly absurd that much of his work might almost be disregarded. But despite this, and despite an excellent and damaging review of his work by Molinier,[3] the work of Delpech is still

---

[1] III, pt. 3, pp. 136–249. [2] H. Delpech, *La Tactique au XIIIème siècle*.
[3] *Revue historique*, XXXVI (1888), 185–95.

used and quoted as an authority. Views on medieval warfare expressed in a modern American history of the subject are taken almost bodily from Delpech,[1] and this is true of the remarks with which Professor Baldwin introduces his admirable study of the battle of Hattin.[2]

The next account of warfare in Latin Syria was given by Professor Sir Charles Oman.[3] In the revised edition of his work Book v is entitled 'The Crusades'. Oman has two short chapters devoted respectively to the march across Asia Minor of the different crusading expeditions, and another on the strategical problems and military geography of twelfth-century Syria; but the longest section of his fifth book is a study of the tactics employed by the Franks. His method is that of Köhler and Heermann: reconstruction of battles, followed by generalizations. In particular he analyses the causes of victory and defeat of the Frankish armies on the battlefield.

Oman wrote for the general reader, and the text is not overburdened with scholarly apparatus. As a result his work has been regarded with suspicion by many critics, and his undoubted carelessness on points of detail[4] only strengthens the opinion of those who regard him as 'a learned amateur'. Nevertheless, besides being the most accessible and acceptable to the general reader, Professor Oman's work remains the best single history of the subject. His conclusions on matters of crusading strategy and tactics are, as far as they go, firmly based on the evidence at present available. They are presented clearly and convincingly and establish important points which have escaped the notice of more obviously painstaking historians.[5]

Contemporary with Oman's work was the masterpiece of one of the greatest of all military historians, Hans Delbrück.[6] As the

---

[1] Spaulding, Nickerson, and Wright, *Warfare*, pp. 323–9.

[2] M. W. Baldwin, *Raymond III of Tripolis and the Fall of Jerusalem*, pp. 97–8.

[3] C. W. C. Oman, *A History of the Art of War in the Middle Ages*.

[4] For example, the chapter heading in *Art of War*, i, p. 320, announces an intention to discuss the battle of Harenc. There is in fact no mention of this battle in the chapter which follows. See also J. E. Morris in *EHR*, xiv, 134 and T. F. Tout in *EHR*, xl, 114.

[5] Below, p. 85, n. 2.

[6] H. Delbrück, *Geschichte der Kriegskunst im Rahmen der politischen Geschichte*.

title implies his history is not a technical treatise on military methods, but a study of military history as a part of general history. The relation of warfare to other human activities is all too seldom attempted by historians, and certainly Delbrück's work stands alone both in scope and excellence.[1] It is therefore the more disappointing that he does not consider the warfare of the Latin states as part of their general history. Such a treatment of the subject by a scholar of Delbrück's learning and insight would have been a notable addition to crusading historiography. He himself draws attention to the opportunity, but at once rejects it for a number of reasons which appear to him to be decisive.[2] The whole series of crusading expeditions took place over a period of 175 years, which is too long for a unified exposition. They were, he thought, so deeply influenced by the mystical aims of the pilgrims that it is not possible to consider them rationally as military campaigns. Furthermore, the few colonists who settled in Latin Syria maintained themselves only with great difficulty, and that the states established by them survived as long as they did was principally due to successive waves of assistance in the form of new crusading expeditions and the formation of the military orders of knighthood. For these reasons Delbrück included in his work only a short 'allgemeine Ansicht der Kreuzzüge' in which little more is discussed than the numerical strength of the crusading armies and the foundation of the Templars.

In his survey of the feudal military class in the central period of the Middle Ages, however, Delbrück quotes from and includes observations on the history of that part of it which settled in Syria. In a penetrating discussion of the emergence of the social caste of the knighthood during the eleventh and early twelfth centuries, and of the military methods and characteristics of the fighting men of the period, he gives his views on many aspects of crusading warfare:[3] on the co-operation between individual

---

[1] B. H. Sumner, *War and History*, p. 18.

[2] For the remainder of the paragraph, see Delbrück, III, pp. 230–5.

[3] Historians seeking Delbrück's views on crusading warfare do not always pay sufficient attention to his chapters entitled 'Das Rittertum als Stand', and 'Das Rittertum militärisch', *Kriegskunst*, III, pp. 239–328; e.g. L. J. Paetow's *Guide to the Study of Medieval History*, 1931 ed., p. 236, gives a reference only to *Kriegskunst*, III, pp. 226–31. M. W. Baldwin in his *Raymond*

knights and foot-soldiers, on mutual support between formed bodies of the same; on the use of mounted archery in the Latin forces; on the tactical effects of a lack of horses; on the organization of marching columns.[1] The longest single section of his work devoted to the Crusades is contained in the last chapter of his consideration of 'das hohe Mittelalter'. This chapter is a series of notes, each of which is on a battle fought in the twelfth or thirteenth century. The notes are not intended as full accounts of battles; they contain only such details and observations as were considered necessary by the author either to support the views he expressed in the foregoing chapters, or to remove misunderstandings or false conclusions concerning them. In the course of the pages he mentions seventeen battles fought by the Franks in Syria, and includes as well criticisms of Heermann's terminology, together with some observations on the role of foot-soldiers during the Crusades.[2]

The most recent contribution to the subject has been made by Professor Lot. Besides attempting to relate the warfare of the crusaders to their general history he concentrates on two further main points—the results of earlier researches, and the numerical strength of crusaders' armies. Because the declared purpose of his book is to provide French-speaking students, for the first time, with a general survey of medieval warfare in their own language, he summarizes for them the main conclusions of older books; of those on crusading history he chooses the works of Delpech and Heermann to which reference has already been made. He also devotes much space to the important topic of the numbers of those who went on crusade or who fought in the Christian armies in Syria. His account of warfare in the Latin East is thus made up of certain limited topics selected from the whole range of the subject.

The basic method adopted by most of the historians whose work has been so far considered is research into contemporary accounts of a number of battles fought in Latin Syria. This leads to reconstructions of these battles, which are used as a basis for

---

III of Tripolis, p. 151, n. 6 refers only to Delbrück's single sentence on Hattin in the unrevised edition of *Kriegskunst*, III, p. 421.

[1] Delbrück, III, pp. 283, 289–90, 305, 317, 417, 430.
[2] *Ibid.* pp. 420–30.

general conclusions on tactical developments. Except for a few pages in Oman on some strategical problems of the crusaders,[1] and a few more on fortification and siege methods,[2] earlier work is almost entirely devoted to this topic. The tactics employed in Latin Syria are treated as part of the general history of tactics in the Middle Ages, and some writers have examined the possible influence of crusading tactics on those practised by the feudal military classes in Europe.[3]

The total achievement of the military historians, impressive as it is, is open to at least one serious criticism: its scope is limited, and study of the subject has hardened within those limits. The specialists have, as it were, drawn boundaries and have accepted the convention that these need not be crossed. They have regarded battles as the principal, almost the only, aspect of warfare which requires investigation, and in their study of Latin Syria they have confined their attention to a selection of engagements which is beginning to assume the authority and rigidity always conferred by customary usage. The similarity between the lists of battles studied by Heermann and Köhler has already been remarked. There is little difference in those studied by Delpech, Oman, and Delbrück. Generally speaking, all make the same selection; and in a recent monumental work on the history of warfare[4] to which a contemporary authority is able to refer with warm approval,[5] the warfare of the crusaders is again summarized in terms of that succession of battles already so familiar from earlier writings.

The aggregate of all the battles which have been so studied is far short of the total number fought in Latin Syria. Except for some inadequate notes by Delpech, military historians have ignored military events which took place between 1129 and 1187. So far as their work is concerned, those two generations are a blank which saw the loss to Zanki of Edessa and much of the principality of Antioch; the failure of the Franks to conquer Damascus and Egypt; the aggressive thrusts of Nur al-Din and

[1] Oman, I, pp 235–69.
[2] Jähns, *Handbuch*, pp. 630–2, 682–4; Oman, II, pp. 24–33 and 48–52.
[3] Delpech, *passim*; H. Prutz, *Kulturgeschichte der Kreuzzüge*, p. 182; Delbrück, III, p. 317 devotes a short paragraph to this topic.
[4] *Handbuch für Heer und Flotte*, ed. G. von Alten.
[5] Erben, *Kriegsgeschichte*, p. 30.

Saladin. They have their reasons for this, and they are best explained in the words of Professor Oman. 'There are', he says, 'many Christian successes worth recording in the years between Marj-es-Safar and the fall of Jerusalem in 1187. But they are not of any special tactical importance....'[1] This appears to be the view of the historians of medieval warfare in general and of crusading warfare in particular: they are historians of tactics, and these they find on the field of battle. It is a standpoint which is discussed in the next section of this chapter.

III. BATTLE AND MILITARY HISTORY

For the purposes of study, it is open to question at what point a battle begins. In the general view of the historians of warfare in Latin Syria, it begins when the opposing armies are drawn up face to face on the chosen battleground. These historians assume the fact that both commanders have decided on battle, or that one commander has so decided and has been able to compel the other to fight. Yet such an approach leaves out of account much that is of military importance. One fact that has always influenced the conduct of war is that the outcome of a battle can never be certain. Success in battle will nearly always achieve the objects of a war more quickly and certainly than any other means, but a commander who aims at victory in battle and its consequences always risks defeat and its consequences. Battle will rarely be undertaken lightly, and will nearly always be the result of a reasoned and deliberate decision.[2] It is true that at the present day the possible effects of unlucky chance in battle have been diminished. Modern communications give the commander maximum information and maximum control. He knows when the battle is going against him, and if he wishes he is able to organize measures by which he gradually breaks off the fight, a process in which he is immensely assisted by the fire power of modern weapons. Medieval conditions were very different. Before battle a commander could make a plan, in accordance with which he could draw up his troops and send them into action. But once he had launched them into the battle, he had little or no control over them, and this

---

[1] Oman, *Art of War*, I, p. 304.
[2] F. E. Adcock, *The Roman Art of War* (1940), p. 106; Delbrück, IV, p. 352.

limitation applied especially to the most effective troops, the mailed mounted knights. If the knights had charged, and then something occurred to upset his plan, the medieval commander could not usually rearrange his forces. The result of the battle must then be left to the interplay of morale, individual prowess, and good fortune. It was these conditions which made doubtful the outcome of medieval battles and in that age the decision to give battle was usually the conscious acceptance of risk. The greater the issues at stake, the more must the thought of the element of chance have influenced the mind of the commander.

The risk involved can, however, be varied by the art of the general, and much of the theory and practice of war turns upon this fact. If a commander can force battle upon an opponent who is unprepared for it, then he has reduced to nothing the risk to himself; and surprise will always remain a cardinal principle of war. Although so complete an elimination of the element of chance is rarely possible, most soldiers and military theorists would agreed that the wise commander who contemplates battle will endeavour to ensure that he does so in circumstances favourable to himself. Yet within such general agreement a wide divergence of views is possible, according to the relative degrees of importance attached to the combat itself on the one hand and to the preparations for it on the other. At certain epochs military theorists have argued that the main emphasis should be on the preparation for combat. The development of such a view can lead not only to the opinion that unless a favourable situation can be prepared, battle should be refused, but even to the extreme doctrine that the ideal in war is preparation so perfect that battle becomes unnecessary. The successful commander will manœuvre himself and his opponent into such a position that combat will result in certain victory for himself.

Such thought and practice was typical of the military leaders who fought in Italy in the late fifteenth and early sixteenth centuries,[1] and of those of the continental armies of the *ancien régime*.[2] It is no coincidence that in both periods the logical con-

[1] Oman, *A History of the Art of War in the Sixteenth Century*, p. 95.

[2] Delbrück, IV, pp. 352–6, 362; B. H. Liddell Hart, Lees Knowles lectures on military science delivered at the University of Cambridge and published as *The Ghost of Napoleon* (London, 1933).

clusion of current views should have found expression in similar terms.[1] It is notable, too, that in both ages the doctrine provoked a similar reaction. Views like those of Pescara were criticized by Machiavelli;[2] those of de Saxe were assailed by Clausewitz, and by other nineteenth-century theorists.[3] To the critics the combat was the important act in war; success in battle could quickly undo the results of strategical manœuvre. As Spenser Wilkinson pointed out, the criticisms brought by the theorists who put emphasis on battle are contained in a single sentence of Machiavelli, 'Una giornata che tu vinca cancella ogni altra tua mala azione'.[4] This controversy was between two sets of extremists. On the one side were the exponents of a 'strategy of overthrow', who emphasized the importance of battle to such a degree that they regarded it as the only important act in war, and one to which a commander in the field should commit himself at the earliest opportunity. At the other extreme were the protagonists of a strategy of manœuvre who enjoined the waging of war without loss and with the aim of paralysing the enemy by skilful movement and occupation of positions in the theatre of war, without recourse to battle. Between the two is a more balanced view, which contemplates the use of battle if advantageous conditions can first be created, but otherwise is prepared to refuse it. Just as war is only one of the means by which a government may pursue the objects of policy, so it regards battle as only one of the means available to attain the objects of a war.[5]

[1] Pescara, quoted by Delbrück, IV, p. 127; and by Oman, *Art of War in the Sixteenth Century*, p. 96: 'May God grant me a hundred years of warfare without a single day of battle.' For similar sentiment in the eighteenth century, see Marshal de Saxe, *Mes Rêveries* (1757), II, p. 148: 'Je ne suis cependant point pour les batailles, surtout au commencement d'une guerre; et je suis persuadé qu'un habile général peut la faire toute sa vie, sans s'y voir obligé.'

[2] Delbrück, IV, pp. 128–9. Oman, *op. cit.* p. 94.

[3] C. von Clausewitz, *Vom Kriege*, erläutert durch W. von Schaerff (1880), pp. 168, 201, 551–2. Foch, *Des Principes de la guerre* (1917), pp. 23–7. These are famous examples, but it was general for nineteenth-century theorists to contrast the excellence of military thought and practice in their own day with the outworn ideas of the eighteenth century. As an example see von Caemmerer, *Die Entwickelung der strategischen Wissenschaft im 19. Jahrhundert.*

[4] H. Spenser Wilkinson, *The French Army before Napoleon*, p. 17.

[5] This whole topic is brilliantly treated by Delbrück, IV, pp. 126–33, and in the chapter on 'Strategie', pp. 333–63. See especially pp. 334–8. For the

Military theorists of the nineteenth century were wedded to the first of these doctrines. It was well suited to the means available for making war in their own day, but many of them claimed for it universal application. They did not always perceive that in other ages and other conditions, other strategic ideas could be more usefully applied, and so they adjudged those ideas to be bad in all circumstances. Signs are not lacking that some military historians, either consciously or unconsciously, have written under the influence of such theories, and their preoccupation with the history of tactics on the battlefield may be regarded as a symptom of this.[1]

The interpretation of the events of one age in the light of the assumptions and prejudices of another can never produce satisfactory history, and the story of medieval military methods told wholly or principally in terms of battle is very far from complete. It was not an age when commanders in war consciously applied strategic doctrine, but they were well aware of the risks involved in giving battle; in adverse circumstances they were prepared to refuse it.[2] Yet even when they decided against combat, conditions in the Latin states were such that by keeping their army in being in the neighbourhood of the enemy they achieved important military objects.

---

purpose of his discussion Delbrück adopted Clausewitz's term 'Niederwerfungs-Strategie' for the first of the strategic doctrines mentioned in my paragraph above. The other two were termed by Delbrück, 'Manöver-Strategie' and 'Ermattungs-Strategie' respectively. For his explanation of these terms see *Kriegskunst*, IV, pp. 440, 127–8, 334–8, 514–21.

[1] E.g. Oman found the tactics of the condottiere 'absurd' (II, p. 305) and a matter for ridicule (pp. 308–9). Elsewhere (*Art of War in the Sixteenth Century*, p. 96) his comment upon them is identical with that of Foch on the ideas of Saxe (*Principes de la Guerre*, p. 27). Both appealed to the example of Napoleon.

[2] This will be demonstrated by facts. If the Syrian Franks were influenced by military theorists, the most widely read work during the Middle Ages was the *Epitoma rei militaris* of Vegetius. See Erben, *Kriegsgeschichte*, pp. 58–66 and Delbrück, III, pp. 669–72. Vegetius more than once stated that battle was an uncertain business, to be rejected in favour of other means unless circumstances were favourable. *Epitoma rei militaris*, ed. C. Lang, pp. 92, 121, 124.

These passages were remarked by Köhler, III, pt. 3, p. 43, but he did not perceive that these eternal common-sense principles influenced far more medieval warfare than the examples he quotes. In Latin Syria there were no illusions about the risks of battle.

Whether to employ battle as a method in warfare was a problem constantly before the rulers of the Latin states. No historian has any difficulty in recognizing that in July 1187 Guy de Lusignan made a fatal error when he decided to relieve Tiberias and to expose his forces to almost certain battle in unfavourable conditions. The fate of the kingdom of Jerusalem was decided by the ensuing defeat at Hattin; but it is to be noted that a military fact equal in importance to the battle was the decision to incur the risk of battle. Throughout the century similar decisions had to be taken on innumerable occasions. Hattin demonstrates the possible consequences of a wrong decision, and it can be understood why battle was sometimes avoided, and why the immediate aims of military policy were pursued by other methods.

The historians of warfare in Latin Syria have treated events on the field of battle as the only raw material for their studies. The subject needs to be taken beyond those narrow limits. Beyond the actions of troops in battle lie conditions and influences which determined those actions and, even more important, military history was made on countless occasions before battle was joined, and even when it was refused or avoided. Once the study of methods of warfare is taken further than the battlefield, its scope is wider than the consideration of tactical developments. Those methods are conditioned by, and must therefore be related to, other aspects of the society which employs them. The use made of their field army by the rulers of Latin Syria depended on many factors: on the policy to achieve which war was undertaken; on the relations between the Frankish settlers and the native population; on the structure of the opposing armies as well as on their tactical combinations and their use of available weapons. Among the chapters which follow, one is therefore devoted to each of these subjects. These conditions combined to impose on the Franks certain methods of warfare, and these are illustrated in a further chapter which is a study of the Christian field army in action.

Historical studies do not always sufficiently reflect the fact that the same man who is a political and economic animal is also a fighting animal, and that organized human violence is conducted by methods and directed to ends which affect and are affected by the other aspects of his existence. Warfare is a related part of the whole activity of any society. So it was in Latin Syria. In many respects the crusader states were no more than 'a rude military settlement';[1] but acceptance of this view involves recognition of the importance of warfare as a factor in their existence. It is a facet of their whole history which has not yet been studied; that task is attempted in the pages which follow.

[1] Sir Ernest Barker in *The Legacy of Islam*, ed. T. Arnold and A. Guillaume, p. 54.

CHAPTER II

WARFARE AND POLICY IN LATIN SYRIA

I. SOME EARLIER OPINIONS

WARFARE in Latin Syria had a double aspect. It was both a profitable pastime for feudal magnates, and an instrument of policy employed by the rulers of the Latin states. This study is concerned with warfare of the second kind,[1] and the subject of this chapter is the effect of the ends on the means, of the aims of policy on military methods.

It is a matter on which views have been expressed by earlier students. It was Delbrück's opinion that the principles of strategy could not be applied to crusading warfare, because the Crusades were born of mystical rather than political motives.[2] Certainly the preaching of the First Crusade appealed to Christian abhorrence of Islam;[3] but from the first other motives were present, and the crusade included, besides a Peter the Hermit, land-hungry Normans and the Genoese, eager to exploit commercial opportunity. For the small body of Latin settlers it was impossible to maintain relations permanently with their Muslim subjects and neighbours in the spirit of the Holy War. A *modus vivendi* was essential, and from an early date diplomatic and political relations were established between Franks and Muslims. On occasions religious fervour might inflame the conflict produced by the clash of mundane interests;[4] but the normal external policies, and therefore the warfare, of Latin and Muslim rulers were inspired by rational motives.

Other historians of warfare have postulated an ideal strategy for the Franks.[5] They have noted that Syria is a narrow strip of

---

[1] In fact every expedition, great or small, exhibited both aspects. A ruler fighting to gain permanent conquests looked also for immediate profit; the feudal raider might by his persistence win territory from the Muslims. But in the major campaigns the needs of policy predominated.

[2] III, p. 231.   [3] D. C. Munro in *AHR*, XI, 231–42.

[4] J. L. La Monte in *The Arab Heritage*, ed. N. A. Faris, p. 197.

[5] Notably Oman, I, p. 254 and H. Belloc, *The Crusade*, p. 101.

habitable territory between sea and desert, and that in history it has served as a bridge connecting the civilizations of the Nile and Euphrates valleys.[1] Occupation of the whole breadth of Syria would have enabled the Latin rulers to prevent all connexion between the Saljuq Sultans of Baghdad and the Fatimid caliphs of Fustat. The Franks never conquered the most important cities of eastern Syria, Aleppo, Hama, Hims, and Damascus, and when this belt of Muslim territory was all possessed by Saladin, together with Egypt and important parts of Mesopotamia, then it became possible for him to crush the Latin states almost out of existence. Such generalizations are in accordance with the facts of history as well as with the principles of strategy; but at the same time it has to be emphasized that the military activities of the Latin rulers were not consciously inspired by the conception of occupying Syria from sea to desert. During the First Crusade there was no single plan of conquest; after the settlement there was no co-ordination of effort in the interests of expansion. The rulers of the four states sometimes combined their forces under the leadership of the king of Jerusalem in time of military adversity; but in the process of conquest each usually went his own way.[2] The occupation of the whole breadth of Syria was an ideal; but it was perhaps never perceived and certainly never pursued by the Syrian Franks.

Strategic motives have been ascribed to the Franks in their occupation of certain areas which lay between Muslim territories. The evidence of the map seems to show that in this way the Franks could prevent co-operation between the rulers

[1] Short accounts of the physical conformation of Syria can be found in the 'Description of Syria' by the Arab geographer Mukaddasi, who wrote in the tenth century. Parts of this work were translated and edited by G. Le Strange, *Translation of Mukaddasi's Description of Syria*, see especially p. 85. For short descriptions by modern writers see Deschamps, *Le Crac des Chevaliers*, pp. 16–17; Oman, I, pp. 253–4; Belloc, *The Crusade*, pp. 91–8.

[2] A single plan of conquest would have been at least possible if the rulers of Antioch, Edessa, and Tripoli had held their lands as vassals of the king of Jerusalem, and had owed him the normal feudal services. After 1109 the counts of Tripoli were the king's vassals; but the counts of Edessa were only occasionally in this position, and the princes of Antioch never. The best treatment of this subject is by La Monte, *Feudal Monarchy*, pp. 187–202. Grousset's attempts to prove a strictly feudal relationship between Antioch and Jerusalem do not succeed.

whose lands they separated. Historians have been led to state
that the Frankish county of Edessa divided Mesopotamia from
Aleppo and Damascus,[1] and that the lordship of Karak divided
Damascus from Egypt.[2] Such expressions have only a very
limited meaning. It is easily demonstrated that the communications of Aleppo and Damascus with Mesopotamia were never
broken. The main route from Aleppo to the Euphrates passed
through Bab-Buza'a and Manbij,[3] and except for very short
intervals the Franks never possessed any place on this road.[4]
Damascus has always been connected with the Euphrates by
desert routes,[5] and that to Rahba, always free from Frankish
control, was used, not only by travellers, but on occasion by the
small military forces of the day.[6] Even routes which passed
through the heart of Latin territory were used by Muslim armies. On many occasions such forces marched through the county
of Edessa;[7] Shirkuh and Saladin each led armies on five occasions through the Transjordan fief.[8]

Dussaud has in this connexion quoted the area controlled by
the Franks from Ma'arrat al-Nu'man and Kafr Tab. He has
shown that these towns lay on the most important road between
Aleppo and Hama.[9] He has stressed their importance as the keys
to Hama, and regarded the capture of Ma'arrat al-Nu'man by
the Franks in 1098 as proof of their intention to take Hama
also.[10] Dussaud's authority in these matters is justly great, but it
must be stated as a matter of historical fact that although the

---

[1] Grousset, III, Pref., p. xxi; L. Halphen, *L'Essor de l'Europe*, p. 77.

[2] Grousset, II, p. 554; Deschamps, *Le Crac*, p. 20, and in *Revue historique*,
CLXXII (1933), 43.

[3] Dussaud, *Topographie*, pp. 451, 474–5, and map XIII; Cahen, *Syrie du
Nord*, p. 165; Le Strange, *Palestine under the Moslems*, p. 406.

[4] According to IA, p. 323, the Franks took Buza'a in 1119; in view of their
heavy defeat by Il Ghazi later in the year they can have held it only for a
very short time.

[5] C. P. Grant, *The Syrian Desert*, pp. 36, 39.

[6] IQ, p. 49, records that when in 1099–1100 Duqaq led an expedition from
Damascus to Diyar Bakr, he went by way of Rahba and the desert route. For
its use on other occasions see IQ, pp. 56, 181–2, 206; *AM*, p. 60.

[7] E.g. the march of Qilij Arslan through the heart of the county in 1106.
See Stevenson, *Crusaders in the East*, p. 84.

[8] Shirkuh twice in 1164, twice in 1167, once in 1169; Saladin in 1174, 1176,
1178, 1181, 1182.

[9] Dussaud, *Topographie*, pp. 187–94.

[10] *Ibid.* p. 189.

Franks, except during brief intervals, continued to hold the town until 1135, they never during that period made a serious attack on Hama, nor was Aleppo ever effectively isolated from Hama and Damascus. Their possession of Edessa, Ma'arrat, and Karak in Transjordan enabled the Franks to control and profit from normal traffic, that of merchants, pilgrims, nomads, and travellers, between Muslim Syria and Mesopotamia, Egypt or Arabia. If they wished they could make such journeys extremely hazardous;[1] but they could not forbid all intercourse between any two Muslim territories, and still less could they prevent the passage of armies. If the need arose for Muslim rulers to maintain political and military relations with each other, intervening Latin territory was never an insuperable barrier.[2]

The war aims of the Syrian Franks were different from those stated or implied by the writers whose views have just been discussed. The effect of those aims on military methods were so important that they will be further considered in the following section.

II. WAR AIMS OF THE SYRIAN FRANKS

When governments cannot settle important differences by negotiation or arbitration, then a state of war may be declared, in which each party seeks to impose his will by force. The use of that force may, however, be limited to the attainment of those objects, or of some part of them, which caused the dispute, or it may be directed to the complete overthrow of the enemy, so that

[1] See general evidence of *AM*, pp. 59–61, and the personal evidence of Usamah, who describes desert journeys between Egypt and Damascus in his Memoirs, ed. and trans. Hitti, p. 35, 53.

[2] It is possible that historians regard the Transjordan fief as an effective barrier between Damascus and Egypt because, until Saladin united both under his rule, the two states rarely co-operated. The real reasons for this appear to lie deeper. The rulers of Damascus always owed allegiance to the Abbasid caliphs and Saljuq sultans, to whom the Fatimid caliphs were unorthodox and schismatic. There is evidence that the rulers of Egypt suggested co-operation against the Franks to those of Damascus, but on every occasion these overtures were rejected. See Usamah, p. 34, Derenbourg, *Vie d'Ousâma*, pp. 223–32; Wiet, *Histoire de l'Égypte*, pp. 280, 287. That diplomatic relations between the two states were maintained during the twelfth century is shown also by IQ, pp. 220, 280. All these facts have been disregarded by those historians who have commented on the 'separation' of Damascus and Egypt.

the victor is able to settle in his own favour not only the questions originally at issue, but to dictate as he pleases to the defeated enemy. During the last forty years there have been two
wars of this kind, almost unlimited both in aims and methods.
The corresponding necessity of seeking out and destroying the
armed forces of the enemy has been axiomatic in modern military doctrine. It is therefore necessary to bear in mind that in
other ages the use of force has not always been carried to the
same extremes. It has been confined to the achievement of known
aims, and has not involved the unconditional surrender of the
vanquished. It was in such warfare of limited objectives that the
rulers of the Latin states were always engaged. Throughout the
twelfth century the principal object of the Latin rulers' external
policy most likely to involve them in war was land, its conquest
or its defence. Force so employed was directly applied, that is, it
was used within the disputed area.

There were exceptions to these generalizations. On occasion
Latin rulers entered into defensive alliances which could involve
them in hostilities of only indirect value to themselves.[1] Furthermore the age well understood how one area could be acquired by
the military conquest of another. The idea that Jerusalem could
be won on the banks of the Nile was born during the First
Crusade,[2] remained alive during the twelfth century,[3] and had a
continuous history into the late Middle Ages. Yet the general
rule remains unaffected by the exceptions: in the warfare in
which the Latin rulers took part, the matter at issue was usually
the possession of land, and consequent military events took
place within the area in dispute.

As early as the First Crusade the Franks were aiming at the
conquest of territory. Not only was it the avowed intention of
men like Bohemond and Raymond of St Gilles to acquire lands
in the East, but the aspiration of the most pious and unworldly

---

[1] E.g. the alliance of Fulk with Mu'in al-Din Unur of Damascus. The
king's object in making this alliance, which could involve war with Zanki,
was not to secure Damascus for himself, but to enable Unur to prevent
Zanki from doing so. See Grousset, II, p. 132.

[2] RA, p. 292.

[3] See provision made by Genoese in the treaty with Baldwin I in 1104.
Regesta, no. 43. The attempt was made by Amalric in the years 1163-9, and
the idea again found expression during the Third Crusade; *Itin.* p. 381.

pilgrim who marched with them, which was the recovery for Christendom of the Holy Places, involved the military conquest of the walled city of Jerusalem. Permanent settlement required the acquisition of further territories. In order to ensure communication with the West the Franks had to establish themselves on the Syrian coast, and to become masters of routes which linked the ports with their inland possessions. Above all, land was required as the material basis of government. Although the Latin rulers had resources in the form of poll taxes and of tolls and dues on trade which were not then available in the same degree in western Europe, their ability to discharge the administrative and military functions of government still largely depended on the extent of their landed possessions.[1] This fact, more than zeal for the Holy War, or thoughts of personal enrichment and prestige, or the needs of trade, was responsible for the aggressive warfare waged by the early Latin rulers. The revenues which accrued annually to the feudal ruler supported at once his personal expenses and those incidental to government. Since he 'lived of his own', the stability of his rule depended principally on his demesne lands, which were his most important asset. He required also lands to assign as fiefs to his immediate vassals, that they might serve him at his court and in his army, and so provide the basis of that armed strength which was the ultimate sanction of Frankish rule over the Oriental peoples living within the Latin states, and the sole means of resisting invasion from without. In the second half of the twelfth century the military strength of the Latin rulers depended to an ever increasing extent on the military Orders of Hospital and Temple, and on mercenary troops; but during the first thirty years of the Latin occupation, when the Franks gained their greatest military successes, the knightly Orders were not yet militarized, and less was heard of mercenaries than during the last years of the kingdom. The backbone of the army was then the knights, brought to the muster by the magnates who owed military service for the lands they held.

[1] La Monte, *Feudal Monarchy*, p. 171. The revenues of the kings of Jerusalem are discussed by Rey, *Colonies*, pp. 257–66; Dodu, pp. 235–60; Chalandon, *Première Croisade*, pp. 346–59; La Monte, *Feudal Monarchy*, pp. 171–83. For Antioch see Cahen, *Syrie du Nord*, pp. 465–71.

The profits most commonly derived from land arose from the exploitation of the peasants who cultivated it. They gave up annually to their lord part of their produce or its money value,[1] and rendered besides certain customary payments and services.[2] Furthermore, the lord of a district took payment for his protection from the merchants and nomadic Bedouin who passed through it.[3] Land was the essential basis of Latin dominion. The policy of the Latin rulers centred on its possession, and war, as an instrument of policy, was employed in the interests of territorial expansion or defence.

It was usual that force was applied within that territory which was the source of contention. Thither a ruler who launched an offensive campaign led his army, and his intention was either to conquer the area or, by devastation of the country-side, so to weaken it that he might acquire it more easily at a later date.

Effective and durable lordship over a district depended on possession of the walled towns and castles which lay within it. An invader could control an area while he occupied it with an army; but if he took no strong place then his control ended with the withdrawal of his forces. The primary objective of an invader who came to annex territory was to take its fortified points. It was not then, as now, to destroy or to paralyse the enemy forces in order that he might impose his will in all things on the ruler whose lands he was attacking. If an enemy field army attempted to interfere with his offensive operations then the invader might be compelled to engage it; but its defeat was not an end in itself, but a means to achieving his principal military object, which was to weaken or conquer the territory which he had invaded. When an aggressor was challenged by a defending army, the nature of the campaign was determined by the invading commander's decision whether or not to offer battle. If the object of the campaign was permanent conquest, and therefore the reduction of towns and castles, it was normally necessary for him to fight. A hostile army, able to attack the besieger's camp

---

[1] Beugnot in *BEC*, v (1854), 3me sér. p. 421; Rey, *Colonies*, p. 243.

[2] Beugnot, *loc. cit.* pp. 418–19; Dodu, p. 242; La Monte, *Feudal Monarchy*, p. 171.

[3] Discussions with references in Rey, *Colonies*, p. 252; Dodu, p. 238; La Monte, *Feudal Monarchy*, p. 173. For the importance of the Bedouin as a source of revenue see *Regesta*, nos. 174, 355, 366, 562, 567, 593.

and to cut off his supplies from the surrounding country-side, always made siege operations difficult and usually impossible;[1] the besieger must therefore attempt to dispose of the threat by success in battle. If, on the other hand, he was prepared to postpone his attempt until a more favourable opportunity, and friendly territory was available into which he could retire, then his likely course was to attempt neither siege nor battle, but to fall back with nothing accomplished.

Conversely, successful resistance to invasion meant the preservation of the strong places. That the invader should cross the frontier and penetrate deep into the disputed territory was undesirable, for the damage which he could do to cultivation and to unprotected villages weakened the resources of the ruler attacked; but this was a temporary disadvantage of minor importance so long as the castles and walled towns remained intact. To achieve this primary object, the defender might put all his trust in the fortifications and garrisons of those places; but a fortress left to its own resources could not indefinitely resist a patient besieger, and the knowledge that no relieving army could be expected always gravely weakened the morale of the garrison.[2] Defence was therefore far more effective if an army was in the field to help the garrison and to hamper the besieger. Here again the main purpose of such a force was not to destroy the invader, but to secure his withdrawal from the disputed area. This could be achieved by adding to the difficulty of his siege operations, and by aggravating his supply problem. To offer battle was usually unnecessary.

Many of the foregoing generalizations can be illustrated from the principal episodes of the military history of the period, which are briefly surveyed in the following section.

[1] The only recorded sieges during the period which were conducted by the Franks in the presence of a force co-operating with the besieged were those of Tyre in 1112, Damietta in 1169, and Acre in 1189–91. Of these only the last was successful.

[2] The condition was sometimes made by a besieged garrison that if relief did not arrive within a certain period it would surrender.

III. SURVEY OF MILITARY EVENTS

In 1097 the Franks left Nicea and invaded the lands of the Saljuq empire. To establish themselves in the Levant it was necessary that they should conquer some great city as a base for future expansion. If the Muslims opposed this process with an army in the field, then the Franks, with no possessions on which to base a patient defensive, must stake the success of their venture on the issue of battle.

Such in fact was the pattern of military events between 1097 and 1099. The crusaders opened a way through Asia Minor by their decisive victory over Qilij Arslan at Dorylaeum on 1 July 1097, and in the following autumn their conquest of Syria began. The first objective was the great city of Antioch, which was besieged between October 1097 and June 1098. When Muslim armies approached to relieve it the Franks promptly joined battle with them on 28 December 1097 and 9 February 1098. Immediately after the conquest of Antioch, the greatest relieving force of all, led by Karbuqa of Mosul, besieged the Franks within the city. Without the resources to sustain a lengthy siege, and without hope of relief, battle against heavy odds was the only course which gave the Franks any hope of survival. Their victory on 28 June 1098 gave them Antioch, and in northern Syria freed them for ten years from military attack on the scale of that led by Karbuqa.

The next major achievement of the crusade was the conquest of Jerusalem. The siege of the Holy City during June and July 1099 was attended by many difficulties; the garrison offered resolute resistance, and the Latins were handicapped by scarcity of wood and water. Yet their problems were slight in comparison with those of the Third Crusade ninety-two years later, for during neither the approach march nor the siege itself were they opposed by a Muslim army in the field.

Jerusalem fell to the Franks on 15 July 1099. In the next month their slender hold on the Holy Places, Jaffa, and the road between was threatened by an army sent overland into Palestine by the government of Fatimid Egypt which, until the Latin invasion, had been overlord of Judea, Samaria, and the Syrian coast-towns as far north as Jabala. The Franks were in the same position as when they had faced Karbuqa: they were not yet masters of their recent conquests. They were not defenders of possessions securely held, but invaders whose mission was not yet accomplished, challenged by a relieving army. Therefore, as at Antioch, they could trust only in battle.

Their victory at Ascalon in August 1099 taught the Franks that the soldiers from Egypt were the equals neither of the redoubtable Turks nor of themselves. Because this knowledge of tactical superiority gave them confidence, and in 1102 over-confidence, in victory, and because the Latin hold on southern Palestine remained precarious until they increased their possessions in Samaria and Galilee, they did not hesitate to meet renewed Egyptian counter-attacks with battle.[1] While repelling these attacks, the Franks of Jerusalem were, by fighting, acquiring new areas. The coastal plain was controlled by the sea ports, which were all-important to the communications of the Latin states with Europe and with each other. These towns were won from their garrisons by the Latin field army; only in 1112 did a Muslim force actively interfere with the siege operations of the Franks.[2] Expansion into the Sawad and the Hauran[3] was, on the other hand, the prize of persistent raiding, of which the greater part was initiated by the princes of Galilee.[4] Resistance was organized by Tughtagin of Damascus, but the main armies on either side were never engaged. Frankish progress was marked by the partition treaties which Tughtagin was soon forced to accept,[5] and by the construction of castles from which the newly won territories were administered.[6]

[1] The situation resulted in a series of battles against the Egyptians in 1099, 1101, 1102 (twice), 1105, and 1123.

[2] In 1112 the activity of Tughtagin's force based on Banyas was one of the reasons why Baldwin I failed to take Tyre in that year; IQ, p. 120.

[3] Dussaud, *Topographie*, pp. 323, 381.

[4] Tancred was first prince of Galilee, and from an early date he showed that he intended to extend his lordship to the east of Jordan; see *Regesta*, no. 36. His two immediate successors were both victims in the ensuing warfare. For a summary of events, in which the accounts of AA and IQ are collated, see Grousset, II, pp. 837–50.

[5] IQ, p. 92. Certain districts were still partitioned when William of Tyre was writing; WT, p. 1090.

[6] According to IQ, p. 72, the Franks were attempting to establish a castle at al-'Al as early as 1105–6. They ultimately succeeded, and further progress eastwards was marked by castles at Habis Jaldak and Khan Rahub. See C. N. Johns's map, *Palestine and the Crusades*, squares C7 and D8; Dussaud, *Topographie*, p. 381. Deschamps in *Revue historique*, CLXXII (1933), 47–57; Beyer, *ZDPV*, LXVII, 214–15.

The course of the warfare in northern Syria during this period was principally determined by the ambitions of the Norman princes of Antioch and by the Muslim reaction to them. After the main crusading army had continued its march from Ma'arrat to Jerusalem, Bohemond continued the work of conquest which they had begun beyond the Orontes. According to the historian of Aleppo, Kemal ed-Din, he was threatening that city as early as 1100.[1] This rapid expansion was checked first by the captivity of Bohemond from 1100 until 1103, and then in 1104 by the defeat of a joint expedition undertaken by the armies of Antioch and Edessa against Harran. Success would have given the Franks a point of departure for further enterprises down the famous route provided by the Khabur valley[2] and so to Raqqa[3] and the Euphrates. Harran was besieged, and was on the point of surrender, when a relieving army appeared. The problem of completing the siege in the presence of this force was resolved by a battle in which the Franks were decisively defeated. It gave an early indication of the possible consequences of defeat in the field to a ruling minority which depended for its position on its military power. It was necessary to abandon nearly all the Norman conquests east of the Orontes. The Greeks reoccupied Cilicia which had been recovered from them by Tancred in 1101, and laid siege to Ladhaqiya.[4] Bohemond judged the situation to be desperate, and departed to Europe in search of reinforcements.

Recovery from the setback of 1104 was the work of Tancred. Left with scanty resources, he patiently regained the losses, and added new conquests of his own. In 1105, when besieging Artah, he was attacked by a force led by Rudwan of Aleppo; Tancred defeated it in battle and then completed the siege. Thereafter in his work of recovering and extending the lands beyond the Orontes, and in the reoccupation of Cilicia, he met nothing but minor opposition.

The first major attempt organized by the Saljuq sultanate to check Latin expansion was launched in 1110. The army for the purpose was raised in Mesopotamia, and the attack was repeated in each of the five following years. In 1110, 1112, and 1114 the

---

[1] KD, p. 589.   [2] Dussaud, *Topographie*, p. 495.
[3] For the importance of Raqqa on the main trade route see Heyd, *Histoire du Commerce*, I, p. 167; Le Strange, *Palestine under the Moslems*, p. 518.
[4] Chalandon, *Alexis Comnène*, p. 235.

city of Edessa was the objective; in 1113 Galilee was invaded, and in 1111 and 1115 the Latin possessions which lay east of the Orontes between Aleppo and Shaizar. The sultan appointed the leader of these expeditions, and ordered certain of his amirs to join the army with their military contingents. It was intended that the force should be strengthened by the addition of the rulers of Muslim Syria; but since these suspected that the sultan's army threatened their own independence as well as that of the Franks, and since the amirs neither fully subordinated themselves to the leader whom the sultan set over them, nor were happy in their relations with each other, the army neither reached the strength envisaged by the sultan, nor was ever an effective instrument for war. In meeting this threat the Franks made it their first objective not to destroy the Muslim army, but to prevent its reconquest of the towns and castles of Latin Syria. In every year except 1112 and 1114, when the attacks were on a reduced scale and were directed only against Edessa, the rulers of the Latin states combined in defence; they did so promptly; they did not seek battle, but held their army in being, ready to interfere with any serious attempt at permanent conquest by the enemy. This general caution did not prevent the Franks giving battle when they could catch the enemy at a disadvantage. On 15 September 1115, Roger of Antioch was able to surprise the army of Bursuq b. Bursuq near Tell Danith, and his victory on that occasion ended the series of counter-attacks which had begun five years earlier.

Freed from opposition, Roger and Jocelin of Edessa renewed their advance in the north, and by 1118 Aleppo was once more in danger. The citizens required a protector, and found him in Il Ghazi b. Urtuq, the ruler of Mardin. He was able to call on the military support of the warlike Turkmen tribes of the Diyar Bakr. When at the head of a strong force he invaded the lands of Antioch, Roger took up the challenge, but in doing so disregarded the precautions on which the hitherto successful Frankish defensive had been based. Without waiting for the arrival of King Baldwin and Pons of Tripoli, he exposed the army of Antioch to the Turkmen attack. On 28 June 1119, in a battle known to Frankish historians as the Ager Sanguinis,[1] Roger was killed and his army annihilated.

[1] Dussaud, *Topographie*, p. 220.

The destruction of the field force was followed by the loss to the Franks of many of their possessions east of the Orontes, Atharib, Zerdana, Sarmin, Ma'arrat al-Nu'man, and Kafr Tab among them. Antioch itself was in serious danger of capture. The patriarch assumed military command of the city, and prepared to defend it with a garrison of Frankish citizens and clergy.[1] Il Ghazi, however, was unable to extract full profit from his victory. His prolonged drunkenness deprived his army of leadership, and left the Turkmens free to indulge their natural tastes and to scatter after plunder. When Baldwin arrived in the north his first task was to rid the threatened principality of the triumphant enemy. In so desperate a situation he could not afford to be patient; the enemy was too confident to withdraw; the result was a battle near Burj Hab on 14 August 1119. It was a long, hard struggle in which neither side was clearly victorious; but the result favoured the Franks, since the Turkmens withdrew, and without opposition Baldwin was able to recapture some of the places lost. From that year until 1126 Baldwin ruled in Antioch as well as in Jerusalem, and for seven years spent more of his time in the threatened north than in the comparatively peaceful south. These years were full of military activity. Both Baldwin and the Muslim leaders, who until 1124 were the Urtuqid family and thereafter Aq-Sunqur Bursuqi, sought possession of the disputed territory between Antioch and Aleppo, and for the Franks the ultimate goal was Aleppo itself.[2] The consequent warfare was typical of the period. Both sides sought conquests by means of sieges, but were usually unwilling to go to the length of battle with a relieving army.[3] Thus on Baldwin's approach Balak, the nephew of Il Ghazi, abandoned in 1122 the siege of Zerdana, and Bursuqi in 1126 that of Atharib. In 1125 Baldwin himself, despite the fact that his three-month siege of Aleppo, the greatest prize the war could offer, was nearing success, retired from the city without fighting when Bursuqi came to relieve it.[4] In the same year the

[1] Galt. p. 95.
[2] Cahen, *Syrie du Nord*, p. 283, entitled his chapter on this period 'Les années tournantes'. Its importance in the history of the Latin occupation was also stressed by Stevenson, *Crusaders in the East*, p. 105.
[3] Typical too is the lack of military events which show tactical interest; therefore the period has not attracted the attention of military historians.
[4] This was the only regular siege of Aleppo undertaken by the Syrian Franks.

two leaders fought a battle before Bursuqi would abandon the siege of 'Azaz, a place to which both sides attached considerable importance, although it is possible that this battle may have been due to one of them seizing a temporary tactical advantage.

When the arrival in Syria of Bohemond II relieved Baldwin of his responsibilities in the north, the king made two attacks on Damascus. These were no mere raids, but were pressed to the immediate neighbourhood of the city. On the second occasion the expedition was planned to take place in conjunction with an Isma'ilian uprising in Damascus, and the army of Jerusalem was joined by those of Antioch, Edessa, and Tripoli, as well as by re-inforcements newly arrived from Europe. Under the Burid rule, however, the resources of the city were so well organized and led that, unlike those of Aleppo, government and populace could defend themselves. In both years the army of Damascus came out to give battle. In 1126 it was beaten, but with such difficulty that the Franks could not continue with their plan to attack the city. In 1129 it took advantage of the fact that shortage of supplies compelled the Franks to send a large part of their army in search of forage. That detachment was attacked and defeated singly; the remainder, still with their supply problem unsolved, and hindered by bad weather, were forced to abandon the invasion.

Two years later Baldwin died, and Jocelin of Edessa did not long outlive him. With the passing of these two survivors of the first conquering generation of Franks, and the failure before Damascus, the first period of the Latin occupation ended. The beginning of a new phase was even more strongly marked when in 1127 Imad ed-Din Zanki was able to succeed Bursuqi, first in Mosul, then in Aleppo. The new atabek soon showed his intention of conquering the rest of Muslim Syria, an ambition which was achieved by his son and successor Nur al-Din, who in 1154 acquired Damascus and made it his capital. The many rulers of Muslim Syria, whose inability to pursue a consistent and co-ordinated military policy had permitted the creation of Latin Syria, were now replaced by one.

The unification of Muslim Syria alone would have aggravated the military problems and reduced the military successes of the Franks, but certain developments within Latin Syria worked towards the same end. As they absorbed Muslim Syria, both Zanki and his son made important conquests from the Franks, and the loss of lands meant the loss to the ruler of military service owed by the tenants of those lands. There is also evidence that the impoverishment of feudal tenants made them incapable of rendering their due service. It was necessary to maintain the strength of the Latin armies from extra-feudal sources, of which the most important were mercenaries and the Orders of the Hospital and Temple. But the employment of either carried serious disadvantages; the mercenaries imposed an additional strain on the always insufficient resources of the Latin rulers, while the militarized Orders, by insisting on considerable independence in military matters, subtracted from that full control over military policy which had been exercised by the Latin rulers early in the century.[1] For these reasons the military effectiveness of the Franks declined during the second period of the occupation. The policy of sustained aggression was replaced by opportunist, and therefore sporadic, attacks, while in defence the ability was lost to meet every Muslim invasion always promptly and often with the combined strength of all the Latin states.

In 1135 Zanki captured Atharib, Zerdana, Ma'arrat al-Nu'man, and Kafr Tab. All had been the cause of much hard fighting during the two previous decades, but they fell to Zanki without a Latin army taking the field to save them. In November 1144 Zanki made a surprise attack on Edessa. On account of the bad relations then existing between Jocelin the younger and Raymond of Antioch, there was no co-operation between the two to relieve the city. A generation earlier a similar situation had been resolved by the authority of the king of Jerusalem,[2] but in 1144 Baldwin III was a minor, and although the queen mother did at length send an army northward, it was too late to save Edessa. On the death of Zanki in 1146 Jocelin attempted to recapture his capital, but his small force was destroyed by Nur al-Din. From that occasion until 1149 the dismemberment of the county of Edessa, and the conquest by the Muslims of important places belonging to Antioch, proceeded without interruption by the

---

[1] The points made in this paragraph are discussed in greater detail below, pp. 99–104.

[2] In 1110, when Tancred and Baldwin II of Edessa were on bad terms; Grousset, I, p. 452.

Franks. In 1149 Raymond of Antioch at last put a force into the field, but like Roger in 1119 he exposed it to surprise attack, and at Fons Muratus, east of the Jisr esh-Shoghr,[1] he sustained a defeat as disastrous as that of the Ager Sanguinis.

Nor did the Franks show their earlier power to recover from defeat. The reverses of the first generation, at Ramla in 1102, at al-Sannabra in 1113, at the Ager Sanguinis in 1119 had been attended by serious consequences, but these had been limited by rapid counter-attack. Sufficient force had been available elsewhere to check the victorious enemy, and to recover the losses. The later defeats resulted in losses which were important and permanent. Fulk's defeat outside Ba'rin in 1137 led to the surrender of that stronghold, which was never subsequently regained. After Fons Muratus in 1149 both Harim and Afamiya fell to Nur al-Din. Harim was recovered in 1157, only to be lost again as a result of Nur al-Din's victory outside its walls in 1164, a success which also gave him Banyas. Such events foreshadowed the danger to the Latin kingdom of the defeat of an army when it possessed no reserve of force with which to restore the situation, and when it was necessary to weaken the garrisons of its strong places in order to muster a field force of sufficient strength to challenge the enemy. The climax of this development was seen in Hattin and its consequences.

Offensive operations, almost continuous during the first period of the occupation, were undertaken only occasionally during the middle years of the century. In 1137 the initiative of the Byzantine emperor John Comnenus led to a major offensive in northern Syria in which Raymond of Antioch and Jocelin of Edessa joined forces with the Greek army. In 1148 the presence in Syria of that part of the Second Crusade which had survived the march into Asia Minor encouraged an attack on Damascus. It may be noted that the offensives of 1137 and 1148 were of such magnitude that the Muslims dared challenge neither in the field; but both remained without result because neither could successfully besiege its main objective, in 1137, Shaizar, in 1148, Damascus.[2]

[1] Dussaud, *Topographie*, p. 167.

[2] Other Frankish offensives of the period were encouraged by the arrival of armed pilgrims from the West, and by dissensions among Muslim rulers. The presence in Syria of Thierry of Alsace in 1139 led to an expedition beyond Jordan; his return in 1157 to a successful attack on Harim. In 1140

Meanwhile the internal anarchy of Egypt invited attack. In 1153 Baldwin III took Ascalon after a long siege during which attempts to relieve the city were made only by sea. Ten years later his successor Amalric began an attack on Egypt itself, and his five invasions in the space of six years represented the most sustained Frankish offensive since the attempts of Baldwin II on Aleppo and Damascus forty years earlier. The main problem of its conquest was the capture of defended towns. The history of Amalric's campaigns, therefore, is principally one of sieges: Bilbeis in 1163 and 1164, Alexandria in 1167, Bilbeis and Cairo in 1168, Damietta in 1169. After 1163 every Latin invasion was challenged by an army sent from Syria by Nur al-Din, who wished as well as Amalric to profit from the weakness and wealth of Egypt. In 1164 that army, led by Shirkuh, did no more than add itself to the garrison of Bilbeis, but in 1167 it remained in the open. As a would-be conqueror, and as the temporary ally of the Egyptians, Amalric had everything to gain by destroying Shirkuh's force, and the story of the campaign in which he attempted to do so is one of the most dramatic in crusading history.[1] In the following year it was Shirkuh who came to Egypt as an ally of the Fatimid government, and on his approach Amalric abandoned without a fight the siege of Cairo he had already begun. The withdrawal of Amalric from Egypt in 1168 virtually left that country to Shirkuh and to his master, Nur al-Din. On the death of Shirkuh a few weeks later, he was succeeded by his nephew Saladin, who consolidated with energy and success his position as ruler of Egypt. In 1169 an attack on Damietta by Amalric, aided by the Greek fleet, was successfully resisted; a rising among the negro troops was suppressed; and in 1171 the Fatimid caliphate was for ever extinguished.

Once more Egypt knew an unchallenged master able to organize her resources in men and wealth to make war on the Franks. As early as 1170 Saladin invaded the districts of Darum and Gaza; in 1171 he recaptured Aila on the Gulf of Akaba; in 1171 and 1173 he attacked the great strongholds of Transjordan at

---

Banyas was recaptured with the assistance of Mu'in al-Din Unur of Damascus; in 1147 the revolt of an amir against Unur gave Baldwin the opportunity to acquire Bosra. The king's attempt was a failure.

[1] See Schlumberger, *Campagnes du roi Amaury en Égypte*, pp. 107–68.

Karak and Shawbak. Until 1174 these attacks were not effective because the relations between Nur al-Din and Saladin were too uncertain to allow full co-operation between them; but the death in that year of Nur al-Din and the immediate action of Saladin to succeed to his Syrian possessions created a new situation and marked the beginning of the third and last phase in the existence of the twelfth-century Latin kingdom. With Egypt as the material basis of his power Saladin applied himself to the conquest both of the Zangid empire and of the Latin states. He entered Damascus in 1174, and in two years was master of all Muslim Syria except Aleppo. In face of a ruler whose dominions enveloped their own the Franks lost all initiative in military policy. The presence in Syria during 1177 of Philip of Alsace and a Greek fleet encouraged them to consider an attack on Egypt, and to undertake an unsuccessful siege of Harim; but with these exceptions they were incapable of a serious offensive. Since Nur al-Din's victory at Harim in 1164 Antioch had ceased to count as a military power, and warfare in Jerusalem and Tripoli was confined to raiding expeditions and defensive campaigns.

The defensive in these years was finely conducted by the young leper king, Baldwin IV. Despite his disability, and the rivalries and conflicts of opinion which developed among his advisers, his leadership ensured that every Muslim attack was met by a Christian army. Except on occasions which appeared to give the prospect of certain victory, battle was avoided, but any attempt to take possession of a town or castle was quickly challenged. Except for a few weeks in 1180, when Saladin's troops ranged unopposed through the county of Tripoli,[1] every attack by Saladin was challenged and, until 1187, frustrated. Saladin's first assault on the Latin kingdom was made between 1177 and 1180, and in the first of those years he invaded Palestine from Egypt by the coastal route. Baldwin took a small force against him, but on Saladin's approach he took shelter in Ascalon. Subsequent events showed that, however small and however far committed to passive defence, no Latin army could be ignored with impunity. Saladin left Baldwin in Ascalon, and pressed on towards Ramla and Jaffa. His troops expected no further opposition and, intent on personal profit, scattered far and wide. At a moment when Saladin

[1] WT, p. 1064.

had thus lost direct control of a considerable part of his army, he was attacked by Baldwin, who had followed in his path. Saladin sustained the heaviest defeat of his career, and because his army had no rallying point, it fled to Egypt in headlong disorder.

In 1179 Saladin attacked the Franks with a fresh army. From a base camp near Banyas he sent raiding parties towards Sidon. Following his invariable rule, Baldwin at once went to oppose him. By descending rapidly on to the plain of Marj 'Ayyun from the west, he was again able to achieve tactical surprise; but the Muslims whom he defeated were only raiding parties detached from the main body. The Franks, already disorganized by their rapid approach, relaxed after their success, and when attacked by Saladin with his main force they were themselves surprised and defeated. In this way Saladin avenged his defeat of 1177 and was able to destroy the new castle of the Templars at Le Chastellet on the upper Jordan. Not until 1187 did the Franks expose themselves again to the risks of battle. In 1180 Saladin granted a truce both to Jerusalem and Tripoli, and so enabled himself to continue his conquests from the Zangids in Mesopotamia. On his return in 1182 he lost no time in resuming his attack on the Latin kingdom. In that year he struck at Karak in Moab; at Galilee by way of Baisan and the valley of Jezreel; at Bairut through the Munaitira pass in the Lebanon. In 1183 he entered Galilee by the same route as in the previous year, and in 1184 besieged Karak. On each occasion the leper king summoned his army and hastened to the area threatened by the invader. Saladin was unable to provoke him to battle, but vigorously pursued his policy of impoverishing the kingdom by sending detachments to lay waste the cultivated country-side. The Franks, with no reserve of strength, could do no more than check the operations of the main army.

In this period the Franks revealed the extremes of strength in defence and weakness in attack. In September 1182 Saladin had left Syria for a final triumphant campaign in Mesopotamia; but, despite the fact that they were free of him for twelve months, the Franks could do no more than raid his territories and recapture one small castle. In October 1182 King Baldwin and the patriarch took the True Cross towards Bosra in the Hauran, and recovered Habis Jaldak. In December Raymond of Tripoli raided in the same direction, while the king took a body of horsemen as

far as Darraya, a few miles from Damascus. Grousset has interpreted these forays as part of a statesmanlike plan to help the
Zangids in distant Mosul,[1] but with equal reason they may be
regarded as symptoms of the impotent anger felt by the Franks
that Saladin should have left Syria without troubling to negotiate a truce.[2] Comments more apt than those of Grousset were attributed to Saladin himself: 'while they knock down villages we
are taking cities; when we come back we shall have all the more
strength to fight them.'[3]

The importance of the defensive achievement in the period
1182–4 was fully demonstrated by the catastrophe of 1187, when
the army of Jerusalem and Tripoli, together with fifty knights
from Antioch, was virtually destroyed in a single battle. In order
to swell the ranks of this force, many garrisons had been so reduced that the towns and castles of the kingdom, undermanned
and without hope of relief, surrendered almost without resistance
to the victorious Muslims. Since no reserve of strength was available, it was impossible until 1189 to organize resistance to Saladin
in the field. As a result, in 1187 and 1188, Saladin conquered the
whole kingdom of Jerusalem with the exception of Tyre, and in
Antioch the only important places which remained to the Franks
were the capital and the castles of Marqab and Qusair. The Latin
counter-attack which followed these disasters was begun by King
Guy. When, after his release from captivity, he was refused ad-
mittance to Tyre, his only remaining city, by its defender, Conrad
of Montferrat, the only courses open to him were to abandon his
career in Syria, or to attempt the reconquest of his kingdom. He
expressed his choice in August 1189 by forming the siege of
Acre.

As a landless adventurer his position resembled that of the
Latin princes in 1097, and the military situation in the three years
which followed had comparable features with that during the

---

[1] Grousset, II, p. 716.

[2] This is reflected in the account of William of Tyre. He speaks of
Saladin (p. 1101): 'nostrorum vires quasi pro nihilo ducens et ad majora
suspirans', and on p. 1102 he refers to the Franks, 'eoque amplius indignati,
quod tantam ejus qui abierat notabant superbiam, quod, contemptis regni
viribus, ut regna sibi vindicaret extera, proficiscens, cum rege nec treugam
nec foedus inierat. . . .'

[3] IA, p. 655.

First Crusade. Guy, and the reinforcements from the west, were almost without resources in Syria; they must win military successes or achieve nothing. Therefore, despite great handicaps, they persevered with the siege of Acre, which provided the only example in twelfth-century Syrian warfare of a major siege successfully conducted in the presence of a field army able to harass the besiegers and to aid the besieged. The role of Saladin's army was to cut off all supplies from the Latins and to destroy them in battle. Although he inflicted famine upon them, they were saved by sea-borne supplies, while their ever-increasing numbers and the fortification of their camp gave them considerable immunity from heavy defeat. The effect of Saladin's presence is best indicated by the fact that the Christian army required twenty-one months to recover a town which in 1187 had surrendered to Saladin in a single day.

After the capture of Acre the Franks passed to the offensive, with Jerusalem as their main objective. As in 1099, so in 1191, they marched south by the coast road. The Third Crusade enjoyed an advantage over its predecessor in the number of ships which supported it; therefore Jaffa was occupied and refortified before any advance on Jerusalem was attempted. Their general plan, however, was hindered by a Muslim army, an obstacle from which the men of the First Crusade had been free. The success of the Third Crusade in achieving the reconquest of the Holy Places depended on the ability of the Franks to defeat Saladin's army so decisively that it could not remain in action. Saladin himself was ready to take advantage of the superiority of his troops in fighting on the march. The result was a conflict which was fought intermittently during the southward march of the Franks, and which reached a climax on 7 September 1191, as they approached Arsuf. The Franks were victorious, but to describe the damage they inflicted on the enemy as 'a crushing blow'[1] is at once to overstate the matter and to forget the objects for which the battle was fought. Despite the retreat and the loss suffered by the Muslims at Arsuf, Saladin was able to reorganize his army and to keep it in being. This fact alone made the siege of Jerusalem almost impossible from the military point of view. The arid Judean plateau on which the city stands, and to which throughout history it has

[1] Oman, I, p. 263.

owed its safety, [1] offered difficulties enough to the First Crusade, when there had been no enemy to oppose them in the field. Richard was confronted by Saladin. He failed in that he neither exploited the crusading ardour of the pilgrims nor sufficiently probed the weakness of the enemy.

The purpose of this section has been, on the one hand, to provide a chronological framework for those military events to which reference will be made in subsequent chapters, and on the other, to illustrate the general nature of warfare in Latin Syria during the twelfth century. It has been seen that this warfare but rarely afforded the spectacle of two armies bent on mutual destruction; the true end of military activity was the capture and defence of fortified places. In its simplest form the struggle could be between an army on one side, and a garrison manning its walls on the other. Many important conquests were made because the only army in the field was that of the invader. [2] The fully effective defence of a territory was possible, however, only if the resistance of the garrisons was supplemented by an army in the field. In such a situation the invading and defending armies did not hurry to attack each other; often they made no attempt to do so. For both, the fortresses remained the most important consideration. The defender might be forced to fight a battle in order to expel the invader, but this end was usually achieved without battle; on the other hand, an invader intent on conquest must rid himself of the threat to his plans represented by an active defence in the field. It is impossible to state a rule, because if the skill or the fault of either commander gave to either side an immediate advantage, and enabled it to give battle with a minimum of risk, and a virtual certainty of victory, then the opportunity was taken; but, with other things equal, decision by battle was more likely to serve the ends of the aggressor than those of his intended victim.

---

[1] G. A. Smith, *Historical Geography of the Holy Land*, p. 255.
[2] For example, the Franks' initial conquests in Palestine, including the all important coastal towns, 1099–1109; those of Zanki in 1135 and of Nur al-Din in 1147 of the territories of Antioch beyond the Orontes; those of Saladin in 1187 and 1188.

CHAPTER III

FRANKS, ARMENIANS, AND SYRIANS

I. 'LA NATION FRANCO-SYRIENNE'

THE crusaders established their dominion over peoples whose numbers far exceeded their own. Many of these native Syrians were Christians, but even more were Muslims and were bound, always by religion, often by culture and race, to the external enemies of the Latin states. For this reason alone the relations established between the Franks and their Syrian subjects were highly relevant to their military situation, and they are the subject of this chapter.

It has been written that 'the researches into this subject of Prutz, Rey, Munro, Duncalf, and Cahen have . . . almost exhausted the subject, at least until new sources of information shall be discovered'.[1] It is possible that this is too optimistic an opinion, and that the problem on which so much has been written awaits fuller understanding. It certainly does not indicate that the historians mentioned do not agree in their interpretation of the evidence. The student is left to choose between two sharply differing conceptions of the nature of Franco-Syrian society. On the one hand are the scholars who have regarded the orientalizing of Frankish manners in Syria, and the instances which appear in the sources of friendly relations between Franks and Muslims, as evidence of the creation of a Franco-Syrian nation and civilization; on the other are those who have assigned greater importance to other aspects of social organization in the Latin states, and to the instances of hostile relations between Franks and Muslims. They consider that the Franks remained a ruling class, separated from their Syrian subjects by language and religion, with force as the ultimate sanction of their dominion. In view of such diverse opinions it is necessary to review the evidence on which they are

---

[1] J. L. La Monte in *Speculum*, xv (1940), 72. His reference to Duncalf's article in note 2 to that page should read, '*Annual Report of Amer. Ass.* (1914), I, 137–45'.

based, and either to reconcile them or to decide which is the better interpretation of the known facts.

The early history of the Latin states shows that the Franks rapidly assimilated some of the customs of the country and established good relations with their Muslim neighbours and subjects.[1] Such developments received marked attention in works as early as those of Rey[2] and Prutz,[3] and they were given fresh emphasis when Frenchmen came to regard the Latin states as the first chapter in their colonial history. Rey himself had written an 'Essai sur la domination française en Syrie'; but the theme was expounded with greater eloquence and given wider publicity by Louis Madelin. This historian believed ardently in the ability of Frenchmen to rule other peoples for their good. Before the outbreak of war in 1914 he was fighting from the lecture platform that 'mentalité de vaincu' which he found among his fellow countrymen; he wished to awaken them to his own splendid view of their country's greatness. In the peace which might follow the victories of World War I he saw France's opportunity to re-enter the provinces and colonies which had once been hers, and once more he strove to influence public opinion to this end. In 1918 he published a series of his earlier lectures with the title L'Expansion française, in which the crusading states are treated as the first chapters in the history of French colonial enterprise.[4] In the previous year he had contributed a long article in similar strain to the Revue des deux mondes.[5]

Madelin's work is discussed here, because in crusading historiography it is something more than propaganda written with reference to a peace treaty. It represents a conception of the Frankish achievement in Latin Syria, and of the Franks' relations with the subject peoples, which has not only influenced a school of

[1] Students have been impressed by the early appearance of Baldwin I in Oriental costume and by coins on which so violent a protagonist of the Holy War as Tancred is shown wearing a turban and perhaps with the title of Great Amir. See Schlumberger, Numismatique de l'Orient latin, pp. 44–5 and plate II, no. 7; Prutz, Kulturgeschichte, pp. 62, 555; Rey, Monuments, p. 9; Madelin, Expansion, p. 21.

[2] E. G. Rey, Les Colonies franques, pp. 4–14.

[3] H. Prutz, Kulturgeschichte der Kreuzzüge, pp. 55–72.

[4] L. Madelin, L'Expansion française.

[5] Entitled 'La Syrie franque', in Revue des deux mondes, 6me sér. XXXVIII (1917), 314–58.

Lebanese historians,[1] but has recently reappeared in René Grousset's history of the Crusades. Madelin, and with him Grousset, regarded the Latin states as a French achievement, and the men who established them as the forerunners of Champlain and La Bourdonnais.[2] The French have a genius for colonization (so runs the argument), and even in those lands they have lost, their name and, above all, the justice of their rule have never been forgotten.[3] So it is in Syria. Twelfth-century French justice guaranteed to each class of its eastern subjects the enjoyment of its own rights and native custom. The French were beloved because they did not, although conquerors, remain aloof from the people over whom they ruled.[4] They adopted their dress and manners, learned their language, maintained with them close and friendly relations. The result was the intermarriage of East and West. The offspring was not only 'une civilization originale',[5] but also 'une nation franco-syrienne'.[6] The Latin states, it is said, were peopled by a cosmopolitan yet integrated society in which the various racial and religious elements were happily blended, and which had an inner life and strength of its own. The logical conclusion of such an interpretation, and this affects the background of the military situation, must be that the destruction of this society cannot have been due to any internal weakness in the social structure, and such a conclusion was, in fact, stated by Madelin.[7] The fatal developments were, he said, the irresistible pressure from without, and the failure to establish a sufficiently strong ruling dynasty within. And it is Grousset's constant contention that the 'esprit colonial' was the principal element of

---

[1] Especially F. Hayek, *Le Droit franc en Syrie pendant les croisades*. This is an authoritative study of its subject and is widely read by students of the Crusades. Another well-known work written from the same standpoint is that of R. Ristelhueber, *Traditions françaises au Liban*.

[2] Madelin, *Expansion*, pp. 2–3. Grousset, I, p. 316.

[3] A recurrent theme in the literature now being discussed. See Madelin, *Expansion*, pp. 27, 160, and *Syrie·franque*, pp. 353, 358. Ristelhueber, *Traditions françaises au Liban*, p. 72.

[4] Madelin, *Syrie franque*, pp. 352–3.

[5] Madelin, *Syrie franque*, pp. 344–5; La Monte, in *The Arab Heritage*, ed. N. A. Faris, p. 666.

[6] Grousset, I, p. 287; Madelin, *Syrie franque*, p. 334.

[7] *Syrie franque*, p. 354: 'Quoi qu'en aient dit certains historiens, je ne crois pas qu'il faille chercher dans le régime même la cause de cette chute. Le royaume a succombé à des événements extérieurs à sa constitution.'

strength in Latin Syria. Policies framed, not in accordance with that element, but with the opposing and incompatible 'esprit croisé' were the original cause of the Franks' misfortunes.[1]

The sources of crusading history give numerous instances in which the manners of the Franks were modified after their settlement in Syria. It can be shown that the Franks employed Syrian doctors, cooks, servants, artisans, labourers. They clothed themselves in eastern garments, included in their diet the fruits and dishes of the country. They had glass in their windows, mosaics on their floors, fountains in the courtyards of their houses, which were planned on the Syrian model. They had dancing girls at their entertainments; professional mourners at their funerals; took baths; used soap; ate sugar.[2] Certainly all these are historical facts, but as symptoms of an 'esprit colonial' it is permissible to believe that they are superficial and of limited value. The Franks' mode of life had changed in some externals; yet how much more remarkable it would have been had such changes not taken place. This would have meant that the Franks had rejected the natural products of the country, as well as domestic habits and personal arrangements which were obviously suited to local climate and environment. Certainly and naturally, the Franks adopted Syrian manners and customs, and Fulcher of Chartres recorded his reflexions on such changes in a passage which repeated quotation has made famous.[3] Yet it seems scarcely justifiable to deduce

[1] Grousset, I, p. 314; II, pp. 141, 225, 264, 518, 615, 754-5; III, Intro. pp. xiv-xv; and pp. 57-9, 61-2.

[2] Rey, *Colonies*, pp. 4-14; Munro, *Kingdom of Crusaders*, pp. 105-6, 120-2.

[3] Fulcher, p. 468: 'Nam qui fuimus occidentales, nunc facti sumus orientales. Qui fuit Romanus aut Francus, hac in terra factus est Galilaeus aut Palestinus. Qui fuit Remensis aut Carnotensis, nunc efficitur Tyrius vel Antiochenus. Jam obliti sumus nativitatis nostrae loca; jam nobis pluribus vel sunt ignota, vel etiam inaudita. Hic jam possidet domos proprias et familias quasi jure paterno et haereditario, ille vero jam duxit uxorem non tantum compatriotam, sed et Syram aut Armenam et interdum Sarracenam, baptismi autem gratiam adeptam. Alius habet apud se tam socerum quam nurum, seu generum sive privignum, necne vitricum. Nec deest huic nepos, seu pronepos. Hic potitur vineis, ille vero culturis. Diversarum linguarum coutitur alternatim eloquio et obsequio alteruter. Lingua diversa jam communis facta utrique nationi fit nota, et jungit fides quibus est ignota progenies. Scriptum quippe est: *Leo et bos simul comedent paleas.* Qui erat alienigena, nunc est quasi indigena, et qui inquilinus est, utique incola factus. Nos nostri sequuntur de die in diem propinqui et parentes, quae cumque possederant omnino relinquentes, nec etiam volentes. Qui enim illic

from them, with Grousset, that the Latin settlement led to the
'formation d'une nation franco-syrienne'[1] nor that 'dans ce
premier quart du douzième siècle, une Nouvelle-France s'était
constituée au Levant et, avec une rapidité et une vitalité sur-
prenantes, avait solidement pris racine dans le milieu indigène'.[2]
The royal chaplain of the twelfth century and the scholar of the
twentieth, Frenchmen both, are equally to be suspected of a taste
and a talent for rhetoric.

Much has been made of the amicable relations which often
existed between the rulers of the Latin and Muslim states. Not
only did policy sometimes lead to alliance, but personal relations
between them were often marked by courtesy and friendship.
Many of the examples quoted in this connexion are taken from
the memoirs of Usamah ibn Munqidh,[3] a fact which is itself a
symptom of the limitations of this type of evidence. Usamah was
a member of the Arab family which between 1081[4] and 1157 ruled
in Shaizar. As a young nobleman two of the principal subjects of
his education were hunting and warfare, and most of his reminis-
cences were concerned with the one or the other of these pursuits.[5]
These were also the primary interests of Usamah's social equals
among the Franks. The most that can be deduced from his testimony is that friendly relations often existed between members of
the small ruling military class on either side, whose outlook and
tastes had much in common by reason of their privileged position
in society, and the enthusiasm they shared for warfare, horses,
and hunting.

It is on evidence of the kind so far quoted that Madelin's thesis
rests, and it enables Grousset to conclude that the Franks struck
root deep in Levantine society. Although from many points of

---

erant inopes, hic facit eos Deus locupletes. Qui habuerant nummos paucos,
hic possident bizantios innumeros; et qui non habuerat villam, hic, Deo
dante, jam possidet urbem. Quare ergo reverteretur in Occidentem qui hic
taliter invenit Orientem?'

[1] Grousset, I, p. 287.   [2] Grousset, I, p. 288.

[3] P. K. Hitti, *An Arab Syrian Gentleman and Warrior in the period of the
Crusades*.

[4] H. Derenbourg, *Ousama ibn Mounkidh*, 1ère partie; *Vie d'Ousâma*, pp.
14, 24.

[5] The Fatimid caliph al-Hafiz once made a comment on Usamah which
was very much to the point. He said 'And what other business has this man
but to fight and to hunt?' (Usamah, p. 225).

view the writings of these scholars may be regarded as embodying
a reasonable interpretation of the evidence, it is at least equally
reasonable to see, both in the orientalizing of the Franks, and in
the friendships of their rulers with their Muslim peers, processes
as superficial as they were inevitable.[1] The historians whose work
has been discussed give no sign that they have recognized the
limitations of the evidence they employ. Consequently their conclusions may be criticized for a lack of the caution and restraint
which those limitations demand. On at least one occasion,
Grousset shows in his work the consequences of a *parti pris*, and
overstrains the evidence of Usamah in favour of his own conception of Franco-Syrian society. He repeats an anecdote concerning
a raid by Tancred against the territories of Shaizar in the autumn
of 1108. After the fighting the opposing leaders exchanged
friendly messages, and Tancred requested the gift of a horse belonging to a member of the Munqidhite household. It was despatched to him, ridden by a young Kurd named Hasanun. Tancred admired the physique and bearing of the youth, and promised him that if ever he became Tancred's prisoner, he would be
set free.[2] Grousset regards this story as a happy example of the
chivalrous relations between Franks and Muslims.[3] But there
was a sequel. A year later Hasanun was captured by Tancred.
Not only did Tancred fail to free his prisoner; he tortured him
and deprived him of his right eye.[4] The sequel shows that there
was another side to Franco-Muslim relations; it is not quoted by
Grousset.

Such evidence sometimes bears conflicting interpretations.
Munro stresses the importance of intermarriage in bringing
Franks and Muslims to a closer understanding of each other. He
also illustrates his point by quoting from Usamah, and repeats
the story of the Frankish girl who became the bride of the Muslim
lord of Ja'bar.[5] Certainly there was intermarriage, yet it should
be noted that the Frankish girl of whom the story is told went to
the lord of Ja'bar not voluntarily, but as part of the spoils of war,
and that despite the exalted position she attained as mother of the

---

[1] Cf. La Monte, *Feudal Monarchy*, Intro. p. xx; C. N. Johns in *Journal
of the Royal Central Asian Society*, XXI (1934), 292.
[2] Usamah, p. 94.   [3] Grousset, I, p. 427, n.1.   [4] Usamah, p. 95.
[5] Munro, *Kingdom of the Crusaders*, p. 119; Usamah, p. 159.

ruling prince of Ja'bar, she ultimately escaped to her own people at great personal risk, and settled down as the wife of a Frankish cobbler. Whatever justification there may be for the use made by Munro of this anecdote, it could with equal or greater reason be used to sustain a contrary thesis: that there was between Frank and Muslim in Syria a wide gulf which could never finally be bridged.

The bearing of this interpretation on the military position of the Latin states is nowhere discussed, but the implication is clear. The closely knit Franco-Syrian society had no internal weaknesses which might demand the use of force. The Franks could safely trust the loyalty and obedience of their subjects by whom they were assisted in military operations. All armed force could be turned against those external enemies who ultimately were to overwhelm the Latin states. This aspect of crusading history will now be more closely considered in a discussion of the relations of the Franks with their Armenian, Syrian Christian, and Muslim subjects.

II. ARMENIANS

The Armenians appear to have been the most numerous and influential part of the population in the county of Edessa and in parts of the principality of Antioch. They had emigrated from their own country during the middle years of the eleventh century, as a result both of Byzantine policy and of the advance of the Saljuq Turks.[1] When the First Crusade entered Syria in 1097, there were, in the Taurus and Anti-Taurus mountains, communities which were independent and under the rule of their own princes. In the plains the Armenian communities were dominated by the military rule of Saljuq garrisons, although some cities, like Malatya and Edessa, were ruled by Armenians who enjoyed a precarious independence in the midst of a Saljuq world. The Armenian welcome to the crusaders as they approached Antioch;[2] the support they gave to Tancred in his rapid occupation of the Cilician plain;[3] their acceptance of Baldwin of

---

[1] Cahen, *Syrie du Nord*, p. 184; Grousset, *L'Empire du Levant*, pp. 157–8, 173 *et seq.*

[2] *Anon.* pp. 62, 64. ME, p. 33 records the supplies sent by Armenian princes to the Latins during the siege of Antioch; same in *Anon.* p. 76, although he also accuses the Armenians of profiteering.   [3] *Anon.* p. 58.

Boulogne as ruler of Edessa and Tell Bashir[1] are all familiar episodes of the First Crusade.

As Christians and enemies of the Turk they were natural supporters of Latin rule. In addition there were two other factors
which brought them closer to the Franks than any other Levantine Christians: they had within living memory been free not only
of Turkish but of Muslim rule, and they were a warlike people.
During the twelfth century they are found both as horse- and
foot-soldiers in the Frankish armies fighting in northern Syria.[2]
On many occasions they gave conspicuous evidence of loyalty
and a high regard for their Latin rulers. The self-sacrifice of the
Armenian band which in 1124 rescued Baldwin II and Jocelin
from Kharput[3] and the sincere and moving Armenian lament on
the death of Baldwin of Mar'ash[4] demonstrate the extent to
which the Franks could rely on their Armenian subjects.

Yet there is also evidence to the contrary. Even when the first
crusaders were besieging Antioch in 1097, the Armenians were
suspected of spying on behalf of the Turkish garrison[5] and were
known to have carried supplies into the city.[6] In 1104 the defeat
of Bohemond and Baldwin at Harran so weakened the grip of the

---

[1] Fulcher, p. 338.

[2] Baldwin of Boulogne first went to Edessa 'cum minimo exercitulo suo
scilicet octoginta militibus' (Fulcher, p. 338). Similar evidence in ME, p. 36,
who says that Baldwin had sixty knights. Since he suffered losses (Fulcher,
loc. cit. says 'plures') in his warfare with the Turks, it may be assumed that
he depended on Armenian military help from the first.

ME, p. 123 records that there were 500 Armenian horsemen with Roger at
the Ager Sanguinis in 1119; and, on p. 143, that there was a similar number
with Baldwin II at the battle of 'Azaz in 1126. Armenian contingents under
their own princes also aided the Franks.

[3] Fulcher, p. 454; ME, pp. 133–5.

[4] *RHC, Doc. arm.* I, pp. 204–22. The attitude of the Armenian author towards Baldwin was probably typical of that of his compatriots towards the
Franks. The fact that Grousset, II, p. 199, is able to deduce that these relations were good, and Prutz, *Kulturgeschichte*, p. 130, that they were based
on antipathy, provides yet another example of the caution with which such
evidence must be used. In fact, Basil reveals a high regard for Baldwin's
virtues, but was not blind to his faults. A typical passage is on pp. 218–19.
On the evidence of the elegy it has to be concluded that while Armenians
could hold their Frankish rulers in high regard, their affection was qualified,
and that if their devotion is to be regarded as a consequence of their affection,
that devotion was not likely to be absolute. On this subject see the following
paragraph.

[5] *Anon.* p. 68.   [6] *Ibid.* p. 98.

Franks on northern Syria that Rudwan of Aleppo was able to re-
occupy several towns. Among them was Artah, to which he was
called by its Armenian inhabitants.[1] In 1108, Baldwin, the second
count of Edessa, found it necessary to repress an Armenian plot
against his authority in the city.[2] Four years later Mawdud's siege
of Edessa was almost successful when certain towers on the curtain wall were delivered up to him by Armenians. Only a desperate counter-attack by a few Frankish knights saved the situation,
and Baldwin took cruel reprisals, against not only the traitors,
but the whole Armenian community.[3] So strongly was Baldwin
impressed by the dangers of Armenian treason, that in the following year he temporarily expelled the whole Armenian population
from Edessa,[4] and soon afterwards annexed certain territories
which were ruled by independent Armenian princes.[5] It may be
remarked that the existence of such rulers on the borders of
Antioch and Edessa created conditions which would divide the
loyalty of many Armenians to their Frankish overlords. There
were enough instances of Armenian disloyalty to show that the
people, whose ties with the Franks were closer than those of any
other Syrian people, could not always be fully trusted, and it is
significant that the weakness often revealed itself when the Franks
were facing military difficulties.

III. SYRIAN CHRISTIANS

Most of the Armenians inhabited an area north of Antioch.[6]
Communities of the Greek Orthodox and of the monophysite
Jacobite churches were found in all parts of Syria, and in their
conduct towards them the Franks showed themselves capable of
friendliness and understanding. When the First Crusade entered
the country it was clearly the policy of Adhemar, who was bishop
of Puy and papal legate,[7] to co-operate with the Greeks. Therefore he acted in concert with the Orthodox patriarch of Jerusalem

---

[1] KD, p. 593.   [2] ME, p. 88.   [3] ME, pp. 101–2.
[4] ME, pp. 104–5. Matthew's account of these events furnishes him with an
opportunity of expressing strong anti-Frankish sentiments.
[5] Grousset, I, p. 493; Cahen, *Syrie du Nord*, p. 275.
[6] Cahen, *Syrie du Nord*, p. 184.
[7] For his appointment as the pope's personal representative, see *HEp*.
p. 136.

to organize supplies for the Christian army, while the Orthodox patriarch of Antioch was restored to that city after its conquest by the crusaders in June 1098.[1] It is thought, indeed, that one of Pope Urban's reasons for preaching the crusade may have been his wish to end the dispute which had divided the sees of Rome and Constantinople since 1054.[2] Certainly during the twelfth century the Syrian Franks regarded their Greek Orthodox subjects as part of an undivided Catholic Church, in contrast to their recognition of the Armenians and Jacobites as separate and autonomous communities. Therefore Orthodox canons remained in the Church of the Holy Sepulchre, and there were Orthodox monasteries in the neighbourhood both of Jerusalem and Antioch. They enjoyed the protective interest of the Emperor Manuel Comnenus which is likely to have been the more effective because, after 1150, the Latin rulers increasingly looked to Byzantium for help, and they were always on good terms with the royal house of Jerusalem[3]. Equal friendliness could exist between the Franks and the monophysite churches. Michael, the Jacobite patriarch of Antioch between 1166 and 1199, has left an account of his cordial reception by the Latin patriarchs of Jerusalem and Antioch, and by King Baldwin IV at Acre in 1179.[4] The Maronites of the Lebanon even resumed communion with Rome.

There are other indications of the value placed by the Latin rulers on their Christian Syrian subjects. After the capture of Jerusalem in 1099, massacre, disease, and the flight of many Muslims had reduced the population of the city. The number of Franks who remained to make good these losses was disappointingly small, and some means of increasing the number of

[1] Runciman, I, pp. 222, 237; Cahen, *Syrie du Nord*, p. 308.
[2] A. C. Krey, 'Urban's Crusade, Success or Failure?' in *AHR*, LIII (1947-8), 235-50.
[3] Runciman, II, p. 321.
[4] *Chronique de Michel le Syrien* (ed. and trans. by J. B. Chabot), III, pp. 332, 379. See also III, p. 222 for his summary of the relations between his own people on the one hand, and the Franks, Greeks, and Turks on the other. He records the tolerance of the Franks ('ils considéraient comme chrétien quiconque adorait la croix, sans enquête ni examen') and of the Turks (who 'n'avaient pas pour habitude de s'informer sur les professions de foi, ni de persécuter quelqu'un pour sa profession de foi, comme faisaient les Grecs, peuple méchant et hérétique'). On p. 225 he expresses a similar opinion of the Greeks. The Armenians, too, regarded the Greeks as persecutors; see ME, p.125.

inhabitants had to be devised. The solution was found by Baldwin I. He brought communities of Syrian Christians from Transjordan and with them colonized the city.[1] As further evidence of Latin favour, the position of 'les Suriens' described in the thirteenth-century law books is often quoted. In his fourth chapter John of Ibelin repeats the tradition that representatives of the Syrian communities had requested from one of the kings of Jerusalem the privilege of being ruled by their own customs administered in their own courts.[2] Their request was granted, and with certain exceptions, causes between Syrians were tried in courts over which a Syrian magistrate presided. This court was normal in rural districts; in commercial centres its jurisdiction was exercised in the 'cour de la fonde', where commercial cases were also heard. In these courts the magistrate was a Frank, but, of the six jurors, while two were Franks, four were Syrians.[3] Had the Syrians been corrupt and untrustworthy, asks Dodu, would the legislator have bestowed upon them such wide privileges?[4]

The answer depends on the extent to which the Franks had any other choice, an aspect of the matter discussed below.[5] Meanwhile there is another side to the picture revealing that the relations between Eastern and Western peoples were not marked only by mutual amity and trust. From the time of their first arrival in Syria there were many Latins who were disposed to regard all local Christians, even the Greeks, as heretics,[6] and throughout the century there were many signs of the mutual antipathy which could exist between Levantines and western Europeans.[7] This was exacerbated by political problems which had their roots in the first contacts between Alexius Comnenus and the earliest crusaders, and in the bitter dispute about Byzantine rights in the principality of Antioch.[8] But the most consistent and enduring source of Greek resentment lay in the very fact that they were regarded as part of, and not separate from, the Latin ecclesiastical

---

[1] WT, p. 500; J. Prawer, 'The settlement of the Latins in Jerusalem', in *Speculum*, XXVII (1952), 490–503.
[2] *RHC, Lois*, I, p. 26.   [3] Hayek, *Droit franc*, pp. 130–5.
[4] Dodu, *Institutions*, p. 210; Rey, *Colonies*, p. 76.   [5] *Infra*, pp. 57–9.
[6] Letter of the crusading princes to Pope Urban II, in *HEp*. p. 164.
[7] See, for example, Odo, p. 29, 43.   [8] Grousset, I, p. 110.

establishment. For they were a subordinate part. The Orthodox clergy were not permitted into the upper ranks of the hierarchy. The Greek patriarch of Antioch, reinstated in 1098, made way in 1100 for a Latin successor, Bernard of Valence, and subsequent restorations, such as that enforced by Manuel Comnenus in 1158, were equally short-lived.[1] Latin Jerusalem never saw a Greek patriarch. The Orthodox were obliged to pay obedience and the tithe to a higher clergy who were of an alien race and who practised a different rite. They had, after all, enjoyed toleration and the protection of the Byzantine emperor in the days of Muslim rule, and they had little incentive to help maintain the domination of the Franks. It is small wonder to learn that, when Saladin was besieging Jerusalem in 1187, the Orthodox community within the walls promised him their help, and that he received the congratulations of the Emperor Isaac Angelus on his conquest of the city.[2]

There had been comparable events when Zanki had captured Edessa in 1144. He had shown no mercy to the Franks, but he treated the Syrian Christians with marked clemency. Grousset has drawn attention to the attitude displayed by an anonymous Syrian author who has left an account of these events.[3] To the Latin west, Zanki was a bloodstained monster, and his capture of Edessa a tragedy sufficient to provoke a second crusade. The anonymous Syrian was able to preserve an outlook which by comparison is neutral. He not only described Zanki's forbearance towards the eastern Christians, but was at pains to record his visits to their churches and his friendly relations with the Jacobite metropolitan.[4] The tone of such historians has its value as evidence of the state of mind of the people to whom they belong. Michael the Syrian and, still more, his anonymous compatriot wrote passages which testify that the common language and race which they shared with many Muslims could be a stronger bond

[1] Cahen, *Syrie du Nord*, pp. 400–2.
[2] Grousset, II, p. 811; Runciman, II, p. 465.
[3] Grousset, II, pp. 866, 882.
[4] 'The First and Second Crusades from an anonymous Syriac chronicle', translated by A. S. Tritton, notes by H. A. R. Gibb, in *Jour. Roy. Asiatic Soc.* (1933), pp. 285, 289, 291. 'He (Zanki) greeted the Christians with joy, kissed the Gospel, saluted the Metropolitan and asked after his health.'

than the Christian belief which they shared with the Franks.[1] All Syrian Christians, orthodox and monophysite, had lived for centuries under the generally tolerant Muslim rule of the caliphs. During the Latin occupation, there were communities of the same faith in the lands of Islam as well as in those of the crusaders.[2] Both in time and space they were part of the Muslim, as well as the Frankish world. Between them and their Latin overlords there was the bond of a common faith, but they were tied also to the Muslims by history, language, and habits.[3] They gave the Franks no trouble, but they could regard the prospect of Muslim rule with equanimity. It was not only the kings of Jerusalem, but also Zangid and Ayubid rulers who saw in them subjects whose loyalty could be secured by favoured treatment.

It would therefore appear that the native Christians provided no firm basis for Latin rule, and that they increased rather than alleviated the Franks' military problems. Dodu, however, considered that the Syrian Christians were an important source of military assistance to the Latin rulers, and he has assembled an array of texts which show, or appear to show, the Syrians fighting at the side of the Franks.[4] He stated further that the infantry force was primarily drawn from native sources.[5] The basis for this statement is by no means clear. It is true of the Armenians in the north, and since he included Armenians when he was consider-

---

[1] In *Jour. Roy. Asiatic Soc.* (1933), 276, 278–9, 293; *Chronique de Michel le Syrien*, III, pp. 267, 270, 314.

[2] During the patriarchate of Bernard of Valence at Antioch the Jacobite Church was disturbed by a quarrel between its own patriarch and the metropolitan of Edessa; see *Chronique de Michel le Syrien*, ed. Chabot, III, pp. 196–8. As the ruling secular power in northern Syria the Franks had an interest in composing this quarrel, and both Prince Roger of Antioch and the Latin patriarch were involved; *ibid.* p. 207. The Syrian patriarch was irreconcilable, was offended by his treatment at the hand of the Franks, and took up his residence at Amida in the Diyar Bakr, far outside Latin territory (*ibid.* p. 212). Michael's own duties as patriarch of the Syriac Church often took him from Antioch deep into Muslim territory: to Amida, Mardin, Nisibin, Malatya (*ibid.* pp. 357–60, 384, 390).

[3] JV, p. 1089. The bishop knew Syria and the Syrians. His summary of their characteristics, based on personal experience, strikingly resembles that given above which is based on available historical facts. He wrote, *ibid.*: 'Suriani . . . secreta Christianorum . . . nuntiant Saracenis, inter quos nutriti sunt, quorum etiam lingua libentius utuntur, quam alia, et quorum mores perversos ex parte magna imitantur.'

[4] Dodu, pp. 205–15.   [5] Dodu, p. 208.

ing native Christians, it is possible that he had this people in mind. As he puts it, however, his generalization applies to all Syrians, and of this there is no good evidence. In the course of several pages he is unable to adduce a single good example of Syrians at war. The best is that provided by Ibn al-Athir, who wrote three generations after the event, that Syrian Christians helped Raymond of St Gilles in his conquest of Tripoli.[1] It is probable that these men were Maronites, who still inhabit the western slopes of the Lebanon. They were distinguished, according to William of Tyre, for their martial qualities, while James of Vitry praised their skill in archery.[2] Dodu also quotes William to show that Syrians were sometimes used for garrison duties. He might have added the evidence of Fulcher, who relates that when the army of the kingdom was besieging Tyre in 1124, the citizens of Jerusalem, aided by Syrians, beat off a raid by the garrison of Ascalon.[3] Syrians had also taken part in the crusaders' unsuccessful attack on Ma'arrat al-Nu'man in 1098.[4] And, as Dodu emphasizes, the Turcopoles, who marched with the Frankish armies throughout the period, were certainly Syrians.[5] The number of active Turcopoles must normally have been small, however, in relation to the size of the whole Syrian community, and due weight must be given to the testimony of William of Tyre and James of Vitry, who both knew the Syrians, that they were an unwarlike people.[6] The evidence appears to show that there were among them individuals of spirit who joined the ranks of the Turcopoles, and certain groups with martial qualities, like the Maronites. The rest, like those at Jerusalem in 1124, might take up arms in a crisis. But they were not, as Dodu argued, a source of military aid as a community, nor was their usefulness in war in proportion to the size of that community.

IV. MUSLIMS

In each Latin state, the majority of the inhabitants were probably Muslims. The establishment of a *modus vivendi* with them was one of the first necessities of settlement. There were many

---

[1] IA, p. 212 quoted by Dodu, p. 211.   [2] WT, p. 1077; JV, p. 1093.
[3] Fulcher, p. 460.   [4] *Anon.* p. 164.   [5] *Infra*, p. 111.
[6] WT, p. 1091; JV, p. 1089. 'Prorsus imbelles et praeliis velut mulieres nutiles.'

reasons why relations could not be determined by the spirit of the Holy War.[1] Oppression as a practical policy demands a numerous administration, and the number of settlers was small; exploitation of the Muslim peasants was an economic necessity for the feudal landholders; daily contact brought a measure of sympathy and understanding; offensive and defensive war against neighbouring Muslim states often required all the force at the disposal of the Franks. There was none to devote to the oppression of their own subjects. So the Franks seem to have left to the Muslims, as they did to the Syrian Christians, considerable rights of self-administration and enjoyment of their own customs. The principal source of information on this matter is the account left by Ibn Jubair of a journey which he made from Damascus to Acre in 1184.[2] On the road between Tibnin and the coast he noted that the Muslims paid to the Franks a proportion of their annual produce, as well as a poll tax, and a tax on fruit trees. Otherwise 'ils sont maîtres de leurs habitations et s'administrent comme ils l'entendent'.[3] Ibn Jubair added that most of the Muslim cultivators appreciated the security and well-being they enjoyed under Frankish rule, which they knew to be more just than that of the Muslim princes.[4]

The extract of Ibn Jubair's work which is translated in the *Recueil des historiens des croisades* has been regarded as especially valuable evidence of the solidarity of 'la nation syrienne', for it shows that the Muslims were happier in being members of that nation than they would have been under Muslim rulers. Here again the limitations of the evidence have not been sufficiently considered. It was gathered as a result of one man's observation within a small space and a short time. Another Muslim could find evidence to the contrary.[5] It is fair to conclude from the translated extract of Ibn Jubair's writing that some Franks did not oppress their Muslim subjects, and that many of these Muslims were content with Frankish rule and were loyal to it. But to take the traveller's words at their face value, and to conclude that all Muslims in the Latin states preferred the rule of the Franks to that of their own amirs and atabegs is uncritical and extravagant. It is natural to suppose that there were within the Latin states

---

[1] Duncalf, *Report of Amer. Hist. Ass.* 1 (1914), p. 137.
[2] In *RHC, Hist. or.* III, pp. 445-56.
[3] *Ibid.* p. 448.   [4] *Ibid.*   [5] KD, p. 625.

many Muslims who did not forget that the Frank was a foreigner and an unbeliever; who maintained connexions in the Muslim states; who looked forward to the day when Syria would be restored to Islam. Probably there were many more who were passively content under the Franks, but who would remember the demands of their faith at the bidding of a successful Muslim invader. If these were the conditions, then no matter how much justice and security marked the rule of the Franks, secret or overt hostility from their Muslim subjects was always a possibility, and a factor to be considered by the Franks when deciding military policy. That such indeed was the background of the relations of Frank and Muslim is illustrated by a series of striking facts.

The potential danger to the Latin states from their Muslim subjects was demonstrated in 1113, when Mawdud of Mosul gained his greatest success against the Franks. During the three preceding years Mawdud had, at the bidding of the Saljuq sultan, left his city of Mosul to lead invasions of Latin Syria. In 1113, as a result of friendly relations established between himself and Tughtagin of Damascus two years before, he joined that atabeg in an invasion of Palestine. He defeated the army of Jerusalem under Baldwin I near the bridge of al-Sannabra.[1] The Franks were not broken, but they were compelled to retreat to a hill position west of Tiberias, where they were closely watched by Mawdud's forces. Even after reinforcements had arrived from Antioch and Tripoli, Baldwin dared not leave the position he had chosen. While the two forces watched each other, detachments of the Muslim army roamed unchecked through Samaria, and sacked Nablus. The best contemporary sources for these events, Fulcher and Ibn al-Qalanisi, both relate how the Muslim cultivators of central Palestine entered into friendly relations with the victorious invaders.[2] It is not without significance that when, two generations later, William of Tyre used Fulcher's account of these events as a source for his own history, he added the quotation 'Nulla enim pestis efficacior ad nocendum quam familiaris inimicus.'[3] Future events were to show that he did so with good reason. After the battle of Hattin in 1187, the Franks in the

---

[1] For a detailed account of these events, see Grousset, I, pp. 268 et seq.

[2] Fulcher, p. 427; IQ, p. 139.

[3] WT, p. 486. See also in this connexion the anecdote of Ibn Jubair in RHC, Or. III, pp. 447–8.

district of Nablus evacuated the area as the Muslim peasants rose
en masse in favour of the victorious Saladin.[1]

William of Tyre records another occasion on which the Arab
inhabitants of an area ruled by the Franks called in the Turks.
The peasants at Ouaïra, in the neighbourhood of Petra, appear to
have taken this step in 1144 or 1145, and the Turks were established in the castle there.[2] The young King Baldwin III at once
led a force to the scene, and after a short siege succeeded in ex-
pelling the Turkish intruders. From that time the castle, well
stocked and provisioned, was held by a Frankish garrison.

The employment by the Franks of Muslims in positions of
trust is among the evidence quoted to demonstrate the existence
of 'une nation franco-syrienne'. But there is also evidence to
show that, however close relations between the two peoples might
become, the Muslims could not forget the call of religion and
culture, and that it could draw them towards the Muslims who
attacked the Latin states from without. The behaviour of the
qadi of Jabala is well known from the account given by Ibn al-
Athir;[3] that of Sulaiman ibn Daoud has been more recently published by Cahen.[4] Stories such as these, taken with the evidence
already quoted, show that the 'familiaris inimicus', especially
during a successful Muslim invasion, was an ever present danger,
and a factor of first-class importance in the military situation of
the Latin states.

The Franks could repose complete trust in none of their

---

[1] See al-Imad in *RHC, Hist. or.* IV, 301–2.   [2] WT, pp. 712–13.

[3] IA, p. 717. The qadi was a trusted servant of Bohemond of Antioch
who had made him, in the words of Grousset (II, p. 825), 'une sorte de min-
istre des affaires musulmanes dans la principauté'. Nevertheless, in June
1188, 'his zeal for the Faith' took him to Saladin, who had begun an invasion
of the country of Tripoli. But when the qadi assured him that Jabala,
Ladhaqiya, and other towns in the north would surrender to his army,
Saladin attacked the principality of Antioch, and the victorious summer
campaign of 1188 followed. See also al-Imad quoted in *RHC. Hist. or.* IV,
p. 352.

[4] C. Cahen in *Syria* (1934), XV, 351–60. Sulaiman was probably born in
Frankish Jerusalem, and subsequently served the Shi'ite caliph in Egypt.
Later he returned to Palestine to be physician to King Amalric; one of his
sons succeeded to this position, and another became riding master to Prince
Baldwin (afterwards King Baldwin IV). During this service they maintained
friendly relations with Ysa, a counsellor of Saladin, and sent a message to
Saladin himself. After the Franks lost Jerusalem in 1187 the family remained
in Ayubid service.

subject peoples, from whom they had most to fear when their own military effectiveness was weakened by poverty, defective leadership, or defeat in the field. An example of such a situation was given by Walter, chancellor to that Roger of Antioch who in 1119 lost his army and his life on the Ager Sanguinis to the Turkmens of Il Ghazi. At that battle the Franks' losses were heavy. The towns and castles of the principality had sent their garrisons to join the army. The Frankish population of Antioch itself was, after the defeat, dangerously few. Responsibility for organizing its defence fell upon the clergy, led by the Latin patriarch. The city was threatened from without by a victorious army, and from within by the possibility of treason among the native population.[1] Accordingly all peoples other than the Franks were disarmed, and might not be abroad at night without a torch.[2] The Latin clergy, monks, and laymen, visited both day and night by the patriarch and his armed escort, maintained a constant guard on the walls, towers, and gates. In this way the city was held until the arrival of King Baldwin II. Both the measures taken by the patriarch and the terms in which Walter described them are the clearest possible demonstration of the precarious foundation of Latin rule in Syria.

V. THE LATIN SETTLEMENT

It may now be asked whether the freedom which both Christian and Muslim Syrians were given to manage their own affairs was in fact the result of an 'enlightened' policy, born of the trust which the Franks were able to repose in their subjects, and the symptom of the fusion of western and eastern elements into a single society with an inner strength of its own. Certainly the Franks were usually able to rely at least on the passive loyalty of most of the peoples over whom they ruled; only on those comparatively rare occasions when the Latin states were threatened by a successful invader did latent hostility reveal itself. But therein lies only part of the answer. An equally important and more immediate

[1] Galt. p. 95: '. . . iam destituto militari officio et iam paene toto amisso Francorum civium auxilio, ea vice in clerum necessario totum redactum exstitit, ita, inquam, ut multo acrius timerent interiorum hostium proditione falli quam vi exteriorum ullo modo intrinsecus posse comprimi.'
[2] *Ibid.*

reason is to be sought in the small number of the ruling feudal class and in the differences in language and manners which divided them from their native subjects. The replacement of native by any other customs in village administration would have required an administrative class more numerous than the Franks possessed, and whose difficulties would have been aggravated by difference of language. To leave to native communities the exercise of their own customs was not only 'enlightened'; it was in keeping with the medieval respect for custom,[1] and it was the most practical policy and the most economical in manpower.[2]

There were other reasons which made changes in local custom unnecessary. A primary need of the feudal class was the economic exploitation of the peoples over which it ruled. For centuries before the advent of the First Crusade a feature of social organization among the peoples of western Asia had been the custom by which peasant cultivators gave up to the tax-farmer, or to the proprietor whose tenants they were, either part of their produce or part of the income derived from its sale. It had been customary for the central government to grant an individual the use of an estate, or even the privilege of administering an area, in return for a remittance by him of an agreed annual sum to the treasury. Such grants were often made to soldiers, and during the second half of the eleventh century an arrangement by which they held land or governed districts in return for their military service alone became a common institution in the administration of the Saljuq empire.[3] A condition akin to feudalism was thus established and there is much truth in the assertion made by Beugnot a century ago that Syria was in 1100 ready to receive feudal institutions.[4] From the point of view of the cultivators, their payments to government or landlord was their principal obligation to authority. Much of the disposal of local affairs was left in the hands of the village community. The essentials of this arrangement were left undisturbed

[1] Cahen, *Syrie du Nord*, pp. 330–1.
[2] Chalandon, *Première Croisade*, p. 301.   [3] See *infra*, Chapter IV.
[4] Beugnot, 'Memoire sur le régime des terres dans les principautés fondées en Syrie par les Francs' in *BEC*, IV, sér. 3, p. 543; Cahen, 'Notes sur l'histoire des croisades et de l'orient latin. II. Le régime rural syrien au temps de la domination franque', in *Bulletin de la Faculté des Lettres de Strasbourg* (1951), 286–310; Cahen, *Syrie du Nord*, p. 193.

by the successive conquerors who ruled in Syria and the Nile delta, and this goes far to explain why the mass of the rural populations remained unmoved by violent and sudden changes in political events, and consequent changes of masters.[1]

The available evidence appears to show that as a ruling race the Franks did not vary the practice of their predecessors.[2] It seems probable that they maintained the system of accounts and registers which they found in existence.[3] As in Europe, grants of land by lords to vassals remained an essential part of the feudal relationship; but these profited from their estates, not by working demesne lands by the labour services of their unfree tenants,[4] but like other races which had dominated Syria before them, by taking from those tenants an annual rent in money or kind.[5] There is significance in the comparatively high proportion of fiefs and gifts which were not in the form of lands, but of money and financial rights over nomads[6] and in the fact that division of territory with Muslim rulers was frequently made in terms of its revenues.[7] In the present state of knowledge it appears, from the facts just quoted and the evidence of the law books to which reference has been made, that the Frankish overlords of Syria maintained a system by which they drew revenue from the native population, and left them considerable freedom in the management of their local affairs.

The 'enlightened' policy was therefore also the most practical in the light of the economic requirements of the ruling class, and of the difficulties which a small military aristocracy must have found in administering an alien people. It is possible to believe, with Beugnot and Cahen, that in social terms the establishment of the Latin states meant the replacement of one ruling military class by another. 'Chefs turcs là, étrangers de race et parfois de langue, eux aussi, chefs francs ici; que ces chefs s'arrangent entre

---

[1] Cf. Lane-Poole, *History of Egypt in the Middle Ages*, p. 18.

[2] Cahen, *loc. cit.* p. 309.   [3] La Monte, *Feudal Monarchy*, p. 167.

[4] La Monte, *Feudal Monarchy*, p. 171, n. 2; Cahen, *Bulletin* (1951), p. 297.

[5] Beugnot, in *BEC*, v, sér. 3 (1854), 421; Rey, *Colonies*, p. 243; Chalandon, *Première Croisade*, p. 301. It was usual for the landlord to take a proportion, often between a quarter and a half of the peasants' crops. See Cahen, *Bulletin* (1951), p. 300.

[6] On the money fief see La Monte, *Feudal Monarchy*, p. 144. On gifts and grants of Bedouin see *Regesta*, nos. 174, 355, 366, 562, 567, 593.

[7] Ibn Jubair, *RHC, Hist. or.* III, p. 446; IQ, pp. 93, 106, 113; KD, p. 651.

eux cela n'importe guère à la vie quotidienne, qui est presque toute la vie.'[1]

The ruling class among the Franks were a military aristocracy whose position in Syria was in many ways comparable with that of the Normans in England in the first generation after 1066. One striking point of resemblance is the dependence of both on their castles to maintain their conquests and this dependence throws further light on the nature of the Latin settlement. These buildings, some inherited and some founded by the Franks, and which remain as their most enduring monument, have been intensively studied by historians of military architecture, but their functions have been less fully considered. They have been most often explained in terms of defending the frontiers, but this is only part of the known truth. On the one hand frontier defence was a role which a castle, or even a group of castles, could only imperfectly fulfil; on the other, the building discharged a wide variety of other functions, and perhaps more effectively. They were used in attack, and played a notable part in the Latin conquest of Antioch, Tripoli, Tyre, and Ascalon.[2] In Transjordan and southern Palestine they were used to establish Latin control in areas of strategic importance, and these castles subsequently became centres of colonization and economic development.[3] They served as residences, as administrative centres, as barracks, and as police posts.[4]

Above all, they were centres of authority. The commander of a castle and its garrison was master of the surrounding district, and

---

[1] Cahen, *Syria*, xv (1934), 359. The matter requires further investigation as Cahen himself remarks in an expression of similar views in *Bulletin* (1951), pp. 288–9, '[ces faits] suggèrent, sous réserve de vérification, que l'établissement de la domination franque n'a pas dû se traduire, pour les paysans indigènes, par un grand bouleversement. Une classe supérieure nouvelle se substitue à l'ancienne pour se superposer à la société rurale antérieure; ignorante des conditions du sol, elle s'en remet naturellement à cette société du soin d'en continuer l'exploitation, au profit des nouveaux maîtres, mais selon ses propres traditions'.

[2] The military role of the crusaders' castles is more fully considered in Chapter VII below.

[3] See the important article by Dr J. Prawer, 'Colonization activities in the Latin Kingdom of Jerusalem' in *Revue Belge de Philologie et d'Histoire*, XXIX (1951), 1063–118. Also R. C. Smail, 'Crusaders' Castles of the Twelfth Century' in *Cambridge Historical Journal*, X (1951), 133–49.

[4] Castrum Arnaldi was built on the road from the coast to Jerusalem 'ad tutelam transeuntium peregrinorum'. WT, p. 617.

had means continuously at his disposal to meet any challenge to his authority. Wherever they stood, fortified buildings provided a base from which power could be exercised, and within which it could be protected and preserved. As in Europe, so in Syria, castles had only occasionally to withstand a siege, but they continuously fulfilled their function as the physical basis of overlordship. On at least one occasion the needs of administration caused the Franks to build a castle. During the reign of Baldwin II difficulty was found in collecting the revenues due from the Muslim cultivators in the Lebanon above Bairut, and the solution adopted was the construction of a castle on Mons Glavianus.[1] Similar difficulties were likely to arise in areas divided between Franks and Muslims. The division appears nearly always to have been made in terms of revenue,[2] and the collection of dues from reluctant Muslim cultivators, encouraged by the proximity of the Muslim power with whom the Franks had divided the district was a possible administrative problem. Such a situation is described by William of Tyre in as-Sawad, and there again the Franks had introduced the necessary element of force in the form of a castle and its garrison.[3] Perhaps the most instructive example is that of Darum, of which the foundation by King Amalric was recorded by William of Tyre. He wrote: 'Condiderat autem rex ea intentione praedictum municipium, ut et fines suos dilataret et suburbanorum adjacentium, quae nostri casalia dicunt, et annuos redditus, et de transeuntibus statutas consuetudines plenius et facilius sibi posset habere.'[4] There is nothing here of defending a frontier.[5] The castle extended the limits of the kingdom by bringing a new area under control. As an administrative

---

[1] Fulcher, p. 473, '... et quia ruricolae Sarraceni tributa locorum reddere antea nolebant, postea vi cohibiti reddibiles exstiterunt'.

[2] See above, p. 59; Beyer, *ZDPV*, 67, pp. 214, 234.

[3] WT, p. 1090, 'nam cum praedicta regio hostium magis esset contermina finibus, quam nostris, et ipsi eam facilius pro suo possent tractare arbitrio, et ejus habitatoribus confidentius imperare, hujus tamen praesidii beneficio multis annis obtentum fuerat, et obtinebatur nihilominus in praesenti, quod nostris et illis ex aequo dividebatur potestas, et tributorum et vectigalium par fiebat distributio'.

[4] WT, p. 975. It must be borne in mind that William wrote with authority. As chancellor of the kingdom, archbishop, and ambassador to Manuel Comnenus he well understood the motives of royal policy.

[5] Deschamps relates Darum entirely to the needs of frontier defence. See *Le Crac*, p. 19; *Défense*, p. 21.

centre it enabled the king to organize more easily and efficiently the collection of dues both from the peasants in the castles, and from the Beduin, and possibly caravans,[1] moving through the district.

The dominion of the Franks was to some extent founded on the goodwill of the subject peoples, but to a greater degree it rested on their possession of fortified places. This was especially true when the Latin states were invaded. A medieval fortress could not halt an attack at the frontier, and many times during the century Muslim armies penetrated deep into the Latin states. The Franks temporarily lost control of any area occupied by the invader. For the time being their dominion could best be represented on a map not as an area bounded by a frontier line but as a series of points, which were the fortified places. When there was no field force to oppose them, the Franks were so narrowly confined to the shelter of their walls, 'ut extra moenia nemo prorsus auderet comparere'.[2]

VI. CONCLUSION

The nature of the Latin settlement affected the military methods of the Franks; but whoever seeks information on that settlement is faced by two very different interpretations of the facts. According to one, the Franks adjusted themselves to their Oriental surroundings and took root among the peoples over whom they ruled. The result was a new nation, in which all elements were thoroughly blended, which was in no way artificial, and which had a life of its own. The other school of thought considers that the basic feature of the organization of the Latin states was the imposition of a numerically small military aristocracy over the mass

---

[1] Historians have confidently stated that the coast route from Gaza to Egypt was used as a caravan route during the Latin occupation. See Rey, *Colonies Franques*, p. 255; Dodu, *Institutions*, p. 239; Derenbourg, *Vie d'Ousâma*, p. 204. Yet the only evidence for the twelfth century seems to be the 'transeuntes' of WT in the passage quoted above. Burchard of Mount Sion, quoted by Rey, was not in Syria until about 1283; see *Peregrinatores Medii Aevi Quatuor*, ed. Laurent, pp. 4, 39.

[2] WT, pp. 486, 784; Fulcher, p. 427.

Note the situation described by WT, p. 1064. Neither Raymond of Tripoli nor either of the military Orders would take the field against Saladin during his attack on the county of Tripoli in 1180. Saladin's forces therefore ranged unopposed through the country-side.

of the native population. This ruling class exploited the subject peoples economically by means of social arrangements which they found in existence, and which were akin to those they had known in Europe. Otherwise they made little difference to the daily life of the Syrians.

This latter interpretation appears to correspond more closely with the facts. Madelin and Grousset have used the available evidence with too much enthusiasm. They have paid too little attention to its limitations and have either disregarded or underestimated the importance of the many facts which are in conflict with it. Consequently they have overlooked the possibility that the 'orientalization' they describe may have been a comparatively superficial process which had a picturesque effect on externals, but little more. The conclusions of Beugnot and Cahen appear to be nearer the truth of the matter.

The security and justice which marked the Frankish rule brought them obedience and a certain loyalty from Syrian Christians and Muslims. It was in time of military crisis that any weakness in that loyalty revealed itself. The connexions of the Syrian Christians with the Muslim world were such that their attitude in the Holy War could be almost neutral. They were 'amici fortunae',[1] inclining to the victorious party. In similar circumstances the Muslims naturally responded to the call of their Faith, and with little encouragement became the active enemies of their Frankish masters. The rule of the Franks had been founded and continued to rest on force. Embodied in the fortified places and their garrisons, it was the ultimate sanction of Frankish dominion, and their sole means of resisting an invader. Although he did not argue the matter, the soundest verdict on the military position of the Franks among the subject peoples was stated long ago by Prutz: '. . . die Franken namentlich bei einem siegreichen feindlichen Angriff sich auf die einheimische Bevölkerung nicht verlassen konnten'; each castle 'gegen die unzuverlässigen Unterthanen so gut wie gegen die mohammedanischen Angriffe dienen musste'.[2]

---

[1] JV, p. 1089.   [2] Prutz, *Kulturgeschichte*, p. 19

CHAPTER IV

THE MUSLIM ARMIES

I. SALJUQ INSTITUTIONS

THE valleys of the Euphrates and the Nile have each been the seat of empire, and Syria, as a bridge between the two, has many times in history been invaded from both. In the twelfth century the power on the Euphrates was the Abbasid caliphate, in which since 1059 the Saljuq sultans had exercised temporal power; that on the Nile was the Fatimid caliphate which had been established in Egypt since the year 969. During the twelfth century both were from time to time involved in war with the Franks, whose military methods were affected by the organization and tactics of the armies sent against them. Those attributes of the Muslim armies which appear to have influenced the Franks are the subject of this chapter.

It is a commonplace that the success of the First Crusade was primarily due to division among the Saljuq Turks. The age of their great sultans, Tughril Beg, Alp Arslan, and Malik Shah had ended with the death of the last named in 1092. Thereafter not only did the dynasty fail to produce a personality equal to that of the great sultans, but their energies were largely absorbed by succession disputes and consequent civil war. In such conditions the control which the sultans could exercise over the institutions of government was weakened. This particularly applied to the administration of those provinces which had been granted as a form of *iqta'* to the great amirs. Since this institution is relevant to both the first and second sections of this chapter it will be shortly considered here.[1]

---

[1] The next two paragraphs are based on the researches of C. H. Becker, 'Steurpacht und Lehnswesen' in *Der Islam*, v (1914), 81–92 and reprinted in the same author's *Islamstudien*, I, p. 243; on the article 'Egypt' in *Encyclopaedia of Islam*, by the same author; on the article 'Ikta'', *ibid.* by M. Sobernheim; on A. K. S. Lambton, 'Contributions to the study of Saljuq institutions', thesis for Ph.D., London, 1939. See also H. A. R. Gibb in IQ, p. 34; Lane-Poole, *Saladin*, p. 15.

Iqta' was land or revenue assigned by the ruler to an individual, and it had existed since the early days of Islam as a form of reward for service to the State. The forms of *iqta'* varied considerably. The beneficiary might be assigned the governorship of a province, with powers which made him almost independent of the central government; or he might have only the right to farm the taxes in the area named in the grant, returning an agreed sum to the government and retaining the remainder for himself; or he might be granted an annual payment from the revenues of an area.[1] A notable development under the early Saljuqs was the militarization of the *iqta'*. In the district assigned the beneficiary retained all the revenues collected, and the only duty he owed to the central government was personal service in the army.[2] If the assignment were an important one, he was bound to take with him a contingent of soldiers, of which the size varied with his status.[3] This system was even more firmly established after Nizam al-Mulk, the great vizier of Malik Shah, had recognized the existence of the system, and had accepted and legalized it.[4]

During the Saljuq period there were still many types of *iqta'*,[5] but that which was of greatest importance in the political and military situation of the Saljuq empire was the administrative *iqta'*. It was a military grant of the type already described, but it included the duties of administering the area assigned. Generally speaking all powers of government were in the hands of its holder. He was tied to the central government only by the sultan's power to appoint and to dismiss him, and by his obligations to include the name of the sultan in the public prayers, and to furnish a contingent to the sultan's armies when he was called upon to do so.[6] The effectiveness of those bonds, and the unity of the Saljuq

---

[1] For these types of early *iqta'* see Becker in *Der Islam*, v, 84–6 and Sobernheim in *Encyc. Islam*, II, p. 461. (art. Ikta').

[2] Becker, *Der Islam*, v, 88.   [3] Lambton, Ph.D. thesis, p. 245.

[4] Becker, *Der Islam*, v, 89; Sobernheim, *Encyc. Islam*, II, p. 462. Lambton, Ph.D. thesis, pp. 209–10.

[5] Lambton, *ibid.* pp. 219 *et seq.* discusses five main types.

[6] Lambton, Ph.D. thesis, pp. 228–9, where the terms of the assignment of Damascus by the sultan to Tughtagin in 1116 are briefly set out. Tughtagin's powers included the administration of justice, the maintenance of internal security, the conduct of war, the levy and collection of taxes, and the appointment and payment of officials. The text of this document is given by Ibn al-Qalanisi, but is omitted from Gibb's translation (cf. IQ, p. 153).

empire, depended on the ability of the sultan to enforce on his great amirs the due performance of their obligations. This was often beyond the power of the descendants of Malik Shah, especially in the distant province of Syria.[1] It is against the background of the administrative *iqta'* that the political weakness of the Saljuq empire can be most clearly understood.[2]

Military weakness arose from the same conditions. The Saljuq armies at this period included two elements: for routine duties and small scale operations a standing force, or *'askar*, of slaves and freedmen was sufficient; but large undertakings demanded the addition of the provincial governors with their contingents and of any other available auxiliaries, among whom the Turkmen tribesmen were always prominent.[3] Thus a full muster of the sultan's army included, besides tribal auxiliaries, the great amirs with their contingents, which were themselves made up of the permanent force maintained by that amir, together with the men to whom he had assigned land or revenue within the greater *iqta'* which he himself held of the sultan. Any large Saljuq army was a composite force.

A basic factor in the military history of the Syrian Franks, and one of particular influence on their methods of warfare, was that any campaign against them which had as its object their expul-

[1] Lambton, Ph.D. thesis, pp. 16–17.

[2] Gibb in IQ, p. 34. The truth of this statement is apparent even in those Arabic sources of crusading history which have been translated. Ibn al-Athir's work on the atabeks of Mosul is the history of a great administrative *iqta'* and of the amirs and atabeks to whom it was assigned. The names of many of them are familiar in the history of the Latin states. *AM*, p. 32, assignment of Mosul to Mawdud in 1108–9; p. 36, to Juyush beg in 1113; p. 44, to aq-Sunqur al-Bursuqi in 1121; p. 65, to Zanki in 1127. IA, p. 240, records an occasion on which the sultan deprived Jikirmish of Mosul and assigned it to Jawali Saqawa.

[3] The change in the relative size of the two elements of the Sultan's army after the death of Malik Shah was at once a symptom and a cause of the diminished power of his successors. Cf. Lambton, Ph.D. thesis, pp. 168–9: '. . . whereas the size of the sultan's standing army after the death of Malik Shah decreased, the military forces of the amirs tended rather to increase . . . finally the sultans came more and more to rely, not so much upon the standing army, as upon the forces of the amirs. This change in the relative strength of the army of the central government and the armies of the amirs led to difficulties, for since the ultimate guarantee for the maintenance of the Great Saljuq empire was military force, by alienating this from their direct control and placing it in the hands of the amirs, the sultans invited the latter to assert their independence.'

sion from the East, or a substantial reduction of their territory, was an ambitious undertaking which required a large composite army. Raid and counter-raid could be carried on with small forces. The forays of Tancred against Shaizar, of Hugh of Tiberias in the Sawad, of Pons of Tripoli in the Biqa', these required only the household knights of the Frankish magnate, and could be resisted by the private 'askar of a single amir; but any important Muslim offensive required the concentration of many such forces, and usually of tribal auxiliaries.

It has been observed that, in twelfth-century Syria, towns and castles were the basis of dominion, and permanent territorial gains could be achieved only by the reduction of such places. In an age of strong fortifications and comparatively weak artillery a siege was normally a difficult operation. If the besiegers were threatened by a field force determined to relieve pressure on the garrison, the problem of maintaining the siege could become insuperable. As the events of 1187 were to show, the pattern of successful conquest was the defeat of the Franks' field army followed by reduction of the strong places. Such an achievement demanded the employment of maximum military strength, especially when the four Latin states were prepared to combine in the interests of self-preservation. With very few exceptions, all those Muslim armies which operated from Mesopotamia or Syria in order to destroy Frankish dominion were composite forces.

The most determined efforts to break the rule of the Franks in Syria were made between 1110 and 1115 and again between 1177 and 1188. During the first of these periods the invasions were ordered by the sultan. The forces which assembled were usually made up of contingents from the administrative districts of the Jazira and Diyar Bakr, and the amir whose assignment was Mosul was often appointed as their leader. The sultan never came in person to lead these armies, and therein lay their principal weakness. In one sense they were a part of the sultan's whole army; but without his leadership they were only a coalition of some of his great subjects.[1] The consequent lack of undisputed leadership

[1] For examples of the conditions described in this paragraph see:
(a) IA, p. 194; KD, pp. 579–80. The army sent to relieve Antioch in 1098 was led by Karbuqa of Mosul. On the same page will be found (i) IA's account of the attitude of the amirs towards Karbuqa, (ii) the list of contingents which made up the army.

frequently paralysed military action. That amirs, as a class, could never successfully co-operate, and, if not strictly controlled, were always rivals to each other, was clearly recognized by at least one Saljuq statesman,[1] and it was abundantly proved by events. The intrusion of the sultan into the affairs of Syria had as its object not only the expulsion of the Franks, but the reduction to obedience of the Muslim amirs of that province. Consequently the rulers of Muslim Syria often refused their co-operation; even when it was obtained the fears of a Duqaq or a Tughtagin for the safety of his assignment could remain a source of weakness.

Relations between the amirs who came from outside Syria were often no happier. In 1104 Sukman b. Ortuq and Jikirmish won a complete victory at Harran over the combined armies of the Franks of Antioch and Edessa. Their success remained without important results, for immediately after the battle they quarrelled over the division of the spoils.[2] Three years later the sultan assigned Mosul to Jawali Saqawa and ordered him to drive the Franks from the lands which they occupied. The new ruler of Mosul was never able to lead such an expedition, for in order to possess himself of his *iqta'* he had to defeat in battle first Jikirmish,[3] its previous holder, then Qilij Arslan of Rum,[4] before he himself was deprived by the sultan's order.[5] The best example of the chaos which could exist in the command of a large counter-crusading army during the first two decades of the twelfth century is provided by the campaign of 1111, which is analysed in a later chapter.[6] Such facts show that as a result of the political situation in the Saljuq empire, of the institutions of government

---

(b) IA, p. 240; IQ, p. 76. In 1107 the sultan assigned Mosul to Jawali and ordered him to expel the Franks from their conquests.

(c) IA, p. 280; KD, pp. 595–6; IQ, p. 101. In 1110 the first counter-crusade was ordered by the sultan, and Mawdud of Mosul was appointed its leader. He commanded the contingents of many amirs; but their names are not given by the writers to whom reference has been made.

(d) IA, p. 292; AM, p. 36. In 1114 the sultan ordered Aq-Sunqur Bursuqi to attack the Franks. His army included contingents from Sinjar, Mardin, and other towns.

(e) For the Muslim invasions of 1111 and 1115 see below, pp. 140–8.

[1] He was Nizam al-Mulk, who recorded his opinion that the amirs 'were a class who were always seeking the loss and disadvantage of one another'. Cf. Lambton, Ph.D. thesis, pp. 100, 171, 175.

[2] IA, p. 222.   [3] IA, p. 241; IQ, p. 76.   [4] IA, p. 247; IQ, p. 79.
[5] IA, pp. 257–8; IQ, p. 83.   [6] See below, Chapter VI.

to which reference has been made, of the size of military force required to achieve conquest at the expense of the Franks, the invading Turkish armies of the early twelfth century were composite and without effective leadership. They lacked cohesion and were liable to disperse of their own accord. As a result the Franks could and did reap the important advantages of a victorious defensive campaign without exposing themselves to the risks of battle.

From 1128, the year in which Zanki acquired Aleppo, until 1174, when his son Nur al-Din died, there was a change in the Syrian political scene. The sultan's authority, and with it his power to intervene in Syria, still further decreased, and the Syrian amirs became independent rulers rather than provincial governors.[1] When Zanki was able to add Aleppo to Mosul he acquired interests in Syria, and there are signs that his attitude towards the sultan approached that of a Rudwan or a Tughtagin.[2] As a result of these changes the sultan no longer directed the Holy War against the Franks. The situation was continued under Zanki's son, Nur al-Din, who succeeded only to the Syrian possessions of his father. Stevenson has drawn attention to the comparatively modest achievement of Zanki, and Nur al-Din's long periods of inactivity, against the Franks.[3] This has sometimes been attributed, on the part of the son, to his timidity and lack of initiative and to his fear of Byzantine intervention in favour of the Latin states. It is suggested that an additional reason is to be found in the military situation. Conquest of any considerable part of the Latin states demanded forces larger than Muslim Syria alone could provide. Nur al-Din sometimes took the field with an ally. On the occasion of his victory at Harim in 1164 and of his attack against the county of Tripoli in 1167, he was aided by the '*askar* of his brother and of other Mesopotamian amirs.[4] On other occasions he invited and obtained the help of

---

[1] Lambton, Ph.D. thesis, pp. 238–9.

[2] When John Comnenus threatened to overrun Syria in 1137, Zanki sent a representative to the sultan imploring military aid. As soon as the danger was past, Zanki sent the strictest instructions that the sultan's army was not to come to Syria. IA, pp. 428–30; *AM*, pp. 110–13, where the opinion is expressed that if the sultan had sent the army, his purpose would have been not only to fight the Greeks, but to resume direct control of Syria.

[3] Stevenson, *Crusaders in the East*, pp. 123, 154, 173.

[4] IA, pp. 537, 551; AS, p. 111.

Turkmen auxiliaries.[1] But an ally was always a potential threat to independence. Nur al-Din usually relied on his own military resources, and this is a reason for his limited, piecemeal conquests from the Franks.[2]

The successes of Saladin against the Latin states grew with his military resources. In 1170 and again in 1177 he invaded Palestine from the south with only Egyptian forces, and achieved nothing; after his conquest in northern Syria and Mesopotamia during the years 1182 and 1183 his military strength became overwhelming.[3] The army with which Saladin won his great victory at Hattin, conquered the greater part of the Latin states, attempted to raise the siege of Acre, and resisted the Third Crusade, was a composite force, built up of quasi-feudal contingents like the armies of Mawdud or Bursuq.[4] In his day the militarized and administrative *iqta'* existed as it had earlier in the century. Under Nur al-Din some soldiers received hereditary assignments in return for which they and their heirs after them were bound to serve in the army.[5] This institution survived under the Ayubids, and was established by Shirkuh and Saladin in Egypt.[6] Local government in his empire was still organized on the basis of the administrative *iqta'*. Saladin had his own permanent guard, but for

---

[1] AS, p. 86; IQ, pp. 291, 305, 315, 341.

[2] It is instructive to note that even these coalitions showed the old weakness. In 1167 Nur al-Din wished to attack Bairut, but owing to quarrels in the composite army, it dispersed (IA, p. 551). The joint expedition against Banyas with a contingent from Damascus in 1153 had the same result (AS, p. 77).

[3] E.g. muster of contingents from all parts of his empire for the attack on Karak in 1184. See BD, pp. 80–1.

[4] For the campaign of 1187 Saladin's army included contingents from 'Egypt and Syria' (BD, p. 91). The contingent of Aleppo was specially mentioned (*ibid.*). Detachments also came from Saladin's recent conquests in Mosul and Mardin (BD, p. 92) and Sinjar (BD, p. 117). Subsequently passages recur in Beha ed-Din's work in which the list of contingents which made up Saladin's army is recited. See BD, pp. 140–1, contingents in battle of Acre, 4 October 1189; p. 148, Beha ed-Din is sent to summon further contingents when news of Barbarossa's imminent arrival was received. On pp. 152–7, BD describes the arrival of contingents at Saladin's camp for the campaign of 1190. See IA, II, p. 7, for muster of 1189; IA, II, p. 21, of 1190.

[5] Sobernheim in *Encyc. Islam*, II, p. 462, art. Ikta'; Lambton, Ph.D. thesis, pp. 263–4; Gibb; 'The Armies of Saladin' in *Cahiers d'histoire égyptienne*, sér. 3, fasc. 4 (May 1951), p. 306.

[6] Becker in *Encyc. Islam*, II, p. 14, art. Egypt. Gibb, 'The Armies of Saladin', *loc. cit.* pp. 304–5.

regular campaigns he summoned the contingents of those amirs to whom cities and provinces had been assigned.

These forces were of similar composition to the counter-crusading armies of seventy years earlier; but there were also important differences. There was in Syria no ruler who could, like Rudwan, refuse to co-operate. Egypt was no longer an isolated power, but soldiers from the Nile valley were present with those of Syria and Mesopotamia. Most important of all, the ruler who summoned the army now commanded it in the field. The amirs were not free to quarrel and disperse, but were subject to an overriding authority. Yet even Saladin often had the greatest difficulty in enforcing his will on his subordinates,[1] and the control he was able to exercise on his army as a whole proved to be incomplete on important occasions. The weaknesses which made his army so defective an instrument for the achievement of his policy were common to all Muslim armies in the twelfth century, and will be discussed in the following section.

II. THE MILITARY CONSEQUENCES

Warfare was seasonal. Once the winter rains had set in the ground became unsuitable for movement.[2] Campaigning was sometimes undertaken during winter, but such enterprises rarely prospered. The failure of the determined attacks on Damascus in 1129[3] and on Damietta in 1170[4] was on either occasion partly due to the weather, and during both the First and Third Crusades the pilgrims suffered considerable hardship on account of the Syrian winter.[5] In the words of one who saw much of the warfare now being studied, 'Il n'est ore mie tans de tenir ost encontre yver'.[6]

---

[1] E.g. his difficulty in keeping Sinjar Shah and his uncle, Imad ed-Din, at the siege of Acre in November 1190; IA, II, pp. 37–9, BD, pp. 192–5.

[2] Cf. G. A. Smith, *Historical Geography of the Holy Land*, p. 64. For a scientific statement of the incidence of rainfall, see Abel, *Géographie de la Palestine*, I, pp. 125–7. On winter mud in Syria see BD, p. 359, when the writer himself was so impeded that he took nineteen days on the journey from Jerusalem to Damascus. See also Usamah, p. 187; BD, pp. 119, 204; IA, II, 17.

[3] WT, p. 597; IA, p. 385.   [4] WT, p. 968.

[5] *HEp.* pp. 160, 159; *Itin.* p. 312.   [6] *Ernoul*, p. 141.

Winter therefore afforded to the amirs and their contingents a convenient opportunity for returning to their homes. It was natural that they should wish to do so. The anxieties of a soldier away from home and family is a factor in morale which no military commander can afford to overlook. Even when men know that the state of the war makes it impossible to release them to their homes, they will not easily endure the continued absence; but if they are denied a clear and reasonable opportunity they become less amenable to discipline and progressively less effective as fighting troops.[1]

Such considerations assume an added importance when the troops concerned are not professional soldiers serving on a long-term engagement, but are, like those of the larger Saljuq and Ayubid forces, summoned to the army in order that major operations may be undertaken. It has been noted that some Turkish troops were permanently held under arms. The remainder saw only occasional service, and for the rest, and greater part, of their time were free to devote themselves to responsibilities of the land assigned to them. Similar circumstances in other historical epochs have shown that where a soldier is given land as a reward for occasional military service in the army, his agricultural soon begin to outweigh his military interests.[2] There is reason to believe that in the Saljuq empire also the soldier could be lost in the farmer. In 1155 the Sultan Muhammad b. Mahmud wished to attack Baghdad. He was unable to carry out his plan because none of the amirs on whose service and contingents he depended would leave their lands during the harvest.[3] This is an extreme example, but similar considerations must sometimes have been in the mind of every beneficed amir. Campaigning was not only dangerous, expensive, and uncomfortable; it was also an interference with the joys of family and possessions and with agricultural routine. Such soldiers would not forgo the annual

[1] Those who served with the British forces overseas for long periods during World War II will appreciate the truth of this statement.

[2] Delbrück, III, pp. 4, 12–13; Frauenholz, *Heerwesen*, pp. 12–13; Helen Chew, *Ecclesiastical Tenants-in-chief*, p. 29; J. F. Baldwin, *The Scutage and Knight Service in England*, p. 15.

[3] Lambton, Ph.D. thesis, p. 160. Later they refused to march because of the summer heats of Baghdad. For other examples of occasions on which 'the 'askaris [were] scattered far and wide in the regions of their iqta's, at the approach of the harvest', see Gibb, 'The Armies of Saladin', *loc. cit.* p. 307.

opportunity of returning home which winter provided. The preoccupations of an administrative amir with his landed possessions were even greater than those of the ordinary soldier. In the early twelfth century his tenure was by no means secure. A rival might attack his possessions while he himself was absent on campaign, or the sultan might assign them to some other amir. In such conditions no Turkish magnate could lightly absent himself from his *iqta'*.

For these reasons those armies which were large enough to threaten the existence of the Latin states never remained in being from the end of one campaigning season until the beginning of the next. In 1111 Tughtagin was anxious that Mawdud's great army should winter in Syria, and should attack Tripoli in the spring of 1112; but despite his efforts he could not persuade the other amirs to consent to this.[1] Even Saladin during his victorious career had more than once to allow his troops to return to their homes at the time he needed them most. In 1176 he fought a successful campaign against the Zangids. After the settlement with Aleppo he led his army into the Jabal Ansariya in order to bring the mountain state of the Assassins under his control. He was unable to carry his plan to a successful conclusion, partly because his soldiers, sated with spoil and weary of the campaign, wished to return to their homes.[2] The victorious general had to permit the dissolution of his army, and the campaign came to an end.

In 1187 the one success needed to crown the achievement of his army was the capture of Tyre; but he did not form his siege until 25 November, by which time the approach of winter and the consequent restlessness of his troops made it impossible for him to continue.[3] In the following year, after a victorious campaign in northern Syria, he had the opportunity to extinguish the Frankish principality of Antioch. Once more his army failed to answer his purpose. Many contingents in his army wished to return home, and he was unable to undertake the siege of Antioch.[4] Any Saljuq or Ayubid army dispersed at the end of the campaigning season, and once again it has to be observed that the Franks could have achieved little more than this by victory in battle.

An additional factor in the situation was plunder. Even in

---

[1] IQ, p. 117. [2] IA, p. 626. [3] IA, p. 711; AS, p. 343.
[4] IA, p. 732; Al Imad in AS, p. 380; BD, p. 117; KD in *ROL*, IV, p. 189.

modern times the individual is able to find personal profit in the spoils of war, and in the Middle Ages his opportunities were far greater. The Turkmens almost always appeared in the large Saljuq armies of the period, and prospects of booty were perhaps the most powerful inducements which brought them to war.[1] The failure of Il Ghazi to profit from his major victory over Roger of Antioch at the Ager Sanguinis in 1119 was due not only to his own subsequent and prolonged drunkenness, but to the scattering of his forces in search of plunder.[2] Throughout the century this was a weakness of the armies which invaded the Latin states. One of the reasons given for Saladin's defeat at Mont Gisard in 1177 was that his forces lost cohesion in their preoccupation with loot.[3] Ten years later the speed of his victorious advance after Hattin was checked for the same reason.[4]

The most important military consequence of these conditions was the growing restlessness of the soldiers if a campaign did not provide the profit they expected. In 1120 Baldwin II took the army of Jerusalem to disengage Antioch from the attacks of Il Ghazi. When he arrived the Turkmen force had largely dispersed, discouraged by the lack of spoils.[5] In 1192 Richard Plantagenet gained a brilliant tactical success before Jaffa. It was due not only to his own skill, but to the lack of fighting spirit among Saladin's troops. A few days before Saladin had negotiated with the garrison of Jaffa, instead of letting his troops take it by storm. They felt that they had been deprived of plunder, and this grievance reduced their morale and their effectiveness as soldiers.[6]

[1] Lambton, Ph.D. thesis, p. 161: 'Their guiding motive was plunder, and wherever this was to be found, there also in all probability were the Turkomans.' There is a striking verbal illustration of her statement in the chronicle of Ibn al-Qalanisi. When that historian mentioned the Turkmens, the word 'plunder' often appeared in the same sentence. See IQ, pp. 161, 176, 199, 221, 226, 239, 311, 332. IA, p. 332–3 describes the arrival of the tribesmen at the muster of Il Ghazi's forces: 'La cupidité seule amenait les Turkomans sous ses drapeaux. On les voyait venir un à un, avec un sac dans lequel étaient de la farine et un mouton taillé en bandes qu'on avait fait sécher.'

[2] IQ, p. 161; KD, p. 619.   [3] WT, pp. 1040–2; AS, p. 185; IA, p. 628.

[4] BD, pp. 98–9; Saladin 'made an attempt upon Tyre, but renounced it because his men were scattered through the districts on the coast, each soldier engaged in pillaging on his own account, and the army was growing weary of ceaseless fighting and continual war.'

[5] KD, p. 624.

[6] BD, p. 337; IA, II, p. 65, has a slightly different version of the same incident.

It has been seen, therefore, that the large armies which threatened the existence of the Latin states were, as a consequence of Saljuq and Ayubid institutions, quasi-feudal in construction and could not be held in the field for long periods. During the age of the *bella Antiochena* they lacked commanders of undisputed authority, and were prone to break up as a result of quarrels among the great amirs. The reigns of Zanki and Nur al-Din were not an age of ambitious invasions; but these were revived under Saladin, whose armies were an aggregate of contingents from all parts of his empire, but whose authority and prestige ensured that unity of command which had been lacking during the early years of the century. Yet even his control over his troops and subordinate commanders was sometimes incomplete and his difficulties in this respect bring into prominence other conditions which throughout the century had the effect of limiting the existence of Muslim armies to a single campaign. The attitude to campaigning of the holders of military and administrative *iqta's* was influenced by the needs of administration and agriculture; nearly every soldier responded to the call of family and home. When winter brought operations to an end that call became irresistible, and even a Saladin in the flood tide of victory must reluctantly allow his contingents to depart. Finally, even the warrior of the Jihad was often moved rather by consideration of earthly profit than of heavenly reward. If the first were not forthcoming, he found no compensation for the danger and discomfort of campaigning. He was left without motives to resist the magnetism of home thoughts which ever sought to draw him from the theatre of war.

III. TURKISH TACTICS

Of all the Asiatic peoples, it was the Turks for whose military qualities the Franks had the greatest fear and admiration,[1] and their tactical methods will be described in this section.

'Erant trecenta sexaginta millia pugnatorum, scilicet sagittariorum. Mos enim eorum est, talibus uti armis. Equites erant omnes.'[2] In this description of the army which met the Franks at

---

[1] *Anon.* p. 50; *Itin.* pp. 226, 228; *Est.* pp. 5067 *et seq.*
[2] Fulcher, p. 334.

Dorylaeum, Fulcher emphasized the two principal characteristics of the enemy which, together with the fierce battle cries[1] and the 'barbarous sound of the Turkish drummes',[2] were always to impress themselves on Western observers. Most Turkish forces of the period did, in fact, include other types of soldier, if only for the reason that there were other western Asian peoples in their ranks. The foot-soldiers were often mentioned by Arab historians, although their military function is never made very clear. Certainly they were required in sieges and for camp and commissariat duties.[3] They proved their worth when fighting in broken country, and when the army of Damascus went out to defend the city against the Franks in 1126, a chosen foot-soldier accompanied each horseman into battle.[4] But generally the infantry was mentioned only because that of the losing side was massacred.[5] There are as well references to horsemen who were not armed with the bow.[6]

It was, however, the tactics of the horse archers which always caused the Franks the greatest difficulty. These methods had been analysed in the Byzantine military writings,[7] and have been described by modern historians, who have made considerable use of two short and similar descriptions, one of which was a free translation into thirteenth-century French of the text of William of Tyre,[8] while the other appears in a late version of the continuation of William's History.[9] Although they did not say so, both

---

[1] *Anon.* p. 44; Fulcher, p. 335; WT, pp. 131, 529; *HEF*, p. 84; *Itin.* p. 117; *HP*, p. 156.

[2] Fuller, *Historie of the Holy Warre* (1640), p. 25; BD, p. 199.

[3] Cahen, *Syrie du Nord*, p. 195.   [4] Fulcher, p. 478.

[5] Gibb in IQ, p. 40.

[6] WT, p. 925, in his account of the battle of al-Babein, says that Shirkuh 'habebat Turcorum duodecim millia, ex quibus novem millia loricis galeisque tegebantur, reliqua tria millia arcubus tantum et sagittis utebantur'. He also refers to the weapons of the Arabs 'lanceis pro more utentium'. *Itin.* p. 262 notes the same division at Arsuf in 1191.

[7] Oman, I, p. 206; Anna, pp. 397–8.

[8] WT, p. 131: 'A la premiere venue, li Turc trestrent as noz si espessement que pluie ne grelle ne poist fere greigneur oscurté, si que molt en i ot de navrez des noz; et quant li premier orent touz vuidiez leur carquois et tout tret, la seconde route vint après où plus avoit encore de chevaliers et commencierent à traire plus espessement que l'on ne porroit croire.'

[9] WT, cont. in *RHC, Hist. occ.* II, p. 606: 'Il [li Sarrazin] aceintrent les noz tout entor et traistrent si grant planté de saietes et de quarriaux que pluie ne grelle ne feist mie si grant oscurté, si que moult i ot de navrez de nos genz et

Oman and Grousset appear to have used this passage as a basis for their own statements of Turkish methods;[1] but neither these nor any other students of the subject have given a comprehensive statement of Saljuq tactics. The description by Delpech is perhaps the best available.[2] He, too, principally relied on the passage just quoted; but because he attached too literal a meaning to the words of the chronicler, the picture he gives is rigidly diagrammatic and therefore unreal. The methods of war adopted by the Franks in Syria were partly determined by the traditional Saljuq tactics, and it is important that these should be correctly stated. The explanation given in the following paragraphs is based on the accounts of Franks who, in the twelfth century, faced Turkish armies on the battlefield; the only important exception will be Albert of Aix, who, although well informed, was never himself in Syria, and whose evidence will be used with caution. It is not certain whether William of Tyre ever went on campaign, but his knowledge of Syria and of all her peoples and their customs was greater than that of any other historian of the age.

The effective part of a Turkish army, like that of the Franks, fought on horseback, but it is clear from all contemporary accounts that the Turks were quicker and more flexible in manœuvre than the Franks. This was ascribed to the pace and agility of their horses and to the lightness of their weapons.[3] Their principal weapon was the bow, but they carried as well shield, lance, sword, and club.[4] There is good evidence that the lance and shield were lighter than those of the Franks. Whenever they were not too heavily outnumbered, the Franks held an advantage in hand-to-hand combat and the adoption by some Arabs of a longer lance, recorded by Usamah, may be significant.[5] The Turkish

---

de leur chevaux. Quant les premierez routes des Turz orent vuidié touz leur carquoiz et tout trait, il se retraistrent arrierez, mes les secondes routes vindrent tentost arrierez ou il avoit encores assez plus de Turz. Cil traistrent encorez plus espessement assez que n'avoient fait li autre.'

[1] Oman, I, p. 274; Grousset, I, p. 33.   [2] Delpech, I, pp. 358–60.

[3] There is evidence for this from observers of different generations in the twelfth century. See RA, p. 243, '. . . quia velocissimos equos habebant, et expediti nec graves armis aliis quam sagittis. . .; Itin. p. 247; Est. 5647 et seq.; RC, p. 628.

[4] See list of Turkish arms given in Itin. and Est. ibid.; HEF, p. 87; Galt. p. 88.

[5] Usamah, pp. 131–2.

lance appears to have been even lighter. It was not, like that of the Franks, 'quercus aut fraxinus',[1] but 'arundineum hastile cuspide ferrata'.[2] Nor was their shield the long kite-shaped defence of the Franks. It appears to have been a small round target, which was a slighter defence, but had the advantage of lightness.[3] The Turks, helped by their horses and weapons, were more mobile than the Franks, and they made four principal uses of that mobility. First, it enabled them to remain at a distance from their enemy and to choose the moment at which they would close with him. In Europe the Franks were used to mounted opponents, but on the battlefield these, like themselves, used the weight and speed of their horses to add impetus to the all-important charge, which was fully effective only against a solid enemy formation. The mounted Turkish archers provided no such target.[4] If a charge were essayed against them, they were ready to retreat: if the attempt were given up, they themselves attacked once more. This characteristic was noted by Latin writers at both the beginning and end of the century. The Turks might be scattered, but always they returned to the fight;[5] now they faced the enemy, now they turned away;[6] they thought it no less creditable to retreat than to pursue;[7] they were like flies who could be beaten off but not driven away.[8]

Second, they employed the device of the feigned retreat. This manœuvre was practised in feudal Europe before the First Crusade, and had helped to decide the battle of Hastings;[9] it is said

[1] RC, p. 631.   [2] Itin. p. 247; Est. 5652, 'de cane bien aceree'.

[3] RC (pp. 621, 640, 645) draws a contrast between the Frankish scuta and the Turkish pelta.

[4] WT (p. 131) speaks of the Turks at Dorylaeum taking action 'ut [francorum] impetus eluderent'. On p. 743 he describes the predicament of the Germans attempting to cross Asia Minor in 1146: 'quibus comprehendendi adversarios nulla erat facultas'. WT was the eyewitness of neither event, but he had every opportunity of knowing the Turks and their military methods, and his clear description of Turkish elusiveness is therefore important.

[5] RA, p. 243.   [6] Fulcher, p. 448.   [7] Itin. p. 50.

[8] Itin. p. 247; Est. 5647–68. William of Tyre, writing of the march of the Second Crusade across Asia Minor in 1147, gives an excellent account of the same tactics (WT, pp. 742–3). His description was founded on the accounts of eyewitnesses, 'ut asserunt qui praesentes fuerunt' (ibid.). Odo of Deuil, an eyewitness of the same events, describes the Turks as 'docti et faciles ad fugam', and says that King Louis VII 'pacem non posset habere, nec pugnam' (Odo, p. 65).

[9] Stenton, Anglo-Saxon England, p. 587. But see W. Spatz, Die Schlacht von Hastings, pp. 55–62.

to have been used on occasions by the Syrian Franks.[1] The Turks used the manœuvre constantly, and in a number of different ways. On occasions their retreat lasted for many days, and was designed both to weary the Franks and to draw them from their bases.[2] Again, it was used as the bait in a prepared ambush.[3] A body of horsemen sufficiently few to invite annihilation was used to provoke attack. When the Franks moved to attack them, the decoys drew the pursuers towards the main body, which remained concealed until the decisive moment. According to the scale on which it was applied, such a plan might gain a slight success, or win a battle.[4]

Third, they used their mobility to attack the flanks and rear of the enemy. Whenever they could they compassed him about like bees,[5] they attacked him 'undique',[6] they attempted to surround him 'quasi corona',[7] like a girdle or the halo of the full moon at its setting,[8] like a globe around its axis,[9] or as if they were besieging a city.[10] If they could not surround, they outflanked, 'ad instar lune corniculate'.[11] Such tactics were sometimes the result of numerical superiority, but they were always an essential part of the Turkish way of warfare, and were always employed in whatever number they appeared.[12] The Franks had always to look over

---

[1] According to RC (p. 715), it was used by Tancred at the battle of Artah in 1105. WT (p. 582) describes an occasion when Baldwin II trapped part of the garrison of Ascalon by the same method. Although military historians take such movements for granted, to issue the necessary orders and then to control the retreat cannot have been easy, and we scarcely know how it was done.

[2] Fulcher, p. 421 (of events in 1110), 'et quum astutia taediosa, per dies plurimos, nolentes praeliari nostros fatigare studuissent'. ME (p. 93) has the same comment on the same campaign: 'Les Turcs reculèrent au delà de Khar'an (Harran) afin d'attirer les Chrétiens, par un strategème, dans un pays inconnu à ceux-ci.' For other examples see Fulcher, p. 423; RC, p. 710.

[3] There are constant references to this stratagem in the writings of Latin and Arab observers. Typical examples in IQ, pp. 242, 331; IA, II, pp. 31–2; Usamah, pp. 74, 85, 87, 133; BD, pp. 127, 202. That the idea was familiar to the Franks when they first came to Syria is shown by *Anon.* pp. 8, 16, 68.

[4] As at al-Sannabra in 1113 (Fulcher, p. 426) and in the fight on 1 May 1187 (*Libellus*, p. 213).

[5] *HEF*, p. 87, quoting Psalm cxviii, 12.   [6] *Anon.* pp. 90, 154.
[7] *Ep. mor.* p. 175.   [8] IQ, p. 138.   [9] IA, p. 685.   [10] WT, p. 772.
[11] *HEF*, p. 84.

[12] RA, p. 244: 'Etenim id moris pugnandi apud Turcos est, ut, licet pauciores sint, tamen semper nitantur hostes cingere suos.' Many other Latin observers record the same characteristic. Typical descriptive words used are, besides 'cingere':

(*a*) circumcingere, *Anon.* pp. 46, 72, 90, 154;

their shoulders. It was a form of attack to which their military experience in Europe had not accustomed them, and against which in the East they had to take special tactical measures.

The fourth use made by the Turks of their mobility was to attack an enemy and to force him to fight on the march. This is possible only when the attacker is able to move faster and further than his opponent. It was a method of warfare new and particularly vexatious to the Franks, who liked before fighting to marshal their squadrons and to undertake the contest in good order.[1] The principal dangers arose from the Turkish habit of attacking 'a tergo'. When they attacked a marching column they always made their main effort against its rear. In such circumstances the problems of the commander in maintaining control are far greater than if the enemy concentrates his efforts on the vanguard. Eyewitnesses have left accounts of the employment of these tactics against the columns of the Second Crusade when they attempted to cross Asia Minor in 1147,[2] and against those of Frederick Barbarossa which undertook the same march in 1190.[3] In Syria itself the Franks had many times to counter the same form of attack,[4] and as a consequence careful attention was paid to the organization and leadership of the rear-guard.[5]

After their mobility, the second tactical characteristic of the Turks was their archery. They used the bow from the saddle, and

---

(b) accingere, RA, pp. 247, 260; Fulcher, p. 478;

(c) circumdare, RA, p. 295; HEF, pp. 84, 85, 87; Libellus, p. 223;

(d) vallare, WT, pp. 718, 772, 1094;

(e) circumvallare, Fulcher, p. 335;

(f) concludere, Itin. p. 117;

(g) circumsedere, Libellus, p. 213.

[1] See Chapter v below.

[2] Odo, p. 65; WT, p. 748, who had his information from eyewitnesses.

[3] HEF, p. 74, 'cum Turci extremam partem Imperatoris incursarent'. For attack 'a tergo' see HEF, p. 80; Ep. mor. p. 177; HP, p. 158.

[4] The attack on the rear of the Christian line of march was one of the most important features of the battles of Hattin and Arsuf. See Chapter v below. See also the account of the attack of the Frankish column between Acre and Haifa on 12 November 1190; Itin. p. 118; below pp. 161–2.

[5] In Asia Minor, 1146; WT, p. 747. Baldwin III's retreat from Aintab, 1150; WT, p. 788. Hattin, 1187; Libellus, pp. 222–3. Arsuf, 1191; Est. 6148; Itin. p. 260.

According to AA, p. 565, the expeditions which attempted to cross Asia Minor in 1101 were attacked 'a tergo', and the rear-guard was the place of danger.

shot without halting or dismounting. As a result they were able to combine their archery with those tactical uses of their mobility which have already been described. Even in retreat they were able to turn in the saddle and to shoot at their pursuers.[1] From the frequent use by Latin writers of words like 'pluvia', 'imber', 'grando', and 'nubes' to describe the volume of Turkish archery,[2] it is probable that a high rate of fire was maintained. The bow and arrow appear to have been light weapons. The arrows penetrated Frankish armour, but often without wounding the body of the wearer.[3] The image of the porcupine was sometimes used to describe the appearance of men or animals who had been under Turkish attack.[4]

The tactical use made of this archery was to destroy the cohesion of the enemy, and this could be achieved by inflicting upon him the loss not only of men, but of horses. Eyewitnesses recorded that the various crusading expeditions which crossed Asia Minor during the twelfth century were always gravely weakened by the loss of horses.[5] Forage and water were sometimes lacking;[6] horseflesh was required as food by the pilgrims;[7] but in addition many horses were killed by the Turkish arrows.[8] This danger remained whenever the Franks took the field during the twelfth century. The Franks relied for victory in battle on the mounted charge, and the Turks were well aware of the value of destroying their horses.[9]

[1] In the words of RC, p. 715, 'illi facile terga vertunt, sperantes, ut est moris, fugiendo gyrare, gyrando sagittare'.

[2] E.g. *Anon.* p. 84; Fulcher, pp. 335, 478; Odo, p. 65; WT, pp. 131, 196, 721, 1040; *Libellus*, pp. 242–3; *Est.* 4047–50, 6067, 6283.

[3] Odo, p. 69, said of Louis VII: 'sub lorica tutatus est a sagittis' (*sc.* Turcorum).

[4] WT, p. 788; *Est.* 11630; AS, p. 269; *Itin.* p. 423.

[5] *Anon.* p. 78; HEp. pp. 157, 169; Odo, p. 69, 74. HEF, pp. 43, 74; *Ep. mor.* p. 176; AA, p. 427.

[6] Odo, p. 71; *Ep. mor.* p. 174; HP, p. 155.

[7] HEp. p. 159, 163, 166; Odo., p. 73; HEF, pp. 79, 81, 83; *Ep. mor.* p. 176; *Itin.* p. 168.

[8] RA, p. 243; WT, p. 131, 1052; Odo, p. 69; *Ep. mor.* pp. 174–5; *Itin.* pp. 118, 263; IQ, p. 199; IA, p. 683.

[9] While he was harassing Richard's march from Acre to Jaffa (Aug.–Sept. 1191) Saladin showed close interest in the casualties inflicted by his archers on the Franks' horses; BD, pp. 249, 262. See also IQ, p. 199; AS, pp. 271–2. The value of inflicting such casualties was well understood by Byzantine commanders; Anna, pp. 129, 185.

Besides the infliction of loss, the arrows imposed a constant nervous strain on the troops at which they were directed. The most certain method of neutralizing any hostile missile weapon is to come to close quarters with the soldiers who are using them;[1] therefore, the Turks by their archery could always count on provoking the Franks to charge, and so to abandon their formation.[2]

The mobility and archery of the Turks alone were usually insufficient to give them victory. By such means they weakened the enemy, but his final defeat on the battlefield could be achieved only by the fight at close quarters with lance, sword, and club. The passages from the *Eracles*, parts of which have already been quoted,[3] show the Turks, when they saw the opportunity of coming to close quarters, hanging their bows from their shoulders and charging in on the Franks.[4] The original Latin of William of Tyre gave the same picture;[5] and it may be said once more that although the archbishop was writing long after the event, he had an unrivalled knowledge of Syria and her peoples. If he therefore wrote down such a detail, even if it did not happen at Dorylaeum, it was probably a normal Turkish custom.

That the Turks began their fights at bowshot range, and later, to force a decision, came to close quarters was observed by Latin eyewitnesses throughout the century. In their accounts of Dorylaeum both Fulcher and Ralph portrayed the Turks attacking first with arrows, then with lances and swords.[6] The same two

---

[1] Delbrück, III, p. 304.

[2] Latin commanders had sometimes to take strong measures to ensure that their men resisted such provocation. Below, pp. 129-30. For evidence of Saladin's intention to provoke the Franks to an untimely charge, see BD, pp. 75, 252, 262; and IA, II, p. 31.

[3] Above, p. 76, nn. 8 and 9.

[4] *RHC, Hist. occ.* II, p. 606: 'Li Tur virent que nostre gent et leur chevaux estoient moult blecié et a grant meschief, si pandirent isnellement leurs arz aus senestrez braz esouz leur rouelles et leur coururent sus moult cruelement as masces et as espees.'

[5] WT, p. 132: 'invalescebant igitur hostium agmina, et nostris pene deficientibus, arcu ab humeris dependente et ejus neglecto officio, gladiis instant cominus.'

[6] Fulcher (p. 335) refers to Turks 'pluviam sagittarum vehementer emittentes', and later, when the Christians were in confusion, 'super nos irruebant'. RC, p. 622: 'Quum subito irruunt, primo sagittis, mox ensibus saevientes Turci.' Fulcher was an eyewitness. RC received his information from Tancred, and later had personal experience of Syria.

stages can be seen at the Ager Sanguinis and Hab,[1] at Hattin,[2] and at Arsuf,[3] and many references to them can be found in the records of the period.[4] The Turks were in no hurry to close with the enemy, for the reason that they wished first to establish whatever superiority they could by means of fire and movement. The Turkish tactics were a natural expression of the common sense maxim that, before irrevocably committing itself to battle, an army should gain every possible advantage over its opponent. Sometimes they gained that advantage by surprise, and preliminary action was unnecessary;[5] or the enemy forced them against their will to immediate close combat.[6] Usually, however, the Turks remained at a distance, retaining their freedom of choice to develop or break off the battle, committing themselves to close combat only when they had created a favourable opportunity by fire and movement.

IV. EGYPT

The Latin kingdom appears always to have been in greater danger from the Turkish than the Egyptian rulers, yet in the first decade of the twelfth century the hold of the Franks on Palestine was more than once threatened by counter-attack from Egypt. With its wealth[7] and well-organized machinery of government,[8] the Fatimid state was potentially a more formidable adversary to the Franks than was the Saljuq empire under the successors of

[1] Galt. pp. 87–8, 103. [2] *Ernoul*, pp. 168–70. [3] *Itin.* p. 265.

[4] E.g. RA, p. 244: Fulcher, p. 472; WT, p. 748; *Itin.* p. 52.

[5] E.g. Nur al-Din's attack on Baldwin III at Lake Huleh in 1157; WT, p. 841; AS, p. 89; IQ, p. 336.

[6] Bohemond was able to do this in defeating the attempt to relieve Antioch on 9 February 1098; see below, p. 171. At 'Azaz in 1125 there was no preliminary archery; Fulcher, p. 472.

[7] Egypt owed its wealth to its agriculture, industry, and above all, to its commerce; see Wiet, *L'Égypte arabe*, pp. 305–7; Heyd, *Histoire du commerce du Levant*, I, p. 167. For a contemporary description of the wealth and commercial activity of Alexandria, WT, pp. 930–1.

[8] In ancient and Byzantine times Egypt had been governed by a strong and centralized state authority (Rostovtzeff, *Journal of Egyptian Archaeology*, vol. VI, pp. 161–71) and the tradition was not broken by the Arab conquest (Moss, *Birth of the Middle Ages*, pp. 163–4; Lane-Poole, *History of Egypt in the Middle Ages*, p. 18). For the organization of government departments in Fatimid times see Lane-Poole, *Hist. of Egypt*, pp. 154–7, for a résumé of Kalkashandi's description.

Malik Shah; and since in 1099 Jerusalem, southern Palestine, and the coast towns as far north as Gabala constituted an Egyptian province, the Fatimids had the incentive to recover their losses.

The ability of their government to expel the Franks depended on the degree of the authority enjoyed by its head, who, by the end of the eleventh century, was the vizier. If that office were in incompetent hands, or in dispute, government, and therefore military policy, was likely to be paralysed by civil war. If, on the other hand, the vizier effectively controlled government and army, he was able to direct the immense resources of Egypt against enemies beyond her borders.

Between 1094 and 1121 Egypt was ruled by al-Afdal, a strong vizier who exercised full authority. For ten years he applied a positive policy to the new situation created by the Latin conquest. After his failure in 1097 to negotiate a partition of Syria with the Franks, he organized almost annually between 1099 and 1107 a series of major expeditions which entered Palestine by way of Ascalon and the coastal plain. Except in 1102 these armies were either defeated in battle, or fell back with nothing accomplished. The one decisive victory of 1102 was not exploited, and after 1107 al-Afdal allowed the effort against the Franks to dwindle to minor raids by the garrison of Ascalon.

After al-Afdal's assassination in 1121 his successor sent an army to attack Jaffa, but that expedition was defeated at Yibneh (Ibelin) as decisively as had been its predecessors. From that time until Saladin became ruler of the country in 1169, Egypt ceased to be a danger to the Latin kingdom. The direction of government was disputed between caliph and vizier, or between rival claimants for the vizier's office.[1] These conflicts divided the loyalties of the army, and the result was civil war.[2] With chaos in the highest ranks of government Egypt, unable to attack other states, was, from 1163 onwards, attacked from Muslim and Latin Syria. In 1169 she became a province of the Zangid, and five years later the foundation of the Ayubid empire. Her series of un-

---

[1] For a summary of events, see Wiet, *L'Égypte arabe*, pp. 267–91. For a personal account of a typical episode in these troubles, see Usamah, pp. 44–54. He played a leading part in an important palace revolution.

[2] Wiet, *L'Égypte arabe*, pp. 273 *et seq.*; Wüstenfeld, *Geschichte der Fatimiden Chalifen*, III, pp. 81, 87.

successful counter-attacks, followed by serious internal divisions, therefore prevented Egypt, between 1107 and 1170, being the danger she might have been to the Latin states.

A further reason was the tactical superiority of the Franks in war. The Egyptian armies of the period sometimes included a Turkish contingent,[1] but in the main they were recruited from Arabs, Berbers, and Sudanese. Many medieval and modern writers have not always made their readers aware of the wide differences in history, race, culture, and language which divided the Arabs from the Turks.[2] These differences extended to the military methods of the two peoples. The Arabs fought on horseback, but they were not, like the Turks, horsemen who made full use of their mobility. Their equipment seems to have resembled that of the Franks[3] and, like them, they fought at close quarters with lance and sword.[4] Archery in the Egyptian armies was provided by the foot-soldiers recruited in the Sudan. These were the 'Aethiopes' mentioned by Fulcher as part of the Fatimid armies against which he saw action,[5] and that they fought on foot as archers was recorded by Latin observers present at the battle of Ascalon in 1099, and at Arsuf in 1191.[6]

It has been noted above that military historians before Oman made no distinction between Turks and Arabs as soldiers. In reconstructing the battles fought between Latin and Fatimid armies they established that the Egyptian troops sometimes outflanked their opponents, and since this was also a Turkish man-

---

[1] As at the battle of Ramla in 1105; see below, p. 177.

[2] For medieval writers, Prutz, *Kulturgeschichte*, pp. 59, 509. In modern times some military historians have overlooked the differences between the two peoples. Even Heermann, whose attention to detail was so close and exact, gives no indication that he understood the difference or its importance; see *Gefechtsführung*, p. 120. Köhler briefly notes the difference in vol. III, pt. 3, p. 138, but makes no further reference to it, and it is not made by Delpech. The first military historian to emphasize the matter was Oman, I, p. 289.

[3] For difficulties of mutual recognition, see Usamah, p. 173.

[4] This appears very clearly in Usamah's memoirs. An Arab himself, he knew no Turkish, appears never to have fought with the bow, did fight with the lance, was interested in its deportment, and told many anecdotes of famous lance thrusts; Usamah, pp. 69–70, 76–80, 132.

[5] Fulcher, pp. 362, 411.

[6] AA, p. 490. Albert was at pains to mention that he had his information about the battle of Ascalon from those who were present. For Arsuf see *Itin.* p. 262.

œuvre, the historians appear to have concluded that all oriental Muslims fought in this way. Fortunately evidence is available which makes it possible to correct this judgement. The Turkish manœuvre of encirclement was natural to a race of mounted archers, who, when in contact with the enemy, never remained stationary but used their mobility to assail the enemy from all sides. They did this in all circumstances, even when they were fewer than the enemy.[1] Mounted archers did not form part of the Fatimid armies; in the battles fought between 1099 and 1123, with one exception, there is no evidence of their presence. The exception was provided by the battle of Ramla in 1105, when a Turkish contingent attacked the Franks in the traditional manner;[2] but it is known that on this occasion Tughtagin of Damascus had sent a contingent to help the Egyptians,[3] and it is almost certain that the Turks described by Fulcher were those whom Tughtagin had sent. The fact that on other occasions Egyptian forces outflanked the Latins was a consequence not of mounted archery, but of numerical superiority. 'Et quia multitudo magna erant, gentem nostram undique giraverunt' said Fulcher of the Fatimid attack outside Jaffa in 1102;[4] and in the other battles fought in the same area the Egyptians were able to outflank the Franks for the same reason.

A further proof of the differences between the Turkish and Arab soldiers was given by the anonymous author of the *Gesta Francorum*. He was himself a fighting man,[5] who appreciated and admired the military qualities of the Turks,[6] and who has left short and vivid descriptions of their tactics.[7] When he came to tell of his first encounter with the Fatimid troops at Ascalon, he was clearly describing a very different opponent: 'Pagani vero stabant parati ad bellum;[8] and a few lines later he used the same verb: 'Stabant autem inimici Dei. . .'[9] The enemy had neither mounted archers nor mobility.

With a mass of bowmen on foot, and horsemen who were capable of awaiting attack, the Fatimid armies provided, as the Turks never did, a solid target for the most powerful tactical

---

[1] RA, p. 244.   [2] Fulcher, p. 413.   [3] IQ, p. 71.
[4] Fulcher, p. 404.   [5] Bréhier, in *Anon.* p. iii.   [6] *Anon.* p. 50.
[7] *Ibid.* p. 46: 'Turci undique jam erant circumcingentes nos dimicando et jaculando et mirabiliter longe lateque sagittando.'
[8] *Anon.* p. 212.   [9] *Anon.* p. 214.

weapon of the Franks: the charge of the mailed and mounted knights. From accounts of the battle of Ascalon we know that the Egyptians were then vanquished 'pro solo impetu nostro'.[1] In other engagements 'dederunt fugam repentinam'[2] and 'continuo in fugam moti sunt'.[3] Such battles were therefore short; they did not last beyond 'horae parvae spatio'[4] and at Yibneh the battle 'non longa hora protrahitur'.[5] For these reasons the Franks never, until the reign of Saladin, feared the Egyptian as they did the armies from Muslim Syria and Mesopotamia. They admired the military qualities of the Turks, but it seems that both Franks and Turks coveted the wealth of Egypt and underrated its men.[6]

[1] *HEp.* p. 172. RA, p. 305 uses the phrase 'uno impetu', in the same connexion, of the same battle.
[2] Fulcher, p. 414.   [3] Fulcher, p. 451.   [4] Fulcher, p. 363.
[5] Fulcher, p. 451.
[6] In describing the Egyptian allies of Amalric in the campaign which the king fought in Egypt against Shirkuh in 1167, WT (p. 925) refers to 'Egyptiis vilibus et effeminatis, qui potius impedimento et oneri essent quam utilitati'. Note the sentiments ascribed by WT (p. 903) to Shirkuh, and by IA (p. 554) to the Franks who persuaded Amalric to attack Egypt in 1168.

CHAPTER V

THE LATIN ARMIES

I. RECRUITMENT

DURING the twelfth century the armies organized by the rulers of western Europe were based on the service owed by feudal tenants of the military class and, in an emergency, on the old public obligation of every free man to serve when required. The forces raised by either means were defective for a number of reasons which will be discussed later, and it was found expedient to supplement or to replace them in part by paid troops. All three sources of recruitment, feudal host, *arrière ban*, and mercenaries, were used in Latin Syria, and to these were added groups of pilgrims and the increasingly important contingents of the military Orders.

La Monte has rightly said that 'the knights who owed service for fiefs—either in land or money—formed the backbone of the army of the Latin kingdom'.[1] The original crusaders brought with them from Europe feudal institutions; therefore those laymen to whom land was granted by the ruler held it on condition of rendering him certain services, of which one was to appear in arms at the appointed time and place to follow the lord on campaign. If the fief owed the service of more than one knight, the tenant took to the muster the number at which his lands had been assessed. All this is made clear in the writings of the jurists, who discuss at length the military service due from vassals, and their accounts are confirmed by charters of the twelfth century which record enfeoffments for knight service.[2]

The records which have survived from medieval Syria do not, however, yield information about the exact number of knights available, nor do they give any clear picture of military feudalism in action. From the contemporary states of western Europe

---

[1] La Monte, *Feudal Monarchy in the Latin Kingdom of Jerusalem, 1100-1291*, p. 158.

[2] For examples of such charters see *Reg.* nos. 447, 465, 517.

administrative documents have survived which bring the system
to life: they reveal the numbers of knights and other troops available, the occasion and manner of their summons, and the duration
of their service during a particular period.[1]

The only comparable information in respect of Latin Syria
is that given by a jurist of the thirteenth century, John of Ibelin.
In his *Livre des Assises de la Haute Cour* he gives details of the
knight service due from the military vassals of the kings of
Jerusalem.[2] The *servitia debita* range from the hundred knights
due from the three greatest baronies to the personal service of
individual tenants. The total is 675 knights.[3]

The list is not contemporary, since Ibelin did not write his
book until 1265.[4] Any information which he gives about the
earlier kingdom must, however, be treated with respect, if only
for the reason that he was a member of a feudal family which
played a distinguished part in the affairs of Jerusalem (and subsequently in those of Cyprus) from the middle years of the twelfth
century. John himself was count of Ascalon and Jaffa. His evidence on knight service gains further authority from its inclusion
of detail which can be checked and corroborated from charters of
the twelfth century. He mentions many tenants by name who
appear as witnesses to documents of the earlier period, and particularly in the years 1170–86.[5] There seems no reason to doubt

---

[1] For studies of military organization based on such records see H. M.
Chew, *The English Ecclesiastical Tenants-in-chief and Knight Service*;
J. E. Morris, *The Welsh Wars of Edward I*; E. Audouin, *Essai sur l'armée
royale au temps de Philippe-Auguste*.

[2] John of Ibelin, *RHC, Lois*, I, pp. 422–6.

[3] Both John of Ibelin himself, and the editor of the *Assises*, give this total
as 577 knights. This number has since been repeated by Prutz, Dodu,
Bréhier, Chalandon, La Monte, Runciman, and all other writers on the subject. If the figures are added, more than one answer is possible. For example,
Ibelin says that the number of knights due from tenants in the city of Acre is
eighty, but addition of the separate items gives the answer as seventy-six.
But, however the figures are added, their total cannot be less than 647. If
discrepancies in detail are overlooked, the total is 675.

[4] Grandeclaude, *Étude critique*, p. 88.

[5] For example, Phelippe le Rous who appears in Ibelin's list on p. 422
is also mentioned as Philippus Rufus or Ruffus in *Reg.* nos. 477 (of 1170),
517 (of 1174), 525 (of 1175), and 608 (of 1181). Lorens de Francleuc (*Ibelin*,
p. 423) appears as a witness in *Reg.* nos. 579 (1180) and 608 (1181). Ansel
Babin (*Ibelin*, p. 423) is Anselinus Babini, witness to *Reg.* nos. 503 (1173),
536 (1176), 653 (1186). For further examples see La Monte, *Feudal Monarchy*,
p. 148.

that John gives a substantially accurate statement of the knight
service due to the Latin kings during the decade before Saladin's
conquest of Jerusalem.

The number 675 does not represent the maximum force available. Rey noted long ago that certain fiefs were omitted from
Ibelin's list, and more recently Beyer has identified a number of
these omissions.[1] The author refers to the service which had
once been due from Banyas and Subeibe before their loss to Nur
al-Din in 1164. He is ignorant of the quantity of that service, and
it is not included in his figures. Nor is the contingent of a hundred
knights which he mentions in an earlier chapter as the service due
from the counts of Tripoli. John probably omits it because it did
not join the feudal host of Jerusalem unless it was specially summoned.

For the principality of Antioch and the county of Edessa even
these slight indications of feudal strength are lacking. It seems
reasonable to suppose that the knight service of Antioch was comparable with that of Jerusalem.[2] Some figures quoted by Walter,
the well-informed chancellor of Prince Roger of Antioch, are not
without interest. He was present when Roger's army was defeated
by Il Ghazi on 28 June 1119, and he states that on that day the
Franks numbered 700 knights and 3000 foot-soldiers.[3] No help
had been received from the other Christian states; and if it is
reasonable to suppose that the whole strength of the principality
had been mustered to meet invasion, then the knight service of
Antioch at that time may have been about 700. But after the permanent losses of territory to Zanki and Nur al-Din during the
middle years of the century it is likely that the number was considerably reduced; and with the disappearance of the county of
Edessa during the years 1144–50, the feudal military resources of
the Franks became more abundant in southern than in northern
Syria.

John of Ibelin states that military service was rendered to the
kings of Jerusalem not only by individual feudal tenants but by
ecclesiastical and urban communities. These owed the service
not of knights, but of sergeants, who were summoned not for any
and every campaign, but only 'quant le grant besoin est sur la

---

[1] Rey, *Colonies*, pp. 110–11; Beyer in *ZDPV*, LXVII, 201.
[2] Cahen, *Syrie du Nord*, p. 328.   [3] Galt. p. 88.

terre dou reiaume de Jerusalem'. In such an emergency the patriarch of Jerusalem, the canons of the Holy Sepulchre, the community of burgesses in Jerusalem and in Acre were each required to send 500 sergeants to the muster. These were the largest single contingents demanded; a more common number was the 150 owed by the archbishops of Nazareth and Tyre, the bishop of Acre, and the abbot of Mount Sion. The sum of such service due from the whole kingdom is given by Ibelin as 5025 sergeants.[1]

He does not state whether these sergeants were required to serve mounted or on foot; modern writers have assumed either or both kinds of service without giving reasons for their decision.[2] It seems more probable that they were foot-soldiers. A man fitted out to fight on horseback was an expensive piece of equipment. Despite the wealth of the Church and the bourgeoisie, and allowing for the fact that the service of two sergeants was commonly regarded as equal to that of one knight,[3] it seems altogether improbable that they would be required to provide so high a multiple of the knights owed by the individual tenants-in-chief. The fact, too, that these contingents were summoned only in an emergency indicates that they were likely to be composed of occasional soldiers who were insufficiently trained to fight mounted.

It may also be allowed that similar but better-known military arrangements in Capetian France throw some light on this dark matter. The contents of two important administrative documents have survived from the reign of Philip Augustus. The first, known as the *Prisia Servientum*, is a record of the sergeants due from various communities on the royal demesne; the second is an account of the French king's receipts and expenditure during the year 1202–3. The original roll was destroyed during the eighteenth century, but it was fortunately transcribed and published by Brussel.[4] These two records combine to establish many

---

[1] All facts quoted in this paragraph are to be found in *Ibelin*, pp. 426–7.

[2] Cahen, *Syrie du Nord*, p. 328, says that they were mounted; Chalandon, *Première Croisade*, p. 324, says 'Les sergents formaient l'infanterie. . .'; so too Rey, *Colonies*, p. 110, and Grousset, *L'Empire du Levant*, p. 285.

[3] For evidence of this common equation see Chew, *Ecclesiastical Tenants-in-chief*, p. 91; Morris, *Welsh Wars*, pp. 44–5.

[4] N. Brussel, *Nouvel Examen de l'usage général des fiefs en France*, Paris. At the end of volume II of the edition of 1750, pp. cxxxix–ccx, Brussel printed the 'gros rouleau en la Chambre des Comptes' which he called

details about the rendering of sergeant service to the Capetian kings.[1] They show that the sergeants, who, like those of Jerusalem, heavily outnumbered the knights, were expected to serve on foot, and it seems likely that the same was true in the Latin East. The Syrian records, however, do not provide the evidence which could reveal the practical value of this kind of service. It is not clear how the phrase 'grant besoin' was interpreted, so that the occasions on which all or some of the sergeants were summoned must remain uncertain.[2] It may be presumed that they were called out during major invasions of the kingdom, like those undertaken by Saladin during the years 1182–7, and the recorded numbers of *pedites* who took the field during those years do something to confirm this view.[3]

There remained the possibility of going beyond the available feudal service and of summoning every able-bodied man to the muster. There were occasions, as La Monte shows,[4] on which such a summons was made; invasion on a large scale,[5] an attack on a city which promised rich spoils,[6] the rapid construction of a castle in the neighbourhood of the enemy.[7] But evidence on the

---

'Compte Général des Revenus tant ordinaires qu'extraordinaires du Roi pendant l'an 1202'. Brussel's version was reproduced and the whole document analysed by F. Lot and R. Fawtier, *Le Premier Budget de la monarchie française.* (Fascicule 259 de la Bibliothèque de l'École des Hautes Études.)

[1] The standard work on this subject is that by E. Audouin, *Essai sur l'armée royale au temps de Philippe-Auguste.* It is based on the author's skilful and productive researches in the two documents mentioned above.

[2] La Monte, *Feudal Monarchy,* makes a number of confident statements in a paragraph which begins at the foot of p. 158, but does not support them with convincing evidence. His reference to the 150 *fideles* throws no light on the matter. The heavy Fatimid counter-attacks of the years 1099–1105 created acute military crisis in a state too newly founded for the formation of fixed laws and customs. Baldwin called on the help of fighting men wherever he could find them.

[3] In the campaign of 1183 the Franks are said to have put into the field 15,000 foot; WT, p. 1122; AS, p. 245. At Hattin in 1187 there were probably about 10,000 foot. Baldwin, *Raymond III of Tripolis,* pp. 102–4.

[4] La Monte, *Feudal Monarchy,* p. 159.

[5] *Ernoul,* p. 156. The *arrière ban* was summoned in 1187.

[6] The *populus* took part in the attack on Damascus in 1126 and on Ascalon in 1153; WT, pp. 582, 795. See also the part they played in encouraging Baldwin III in ˙˙47 to break the treaty with Damascus and to attempt the acquisition of Bosra; WT, p. 718.

[7] Construction of Bait Gibrin (WT, p. 639); of a castle at Gaza (WT, p. 778); of Tell es-Safi (WT, p. 698), 'et vocatis artificibus simul et populo universo necessaria ministrante'.

use of *universus populus* is too scanty to allow analysis of its incidence or of the conditions which governed its use.

It is a commonplace that the manpower yielded by the feudal levy was never sufficient for the military purposes of the Latin rulers, who had therefore to take mercenaries into their service. Both Dodu and La Monte referred to this development, although neither reviewed the available evidence for the twelfth century.[1] During the age of feudal institutions, the soldier who served for pay never disappeared from historical records. From all parts of Europe there is evidence of the use of mercenary troops during the tenth and eleventh centuries, and in the second half of the twelfth century they were used on an ever-increasing scale by most European rulers.[2] These same generalizations may be applied to Latin Syria.

The first mercenary in crusading records was Tancred, who during the siege of Antioch in 1098, was paid by the Latin princes in order to garrison the convent which was fortified to blockade St Paul's gate.[3] In the following year, before the army left Marra to march on Jerusalem, Raymond of St Gilles offered to take most of the other leaders into his pay.[4] Albert of Aix recorded a number of 'conventiones solidorum',[5] and although he was never in Syria, the readiness of the crusading leaders to enter into the mercenary relationship lends probability to his assertions.

[1] Their statements are sound, but are supported by unconvincing evidence, although good evidence exists. La Monte's main evidence, outside the *Assises*, was taken from WT (La Monte, *Feudal Monarchy*, p. 160, n. 3, p. 162, n. 4). The first of these references is an alleged statement by WT (p. 581) that in 1125 Baldwin II raised an army 'interventu pecuniae'. The complete sentence from which this phrase is taken reads: 'Per idem tempus elapso pacis temporalis et initi foederis spatio, quod inter dominum regem et Doldequinum, interventu pecuniae, prius convenerat, sociata sibi de universo regno militia, in terram Damascenorum rex ingreditur.' It was the treaty which was arranged 'interventu pecuniae'; the phrase does not refer to the army.

[2] Frauenholz, *Heerwesen*, pp. 85, 117; Delbrück, III, pp. 329–37. For its continued existence in medieval Germany and development in the reign of Barbarossa, see P. Schmitthenner, *Das freie Söldnertum im abendländischen Imperium des Mittelalters*; also J. Boussard, 'Henri II Plantegenet et les origines de l'armée de métier' in BEC, CVI (1945–6), 189–224.

[3] *Anon.* p. 98; RA, p. 250; RC, p. 643.

[4] RA, p. 271; Runciman, I, pp. 336–41, has made Raymond's information the basis of an ingenious and convincing calculation on the numbers who took part in the First Crusade.

[5] AA, p. 361, 'conventionem solidorum militibus suis solvens' (*sc.* Baldewinus). See also AA, p. 633.

In his comments on the poverty of King Baldwin I, William of Tyre stated that the king had scarcely enough to pay the 'stipendia equitum'.[1] The probability that these were mercenaries and not tenants of money fiefs is strengthened by Fulcher's account of conditions in 1124, when it was necessary to take special measures to raise money for the payment of mounted and foot-soldiers to take part in the siege of Tyre.[2] William's account of the same events refers to 'stipendiarii pedites' in the Latin army,[3] and later he refers to the presence of 'stipendiarii equites et pedites' in the garrison of Banyas.[4] In 1153 the pilgrims who were pressed by the king to join him in the siege of Ascalon were promised pay for their services.[5] In later years the dependence of the Frankish rulers on mercenaries appears to have become greater. In 1183 a tax almost revolutionary in its incidence and principles of assessment, and unprecedented in its scope, was levied throughout the kingdom; its purpose was that 'equitum peditumque copias habere possemus'.[6] The kings of France and England, unable to lead forces to Syria, sent instead money with which troops could be hired.[7] The army which fought at Hattin was raised partly by money sent to Syria by Henry II of England.[8]

A further and constant source of military strength were the pilgrims from Europe. Since their goal was the Holy Places, they were of greater help to the kings of Jerusalem than to the other Latin rulers, and the essential part played by the Genoese, Pisan, and Venetian fleets in the reduction of the ports has been clearly explained in the sources and by modern historians.[9] From the First Crusade onwards the Latin states were always in need of help from the West, both in the form of general reinforcements,[10]

---

[1] WT, p. 488.

[2] Fulcher, p. 459, 'sed quia pecuniae nos inopia universos tunc arcebat, colligitur multa viritim militiae et clientelae conductitiae impertienda'.

[3] WT, p. 568.   [4] WT, p. 631.   [5] WT, p. 799.

[6] The words were written by WT, p. 1110, who was then chancellor of the kingdom.

[7] Cartellieri, *Philipp II August*, II, pp. 5–14.   [8] *Ernoul*, p. 156.

[9] Heyd, *Commerce du Levant*, I, pp. 133–46; La Monte, *Feudal Monarchy*, pp. 227–32.

[10] Letters asking such help were written even before the First Crusade had reached Jerusalem; HEp. pp. 148, 164–5, 167, 175. Similar demands were made from time to time during the course of the century; see *Reg.* nos. 261 (anno 1150), 383 (1163), 394 (1164), 396 (1164), 404 (1164), 497 (1173). Special missions were led to the West by Bohemond in 1105 (RC, p. 713);

and of individual princes as husbands of heiresses for whom suitable partners could not be found in Syria.[1] The arrival of any magnate from Europe with an armed following was an occasion for general rejoicing and, in order that his visit might be put to practical use, an expedition against the enemy.[2]

Still more constant was the annual arrival of pilgrims who, nearly every year, took advantage of the *passagium vernale* offered by the ships of the Italian cities,[3] and came to celebrate Easter at the Holy Places. Their presence was not often remarked in contemporary annals; presumably it was too normal to require special mention. But that they were there, and that their help was available if required, was shown by the striking number of occasions on which they came to the rescue during a military crisis in the kingdom.[4] It is reasonable to suppose that in more normal years a proportion of them took part in any expedition organized by the kings of Jerusalem during the period of their pilgrimage.

The fourth main source of troops in the Latin states was the military Orders of St John and the Temple. Originally founded to serve the needs of pilgrims in the Holy Land, their increasingly rapid militarization during the twelfth century can be traced in the records of the period.[5] As early as 1137 the Hospitallers

---

Hugh de Payen in 1127 (WT, p. 595); the master of the Hospital in 1164 (*Reg.* no. 410); Frederick archbishop of Tyre in 1168 (WT, p. 960); the Patriarch Heraclius in 1184 (*Reg.* no. 638).

[1] Fulk came from Anjou to be heir and successor to Baldwin II, and Raymond of Poitiers to be prince of Antioch. For efforts to find husbands for Sibyl, sister and heiress of Baldwin IV, see WT, pp. 988, 1025, 1059.

[2] WT, p. 665, when Thierry of Alsace was received by people 'multa cum hilaritate' and an expedition into Transjordan was organized. See also WT, p. 1027, for reception of Philip of Alsace in 1176 and p. 1058 for that of Henry of Troyes and Peter of Courtenay.

[3] Heyd, *Commerce du Levant*, I, p. 180.

[4] In 1102 pilgrims awaiting a return passage at Jaffa were called upon to help the king at the second battle of Ramla; Fulcher, p. 397.

In 1105 Fulcher (p. 411) thought that the Egyptians were encouraged to attack because the Franks were 'sine succursu solitorum peregrinorum'. In 1113 they came to help the king after his defeat at al-Sannabra; Fulcher, p. 428. In 1153 pilgrims were pressed into service at the siege of Ascalon; WT, p. 799. In 1183 they joined the army which faced Saladin in the valley of Jezreel; WT, p. 1121.

[5] That of the Hospitallers was traced by Delaville la Roulx in *Les Hospitaliers en Terre Sainte et à Chypre*. See also Prutz, *Die geistlichen Ritterorden*.

received from King Fulk the custody of the newly constructed castle at Bait Gibrin.[1] Five years later the count of Tripoli gave them two of his principal castles, together with the important right of conducting their own military relations with the Turks.[2] In 1147 the Templars distinguished themselves in the fighting march of Louis VII and his French crusaders across Asia Minor; when the expedition decided on the necessity of leadership and discipline, the authority of the master of the Temple was regarded as standing next after that of the king.[3] During the second half of the century the contingents of one or both of the Orders appear to have been an important part of every army summoned by the kings of Jerusalem. In 1153 the Templars played a notorious part at the siege of Ascalon.[4] In 1157 the Hospitallers, who had been granted half of Banyas by Humphrey of Toron,[5] organized a column which made an unsuccessful attempt to relieve that place when it was besieged by Nur al-Din.[6] The siege was later raised by Baldwin III himself. As he was returning from Banyas to Jerusalem his force was ambushed by Nur al-Din in the upper Jordan valley, and on that occasion the Templars who had marched with him suffered heavy losses.[7] The Hospital saw in Amalric's attempts to conquer Egypt an opportunity to gain rich possessions and it guaranteed military assistance on a large scale on the promise of suitable concessions in Egypt when it had been conquered.[8]

In 1177 the force with which Baldwin IV won his complete victory over Saladin at Mont Gisard included the Templars normally stationed in Gaza.[9] Contemporaries blamed the leadership of two successive masters of the Temple for the disasters at Marj Ayyun in 1179 and at 'Ain Gozeh on 1 May 1187.[10] In the

---

[1] WT, p. 639.   [2] *Reg.* no. 212; *Cart. Hosp.* no. 144.

[3] Odo, pp. 71–2. On one occasion the permission of the commander nominated by the Templars was asked before the attack was made: 'unde data licentia a magistro omnes unanimiter illos invadunt.'

[4] WT, p. 805. See below, pp. 102–3.

[5] *Reg.* no. 325; *Cart. Hosp.* no. 258; WT, p. 837.   [6] WT, *ibid.*

[7] Letter of Pope Hadrian IV to the archbishop of Rheims; *Reg.* no. 326. Full text in Bouquet, *Recueil des historiens des Gaules*, xv, 681, no. 34.

[8] *Reg.* nos. 452, 466; *Cart. Hosp.* nos. 402, 409. The Hospital was to provide 500 knights and 500 well-equipped Turcopoles. In 1167 Amalric had fought in Egypt the battle of al-Babein with only 374 knights; see WT, p. 925.

[9] WT, p. 1041.

[10] Odo of St Amand was blamed for the first (WT, p. 1057) and Gerard of

military events of the last years of the kingdom the Orders played a distinguished role; at Hattin and at Arsuf they acquitted themselves nobly in the most responsible positions of the line of march. Like that of the mercenaries, the importance of the Orders as part of the Syrian Franks' military resources increased as the twelfth century grew older.

II. DEFECTS OF THE MILITARY ESTABLISHMENT

The sources of recruitment just surveyed provided the armies which were among the main foundations of Latin power in Syria. At the same time they engendered certain weaknesses in military organization which reduced the effectiveness of the Franks in warfare, and which must be considered here.

No Christian ruler of the twelfth century had an army at his disposal which met his needs in full. In most parts of Europe knight service was, by feudal custom, limited in duration and even, on occasion, confined to a certain territory. Thus circumscribed, it served the purposes of raiding and private warfare far more effectively than those of protracted campaigns fought on a large scale. The *arrière ban*, or any form of popular levy, however useful in a crisis, was unsuitable for normal requirements, since it produced troops who were likely to be inexperienced and ill equipped. Mercenaries had none of these defects. They were often seasoned veterans who would serve for as long as they received pay or could reasonably expect it; but the organization of such a force in any strength and for a prolonged period imposed too severe a strain on the rudimentary financial organization of the medieval state.

Most of these weaknesses were apparent in Latin Syria, and modern historians have emphasized as well that the Frankish rulers, and in particular the kings of Jerusalem, did not enjoy full authority as commanders of their military forces. So far as the twelfth century goes, this point has been overstressed. Dodu quotes in support of it a number of occasions on which the kings of Jerusalem failed to control ruling princes and magnates from western Europe who brought forces to fight in Syria for a season

---

Ridefort for the second (*Ernoul*, p. 152). For the identification of the fountain of Cresson with 'Ain Gozeh, see Abel, *Géographie de la Palestine*, I, p. 445.

at the side of the Franks.[1] La Monte refers as well to the Templars'
refusal to co-operate with Amalric in his invasion of Egypt.[2]

These examples show only that the Latin kings lacked control
in particular circumstances. Distinguished pilgrims were not,
after all, bound in subjection to them, and the military Orders
only to a limited extent. Dodu quotes no instance of Latin rulers
failing to control their own vassals in war. There were such
occasions, and the absence of effective military leadership was
especially evident during the five years which culminated in the
tragedy of Hattin. But this was a period during which Baldwin IV
was overcome by the progress of his leprosy, and was succeeded
first by an infant and then by a sister. Problems of regency and
succession bred faction and so reduced royal authority. Viewed
against the background of the three preceding generations, the
defiance encountered by Guy de Lusignan was an exception. As
a rule the first six kings of Jerusalem seem to have enjoyed a full
measure of authority over feudal and military forces, and this is
borne out by the analysis of military events in the following
chapter. It remains true, however, that they had not the same
command over pilgrims and the military Orders. To that extent
they were handicapped in war by lack of control.

The true military weakness inherent in the sources of recruitment can be more fully stated in this way. In the first generation
of Frankish conquest their princes achieved success in war
mainly by use of their feudal resources. The Orders of the Hospital and Temple were not yet militarized, and less was heard of
mercenaries than in later years. Knightly vassals were available
in numbers sufficient to protect and to extend Latin territories;
they were generally loyal and obedient; their service was not
subject to the limitations common in the West, but they were required to serve for the whole year if need be.[3] During the course

---

[1] Dodu, *Institutions*, pp. 173–7.

[2] La Monte, *Feudal Monarchy*, p. 140.

[3] Dodu, *Institutions*, p. 184; La Monte, *Feudal Monarchy*, p. 141; who on
p. 142 quoted the remark of WT (p. 904) that the army with which Amalric
invaded Egypt in 1167 (not 1166 as stated by La Monte) carried supplies 'ad
dies constitutos'. In La Monte's view (p. 141) 'this would indicate that some
definite time limit (i.e. for the length of the campaign) was set'.

It appears unnecessary to assume, however, that William meant more than
he said. When the Carolingian armies were mustered, they were sometimes
ordered to bring food for a specified period; when this was exhausted sup-

of the century the military problems of the Syrian Franks became more difficult. Earlier successes had been made possible by the divisions and political weakness of Islam. As Muslim Syria was first reunited and then joined with Egypt, the Franks needed increased military strength even to maintain the conquests of their predecessors; but the feudal *servitium debitum* certainly never expanded enough, and may even have contracted. The rulers were therefore obliged to rely more upon mercenaries, whose cost imposed an intolerable strain on their always insufficient financial resources, and upon the military Orders, whom they could not fully control.

The feudal military resources of the Franks were directly reduced by Muslim reconquests. Between 1135 and 1150 Zanki and Nur al-Din permanently detached from Latin rule the northern territories of Antioch, those beyond the Orontes, and the whole county of Edessa. In 1164 he conquered Banyas and the surrounding districts from the kingdom of Jerusalem. In this way the Christian rulers lost the military force which those lands had supported.[1]

It is possible that some compensation was found for such losses by the creation of money fiefs.[2] Another possible source was to

---

plies were found in the theatre of war. Similar arrangements were also on occasions made in feudal times. See Frauenholz, *Heerwesen*, pp. 33, 104; Baltzer, *Zur Geschichte des deutschen Kriegswesens*, p. 66. Amalric's army needed to carry supplies for a given period because of the desert crossing between southern Palestine and Egypt.

WT himself refers to several other occasions on which it was decided to begin an expedition or march with food and forage for an agreed number of days (p. 586); 'ad dies aliquot' (p. 739); 'ad certos dies' (p. 767); 'ad paucos dies' (p. 1108); 'ad dies quindecim'.

[1] The army of Edessa played a prominent part in warfare in Latin Syria down to the death of Jocelyn the Elder in 1131. Most of the feudal contingents mentioned by AA (pp. 682–3) were due from lands lost by the Franks before 1150. WT (p. 789) has these comments on the loss of lands in northern Antioch: 'Sic igitur provincia opulentissima, rivis, sylvis, et pascuis laetissima, ubere gleba dives et omnibus redundans commoditatibus, in qua quingenti equites sufficientia habebant beneficia . . . in hostium manus devenit.' For the military consequences of the loss of Banyas, see above, p. 90.

[2] This suggestion, for it is nothing more, is based upon two considerations. First, that the funds on which money fiefs could be secured became more available in Latin Syria as commerce developed during the century; second, that the money fief in English feudal society 'was essentially military in

increase the *servitium debitum*, but there is no evidence that this was ever attempted. On the contrary, there are signs that the military tenants of Latin Syria, so far from being able to bear heavier services, were often hard pressed to render all that was due from them. They were weakened by poverty inflicted on them both by man and by nature. All sources of our knowledge of the period record the recurrence in Syria of earthquakes, drought, plagues of locusts, and small-scale feudal warfare between Frankish seigneurs and Muslim amirs.[1] Fulcher, reflecting on the means by which God justly punished the sins of the Franks, names Saracens, rats, and locusts as instruments for their impoverishment.[2] The consequences were the failure of crops, the laying waste of cultivated land, the interruption of commercial intercourse. Peasants and other tenants could not pay their dues to their lords whose revenues, on which depended the organization of effective government and military action, could be seriously diminished. These hard realities were recognized in a business agreement confirmed in 1163 by Raymond of Tripoli.[3] The abbot of Mount Thabor leased for twenty-five years to two brothers named Peter all property held by his house in the town and county of Tripoli together with a named village 'in territorio Montis Peregrini'. The lessees were to pay 900 besants down, and an annual rent of 100 besants, but they were to be excused the rent in any period during which the crops were laid waste by the enemy.

In Latin Syria the exploitation of property was a precarious business. It is significant, especially against the background of conditions reflected in this lease, that the jurists considered the circumstances in which the poverty of lord or vassal temporarily

---

nature'. See B. D. Lyon, 'The money fief under the English kings, 1066–1485', in *EHR*, LXVI, 186.

[1] In 1114 there were, for example, both a major earthquake and a plague of locusts; Fulcher, p. 428; Galt. pp. 61–2, 122. For evidence of a series of similar misfortunes during the years 1116–20, see WT, p. 531. There were serious earthquakes in 1138, 1157, 1163, and 1170; see *RGKJ*, pp. 212, 290–1, 319, 348–9. The military consequences of drought could be sufficiently grave for rulers to arrange a truce; Saladin accepts a truce in 1180, WT, p. 1063; Raymond of Tripoli arranges a truce, probably early in 1185, *Ernoul*, p. 124. For its date, see Baldwin, *Raymond III of Tripolis*, p. 70.

[2] Fulcher, pp. 434, 485.

[3] *Reg.* no. 389. Full text in *Cart. Hosp.* II, no. XIII, pp. 904–5.

destroyed the normal feudal relationship. The fact that such a situation is discussed in the oldest of the law books, the 'Livre au Roi', written soon after the loss of Jerusalem, suggests that it was a reality during the twelfth century. Reasons for such poverty are mentioned in terms almost identical with those used by Fulcher: 'aucune mauvaise année, pestilence, Sarasins.'[1] There was yet another reason—the payment of ransoms. In 1158, Hugh III of Ibelin, 'captivitatis redemptione compulsus', sold two *casales* to the canons of the Holy Sepulchre, and at the same time Ralph, one of his knights, 'de capitivitate Turcorum rediens' also sold property 'ut pretium redemptionis solvere possit'.[2] Three years later John Gothman sold five *casales* to the same purchasers for 1400 besants, 'urgente necessitate videlicet redemptione de paganorum captivitate'.[3]

The principal beneficiaries of the situation were the military Orders; feudal poverty created a market in land of which the Knights took increasing advantage. When in 1186 the castle of Marqab, one of the largest and most powerful in all Syria, was sold to the Hospital, its lord did so 'prae nimiis expensis et nimia infidelium vicinitate'.[4] Land near Muslim-held territory entailed the heaviest responsibility and was the most uncertain as a source of profit. In 1142 the count of Tripoli ceded to the same Order the castle which was to become known as the Crac des Chevaliers, together with all his rights in an area to the north and east, including Rafaniya and Ba'rin.[5] These two places had been taken by Zanki five years earlier, and the castles and lands named in the grant had become an area exposed to frequent enemy attack. This is the first of many grants of extensive border areas to be made to both Orders during the rest of the century.[6] Feudal rulers could no longer discharge their responsibilities, and this weakness is further reflected in the grant to the Hospital of the castles of 'Arqa

---

[1] 'Le Livre au Roi', in *RHC, Lois*, 'Les Assises de Jérusalem', 1, 625. See Grandeclaude, *Étude critique sur les livres des assises de Jérusalem*, pp. 46–50, where this work is assigned to the years 1197–1205.

[2] *Reg.* nos. 332, 333, 335.   [3] *Reg.* no. 369.

[4] *Reg.* nos. 647, 649; *Cart. Hosp.* no. 783.

[5] *Reg.* no. 212; *Cart. Hosp.* no. 144.

[6] On this series of grants, see Cahen, *La Syrie du Nord*, pp. 511–17; Richard, *Le Comté de Tripoli*, p. 63. See also Beyer, 'Die Kreuzfahrergebiete Südwestpalästinas', in *Beiträge zur biblischen Landes- und Altertumskunde* (herausgegangen aus der *ZDPV*), 1951, p. 272.

and Jebel Akkar when they were destroyed by an earthquake;[1] in the sale of other castles, of Sarc by William of Maraclea,[2] of Safad by Payen of Haifa,[3] of Belvoir by Ivo Velos.[4] Nor were 'castella cum pertinentiis' the only objects of market value. The cartularies of the military Orders show that the gifts of land made to the Knights in the early days of their existence gave way increasingly to sales.[5] Laymen appear less in these documents as pious donors and more frequently as parties in a business transaction who exchanged land for a pension or for cash down.

As the military problems of the Latin states increased, the ruling feudal class showed itself insufficient to meet them in two respects. First, as the long series of appeals to the West for reinforcements clearly shows,[6] that class was never large enough. Second, the evidence just passed in review shows that it lacked adequate material resources. The Latin princes had therefore to look elsewhere for the military strength which the feudatories could not provide, and they found it among mercenary troops and among the military Orders. The payment of mercenaries, however, imposed a financial burden on the rulers which could be borne, when at all, only with the greatest difficulty. No precise information on the income and expenditure of the Latin rulers has survived, but the insufficiency of their resources was attested by many contemporaries.[7] The lack of sufficient feudal or mercenary forces was partly made good by the militarization of the Orders of St John and the Temple whose contingents, in the later half of the twelfth century, were always a welcome reinforcement to the Christian armies of the period. These contingents, however, had their price; they cost the feudal rulers full military command of their forces in the field. The military Orders were

---

[1] *Reg.* no. 477; *Cart. Hosp.* no. 411.

[2] *Reg.* no. 378; *Cart. Hosp.* no. 317; Dussaud, *Topographie*, pp. 145–7.

[3] *Reg.* no. 447.   [4] *Reg.* no. 448; *Cart. Hosp.* no. 398.

[5] See *Cart. Hosp.* and Marquis d'Albon (ed.), *Cartulaire général de l'ordre du Temple, 1119?–1150.*

[6] See above, p. 94, n. 10.

[7] Much of this has been quoted in the preceding section when the employment of mercenaries was under discussion. See above, pp. 93–4. WT (p. 836) states that it was the debts of Baldwin III which led him to break his truce with Nur al-Din and to raid the flocks and herds of Muslim nomads at pasture in the forests of Banyas. He also refers (p. 846) to the same king's need to enrich himself as a reason for his seeking a wife at the Byzantine court.

not fully subject to any Latin magnate, either secular or ecclesiastical, and they dearly prized their independence. William of
Tyre recorded important occasions when they behaved, even towards the kings of Jerusalem, as independent allies,[1] and another
aspect of their opportunism in gaining freedom from control can
be seen in a number of agreements which they made with Latin
princes. They always sought the power to conduct their own
military policy with neighbouring Muslim rulers. If the Orders
declared war or concluded a truce, the Latin ruler was bound to
observe it; he, on the other hand, might not conclude a truce if
the Orders were unwilling, and if he did, they were not to be considered bound by it.[2] Nor did they wish to follow the normal
medieval practice by taking part in the general division of spoil at
the end of an expedition or campaign.[3] They took every opportunity of exacting the privilege of retaining everything which
they themselves had taken.[4] In the military Orders, therefore,
the Latin princes found soldiers of high quality who helped to
offset the numerical weakness of the feudal host and their inability to hire sufficient mercenaries; but the Knights of Saint
John and the Temple came as allies, and as a result the secular
rulers lost the complete control of military operations and policy

[1] WT, p. 805. The siege of Ascalon in 1153 was directed by Baldwin III;
yet when the Franks succeeded in breaking the wall, the Templars attempted
to monopolize the breach and to allow none but their own men into the city.
WT, p. 949. In 1167 the same Order refused to take part in Amalric's
invasion of Egypt. For their military assistance on the same occasion, the
knights of St John exacted immense concessions in the territory to be conquered. For the agreement with Amalric, which was in effect a treaty between
two equal powers, see *Reg.* nos. 452, 466; *Cart. Hosp.* nos. 402, 409.

[2] *Reg.* nos. 212, 428, 649; *Cart. Hosp.* nos. 144, 391, 783.

[3] The division of spoil among all those who had taken part in an expedition was, to twelfth-century writers, so right and normal a proceeding that it
could be called a 'lex belli'; WT, p. 1046. Spoils were distributed 'sub
ratiocinio', 'aeque', and 'solito jure'; Fulcher, p. 414. Magnates made gifts to
religious institutions in the form of a fixed proportion of their share of the
booty; *Reg.* no. 279; Maurice of Mont Royal to the Hospital in 1152; *Reg.*
no. 397; Amalric to the Church of St Lazarus in 1164.

[4] *Reg.* no. 212; *Cart. Hosp.* no. 144. The Hospitallers of Tripoli need not
divide the spoils taken with anyone, unless the count were present in person.
Reg. no. 428; *Cart. Hosp.* no. 391. They need not divide spoils taken in the
principality of Antioch with anyone.
Reg. no. 452. *Cart. Hosp.* no. 402. They need not divide the spoils unless
the king were present in person. See also *Reg.* no. 477; *Cart. Hosp.* no. 411.
Reg. no. 649; *Cart. Hosp.* no. 783.

that they enjoyed in the earlier decades of the twelfth century.

The final weakness of the Franks' military organization to be discussed in this section was, in many ways, more serious than any, for it closely affected the twin pillars of the Latin occupation, the field army and the strong places. Troops summoned to the army were normally brought from the castles and walled towns,[1] for these were the residences of the feudal magnates and their households, of the Hospitallers and Templars, and probably of the mercenaries who were maintained in time of peace. It was upon these places also that the dominion of the Syrian Franks was based and their preservation in time of Muslim invasion was essential to the existence of the Latin states. Such invasion was best resisted by means of a field army; but should that force be defeated, it was necessary that the walls of the strong places should be defended until a new army could be raised or until the enemy withdrew.

With their limited resources the Franks were faced by a difficult dilemma, of which the correct solution was all important to their existence in Syria. An unopposed invader destroyed for the time being all social and commercial intercourse; by laying the country-side waste he diminished the revenues on which power to govern and to organize military defence ultimately depended. It was therefore necessary to send an army against him, and this was possible only by drawing on the garrisons of the towns and castles. There are many indications that, both in the early period of the occupation, before the military resources of the Franks had been fully developed, and in the late, when those resources became progressively insufficient to resist the mounting power of Muslim Syria, the co-existence of a strong field army and adequate garrisons was not possible.

Whenever in the early days of the kingdom the Latins put an army into the field, they knew that they were endangering the strong places which had thus been deprived of defenders.[2] When

[1] WT, p. 1093. The garrisons of Safad, Kawkab (Belvoir), and Tiberias provided contingents for the army which opposed Saladin's invasion in 1182.

Ernoul, pp. 145–6; *Eracles*, p. 39. The force which was destroyed by the Muslims at the fountain of Cresson on 1 May 1187 was gathered by Gerard of Ridefort from the Templar garrisons at Qaqun (Caco) and al-Fule (La Fève), and the king's knights at Nazareth.

[2] Fulcher, p. 383: 'Milites etiam nostros vix adunare audebamus, pump

the forces of Jerusalem were engaged in the north, the Muslim garrison of Ascalon often raided towards the city, since they knew that the knights who normally lived there were with the army.[1] During his victorious campaign against Antioch in 1119, Il Ghazi decided to attack Atharib, for he had heard that its lord together with his knights, as well as those from other Frankish castles, had nearly all obeyed the king's order to muster at Antioch.[2] Two generations later, when the kingdom needed its maximum strength to meet the constant attacks of Saladin, a similar situation was apparent. It was well summarized by the author of the *Itinerarium*,[3] and the evidence of contemporary records corresponded to his generalizations.[4] When, on 30 April 1187, Gerard de Ridefort, master of the Temple, learned that next day a Muslim force, by permission of Raymond of Tripoli, would range unopposed through Galilee, he determined to attack the intruders. He summoned the garrisons of Qaqun, al-Fule, and Nazareth. Next day Ernoul himself, sent by Balian of Ibelin to discover who was within al-Fule, found the castle empty but for two sick men.[5] Historians have been impressed by the drama of this incident, but have not remarked its significance as a symptom of one of the principal sources of the Franks' military weakness. In order to face the Muslims in the field, a castle had been left literally empty.[6]

Two months later the battle of Hattin was fought to save

---

insidias aliquas inimicis nostris moliri volebamus: timentes ne interim munitionibus vacuatis damnum facerent.' Fulcher, p. 412 (Muster of 1105): 'Metuebamus enim ne aut de civitatibus nostris aliquam gente vacuatam caperent. . . .'

[1] See occasions recorded by Fulcher, p. 427 (1113), 'Milites quippe civitati deerant, quia in hostem iverant'; p. 429 (1115); 460 (1124), 'Equitatus enim noster in exercitu erat'.

[2] Galt. p. 99; 'Algazi . . . ad obsidendum Cerepum profectus est. Audierat namque, fama multorum enarrante, Alanum, illius castri dominum, cum suis militibus, Edessenos etiam milites ac de aliis castris fere omnes iussu regio Antiochiam advenire.'

[3] *Itin.* p. 17; 'Adeo sane totius regni robur edicto regio ad bellum illud funestum confluxerat, ut illi tantum in castrorum et urbium resideret custodia, quos aetatis et sexus infirmitas armorum prorsus habebat immunes.'

[4] *Libellus*, p. 218, describing muster of Christian army for Hattin campaign: 'Non remansit homo in civitatibus vel vicis vel castellis, qui ad bella posset procedere, quin jussu regis urgeretur exire.'

[5] *Ernoul*, pp. 149–50.

[6] On the importance of the castle, see Beyer, *ZDPV*, LXVII (1944–5), 231.

Tiberias, which if not relieved by the army would certainly fall to Saladin because its knights were with the army.[1] When after the battle Balian of Ibelin went to defend Jerusalem, he found but two knights there; as a desperate remedy he admitted sixty sons of burgesses to knighthood.[2] Acre was one of many other places which because of the needs of the field army had been left without an adequate garrison. When that army had been destroyed at Hattin the citizens surrendered without resistance.[3]

The existence of a Christian Syria depended ultimately on the simultaneous existence of an adequate field army and garrisons. This was the problem which the Latin rulers, handicapped by the military weaknesses examined in this section, were finally unable to solve.

III. 'MILITES PEDITESQUE'

Now that the sources of recruitment have been discussed, consideration must be given to the military ability of the recruits. From the tenth century and into the twelfth, Latin writers normally reported the numbers and composition of armies in terms of *milites peditesque*,[4] and the historians of the crusader states provided no exception. The contrast was, however, not simply that between the fully armoured knight, as depicted in the sculpture, seals, coins, and illustrations of the period,[5] and the well-equipped *pedes* described by the author of the *Itinerarium* and Beha ed-Din.[6] Each term in the phrase had a wide meaning.

Until the end of the eleventh century the *miles* was the warrior who, protected by mail shirt, steel cap, and shield, fought on horseback with sword and lance. In the late eleventh and in the twelfth centuries, there were two important developments. First, knighthood became a social distinction, synonymous with nobility. The *milites* were recognized as a class, almost as a caste, of society. The reception into it of a young man of an age to bear arms was marked by a ceremony in which he assumed them, and

---

[1] *Ernoul*, p. 158.

[2] *Ernoul*, p. 175; *Eracles*, p. 70. Some versions of *Eracles* say that he dubbed the sons of knights as well as of burgesses.

[3] *Libellus*, p. 235.   [4] Delbrück, III, p. 255.

[5] For the best collection of contemporary illustrations of twelfth-century armour see G. Demay, *Le Costume au moyen âge d'après les sceaux*.

[6] *Itin.* p. 99; BD, p. 251.

in the literature of the twelfth century statements appear from which it is clear that only those men might become knights whose parents had been also of knightly, that is noble, birth.[1] In the second place, defensive armour became more elaborate. The knee-length mail shirt developed to give protection to the extremities of the man who wore it; the sleeves and skirt lengthened and narrowed, until forearms, wrists, hands, legs, and feet were all covered. The addition of a mail coif guarded his neck and most of his face. At the end of the century men who could afford to do so had replaced the conical helmet with nasal by the pot helm. Armour, and therefore the horse required to carry it, became heavier and more costly.[2]

These two developments meant that the term *miles*, once used to designate the whole body of mounted warriors, came during the twelfth century to be applied to only part of that body which was distinguished from the rest by nobility of birth and excellence of equipment. By the end of the twelfth century this separation was so well marked that contemporaries made a clear distinction between *milites* on the one hand, and the rest of the mounted soldiers, the *servientes loricati* or *serjans à cheval* on the other.[3] In Latin Syria such terms were not used until the end of the period now being considered, and then only occasionally. Generally speaking, the Latin armies were nearly always described in terms of *milites peditesque*, and since during the century

[1] For this transition see Guilhiermoz, *Essai sur l'origine de la noblesse en France au moyen âge*, pp. 370, 462; M. Bloch, *La Société féodale: les classes et le gouvernement des hommes*, pp. 46–77; Delbrück, III, pp. 243–9.

[2] For this development, see Demay, *op. cit.* and G. F. Laking, *A Record of European Armour and Arms through Seven Centuries*.

[3] The description of the mounted part of a medieval force in terms of knights and sergeants did not appear until the later twelfth century. Even then the earliest, and oft quoted, examples are all from the chronicle of one writer, Giselbert of Mons (*Monumenta Germaniae Historica, Scriptores*, XXI, pp. 520, 543, 552, quoted by Baltzer, *Zur Geschichte des deutschen Kriegswesens*, p. 57; Köhler, III, 2, 38–9; Delbrück, p. 259; Guilhiermoz, *op. cit.* p. 229, n. 15). The terms do not appear to have been commonly used until the early thirteenth century; Guilhiermoz, *ibid.*

Another consequence of the greater weight and costliness of armour was that, in thirteenth-century feudal society, tenants owing knight's service could not always afford to send a fully equipped knight, and sent instead two mounted sergeants. The equipment of the sergeants was less elaborate, and probably corresponded to that of a knight in the early twelfth century; Chew, *Ecclesiastical Tenants-in-chief*, p. 90; Morris, *Welsh Wars*, p. 50.

the sense of *miles* was changing, it is not easy to ascertain the meaning attached to each of these words.

It is a matter which has a bearing on the strength of the armies which fought in Syria. Historians are agreed that twelfth-century estimates of the number of pilgrims who accompanied the great crusading expeditions were consistently exaggerated; but when faced with the very small numbers of *milites* and *pedites* put into the field by the Latin rulers, they have recorded these with little comment.[1] Yet from the available evidence it appears that these, like the large numbers, sometimes require adjustment in order to bring them nearer the true fighting strength of the Latin armies.[2]

It is reasonable to suppose that at all times the *miles* was accompanied by one or more servants, and the records support this view. There has been considerable discussion as to whether these attendants followed their master into battle, and the general opinion of military historians is that they did not.[3] A study of the scanty evidence afforded by the sources of crusading history leads to the same conclusion. The *armigeri* and *ecuyers* were recorded as foragers, for whom an armed escort was often pro-

[1] Prutz, *Kulturgeschichte*, p. 182; Dodu, *Institutions*, p. 218.

[2] Delpech, I, p. 410 saw the necessity for such an adjustment, but for the wrong reasons. It is certain that in the thirteenth century a knight was attended by mounted troopers who followed him into battle. When the strength of a force was given in *milites*, therefore, it required multiplication by at least three in order to arrive at the true mounted fighting strength (Morris, *Welsh Wars*, pp. 54–5). Delpech applied the same rule to the armies of twelfth-century Latin Syria. He found a number of examples which showed that in Europe a force contained a number of knights, and a given number, four or five times greater, of mounted sergeants. He therefore arrived at the opinion that when an army was described only in terms of *milites*, their number should be multiplied by four or five, the product being the number of mounted sergeants. All his examples, however, were taken from the thirteenth century, when the distinction between knights and sergeants had become clear. In the twelfth century it was not normally made, and Delpech's rule cannot be applied with any confidence.

[3] Baltzer, *op. cit.* p. 85. Delbrück (III, p. 328) agreed that this was the position at the beginning of the twelfth century; but that during its course the attendants of the knights 'nehmen allmählich mehr Kombattanten-Charakter'.

One difficulty in the problem is that the terms employed during the twelfth century had no precise meaning, and were used by different writers in different senses. When a modern historian, like Köhler, has attempted to assign an exact meaning to each, he has involved himself in a series of self-coutradictions. See the ruthless commentary on this part of Köhler's work in Delbrück, III, pp. 321–8.

vided;[1] during the engagement they had charge of the baggage, and did not normally take part in the action.[2]

There are two further pieces of evidence, one provided by Fulcher and the other by the Rule of the Templars, which appear to show that the attendants of the knights were non-combatant in normal circumstances. In 1101 the need for troops to oppose the Egyptians was so great that, on the orders of King Baldwin, 'quicumque potuit de armigero suo militem fecit'.[3] But for the abnormal crisis, the *armigeri* would not have been required to fight. The Rule records that when the squadrons of the Templars were formed up for battle, each knight kept with him two *ecuyers*. Of these one stood before him and carried his lance; the other stood behind his master and led the spare horses.[4] Before the battle began the *ecuyer* with the horses led them to the rear and came under the orders of the *confanonier*, and it must be supposed that the *ecuyer* who carried the lance handed it to his master, and, in order to leave the front clear, also withdrew to the rear.[5]

The question remains whether the numbers of *milites* given in the records denoted the whole number of mounted soldiers. Again, the evidence is slight, but it appears to show that in Latin Syria the number of *milites* mentioned might be only a part of the whole mounted strength. For example, after Baldwin I had been defeated in 1102, the military situation in the kingdom of Jerusalem was desperate. The forces which the king had taken into battle had been annihilated; Jaffa was closely besieged by the victorious Egyptians; communications between that town and Jerusalem were uncertain.[6] The situation could be restored only if more troops could be raised to defeat the besiegers of Jaffa. Baldwin sent a single messenger to Jerusalem, and his call for reinforcements was answered by ninety men, 'tam de militibus quam de illis qui equos habere potuerunt vel jumenta'.[7]

---

[1] *Anon.* p. 16, *armigeri* foraged with armed protection; AA, pp. 461, 692–3; *Est.* 7233.
[2] *Ernoul*, p. 147.   [3] Fulcher, p. 391.   [4] *Règle*, no. 161.
[5] *Règle*, no. 179; Frauenholz, *Heerwesen*, p. 135.
[6] Grousset, I, pp. 231–7; *RGKJ*, pp. 36–40.
[7] Fulcher, p. 404. The arrival from Jerusalem of reinforcements who were not knights was also recorded by WT, p. 977. In 1170 the army with which Amalric went down to Darum to oppose Saladin was joined by sixty-five young men from a district in Jerusalem. 'Ernat porro ibi juvenes expediti et

On this occasion men who were not knights came mounted to
the army, and it is known that three years later they were again
present. In the muster of 1105, 'milites nostri erant quingenti,
exceptis illis qui militari nomine non censebantur, tamen equitantes'.[1] Once again the *milites* were only part of the mounted
array. This example is particularly instructive, because when
William of Tyre used Fulcher's work in writing his own history
and recorded the same incident, he repeated Fulcher's numbers,
but said nothing of those horsemen who could not be reckoned
as knights.[2] William was interested in giving the numbers only in
terms of *milites peditesque*. He ignored the existence of the other
mounted men, and it may be presumed that this was not the only
occasion on which he did so.

In the examples which have been quoted, Fulcher and William
were using the term *miles* in its twelfth-century sense, to denote
the fully armed, well-mounted knight who was a member of a
social class recognized as noble.[3] That there were other men who
fought on horseback was revealed only rarely, as in the examples
quoted, and in the occasional use of terms like *milites gregarii*[4]
and *milites plebei*.[5] It is also clearly shown in William of Tyre's
description of the numbers and composition of the hosts which
marched from Europe on the Second Crusade.

Nam ut constanter asserunt qui in eadem expeditione praesentes
fuerunt, in solo domini imperatoris comitatu, ad septuaginta millia

ad arma prompti. . .' From the text it is not clear whether or not they were
mounted; but since they attempted 'viam ferro aperire' through the enemy,
and since other reinforcements mentioned in the penultimate sentence of the
same chapter were described specifically as *pedites*, it is probable that the
young men, like those mentioned by Fulcher above, had secured mounts of
some kind.

[1] Fulcher, p. 413.

[2] WT, p. 455: 'Inventi sunt habere equites quingentos, peditum duo millia.'

[3] The ceremony of admission to knighthood was established in Latin
Syria early in the century. When in 1124 an *armiger* of Jocelin the Elder
brought the news of the death of Balak b. Urtuq to Pons of Tripoli, the
elated count rewarded him by admitting him to the order of knighthood.
Fulcher, p. 463: 'Armiger quippe Goscelini erat ipse. Et quia nuntium attulit
desideratissimum in exercitu nostro ante Tyrum astante, acceptis armis, ab
armigero in militem provectus est.'

[4] RA, p. 242; AA, p. 698. Although RA was describing a Turkish force,
he was doing so in terms which would be readily understood by his Latin
readers.

[5] RA, p. 274.

fuerunt loricatorum, exceptis peditibus, parvulis et mulieribus, et equitibus levis armaturae. In exercitu vero domini regis Francorum, virorum fortium loricis utentium numerus ad septuaginta millia, excepta classe secunda.[1]

Because the composition of the force was given in greater detail than usual, the *miles* is described as *miles loricatus*, and with him were the *equites levis armaturae* or *classis secundae*, normally specified in thirteenth-century texts as *servientes* and *equites loricati* or as *serjans à cheval*, but not always considered worthy of special mention by twelfth-century chroniclers in Syria.

The essential role of the light-armed horseman in combat was not different normally from that of the knights. The term *levis armatura* meant only that they were not so well equipped as the wealthier *milites*; it did not mean that they were normally used as light, and the knights as heavy, cavalry, with all the tactical implications which such a contrast would imply to a modern reader. Occasionally the fact that they were lightly equipped was put to some special military purpose;[2] they were sent as 'speculatores' on reconnaissance, or they were employed as skirmishers.[3] Usually, however, they are not associated in the texts with specialized functions, and they appear to have gone into action with the knights.[4]

In Syria the Franks recruited from the native population.[5] These troops, often the offspring of parents of different religions, were known as Turcopoles.[6] In time they became so normal a part of the Latin forces, that contemporaries named them together with *milites* and *pedites* as part of the conventional description of an army.[7] When the master of the Hospital undertook to provide Amalric with a contingent for the invasion of Egypt, he promised 'quingentos milites et totidem Turcopolos bene armatos'.[8] These native levies became a regular part of both military Orders, and both came to include the turcopolier among the great officers.

[1] WT, p. 738.
[2] WT, p. 582. *Equites levis armaturae* were used to bait a prepared ambush.
[3] Oman, I, p. 372.   [4] Frauenholz, *Heerwesen*, pp. 119–20.
[5] Dodu, pp. 205–15.   [6] RA, p. 246; AA, p. 434.
[7] See, for example, letter of Gaufredus Fulcherius, procurator of the Templars to Louis VII in Bouquet, *Recueil des historiens des Gaules*, XVI, no. 195, p. 60.
[8] *Reg.* no. 452.

The Turcopoles included mounted men, and some used the bow.[1] Historians have added these scraps of information and have referred to Turcopoles as if they were all mounted archers who were specialists in certain military functions. It has been said that they were specially used for reconnaissance,[2] and that they employed, on behalf of the Franks, Turkish methods of mobile mounted archery.[3] On occasions they were employed for such purposes; yet there seems to be little justification for assuming, on the basis of the scanty information normally quoted, that all Turcopoles were both horsemen and archers. Certainly they cannot have been recruited solely, or even mainly, for reconnaissance. The Franks did not always excel in this branch of the military art,[4] and its needs were insufficient to explain the importance to which the Turcopoles attained in the Latin armies. Nor were they needed to act as mobile mounted archers against the Turks. This form of skill was peculiar to the Turkish peoples, and there is no reason to suppose that many natives of Syria were adept in its use. Usamah and his friends did not fight in that way, and neither did the Egyptian troops.[5] Further, the Frankish counter-measures against Turkish attacks were based on the military methods which their own equipment and training made possible. Those methods were modified to meet the problems presented by mobile archers, but they were never abandoned in favour of Turkish methods. The Turcopoles seem to have been the *equites levis armaturae* of the Latin East, and William of Tyre described them by just that phrase.[6] They were recruited to supplement the ever insufficient number of Frankish knights, and were a normal part of armies which employed modified western tactics. Those who fought on horseback added to the number and weight of the Latin *milites*, with whom they were marshalled and with whom they normally went into action.

The principal offensive weapons of the knights and other mounted troops were the lance and sword.[7] The first attack was

[1] Usamah, p. 79. Galt. p. 74, describing the battle of Sarmin, has the phrase, 'Turcopoli contra ipsos [*sc.* hostes] sagittantes'.
[2] Frauenholz, *Heerwesen*, p. 120.
[3] Prutz, *Kulturgeschichte*, p. 186; Munro, *Kingdom*, p. 106.
[4] Below, p. 249. The Franks were also taken by surprise in 1119 (below, p. 179), 1149 (p. 183), and 1179 (p. 186).
[5] See above, p. 86.   [6] WT, p. 925, 1097.
[7] This is evident from all sources of the period. For the arms with which a

made with the lance, of which the effectiveness depended on both horse and rider. The animal supported the weight of the armed and armoured rider, and by its momentum provided the necessary force behind the lance thrust. With his left hand the knight held reins and shield; with his right he either wielded his lance with a swinging thrust, or held it rigid beneath his arm.[1] We do not know the speed of the Latin knights riding into action; but the dash and fury of their charge was vividly illustrated in the texts,[2] and it is likely that its pace was the greatest of which the horse was capable.[3] If the lance was shattered in the

---

feudal ruler expected his knights to be equipped, see Henry II of England's Assize of Arms in Stubbs's *Select Charters* (9th ed. by H. W. C. Davis), p. 183, and Frederick Barbarossa's 'Lex pacis castrensis' in Frauenholz, *Heerwesen*, p. 254.

[1] The usual deportment of the lance in battle during the early twelfth century is by no means clear. It could be (*a*) thrown like a javelin, or (*b*) thrust at the adversary by a movement of the rider's arm, or (*c*) held rigid beneath the rider's arm, so that force was imparted to the blow solely by the forward movement of the horse. The Bayeux tapestry shows all three uses. Spears are shown as missile weapons (though it is not altogether clear that it is the knights who have thrown them); they are also shown being wielded by the knights, who have drawn back their right arm preparing to strike or to throw; they are shown held rigid by the knight, and it is with his lance in this position that Robert of Normandy was depicted in the twelfth-century windows of St Denis. For illustrations of the Bayeux tapestry, see R. P. Dom Bernard Montfaucon, *Les Monumens de la monarchie françoise* (1729), II, pp. 26, 28, pls. 7, 8; or Sir Eric Maclagan, *The Bayeux Tapestry*, 1943, pls. 62–9. For the windows of St Denis, see Montfaucon, *op. cit.* I, pp. 390, 396, pls. 50, 53.

I know of no evidence that in Latin Syria the lance was ever thrown by Western knights. The Turks did so (see *Anon.*'s use of *jaculari* on pp. 46, 90, 154) but there is no mention of similar action by the Franks. The verb most commonly used to describe the conduct of the lance was *vibrare*, and sometimes *palpare*. Heermann (*Gefechtsführung*, p. 118) thought that this word described a swinging blow which was aimed by the knight at his enemy, but the reasoning is far from conclusive. Only a light lance could be swung by an armoured rider. A heavy lance like that described by Usamah (p. 131) could only be held rigid beneath the arm. As arms and equipment became heavier during the course of the twelfth century, so it appears that the normal conduct of the lance became that described in (*c*) in the first paragraph of this note. See Hagenmeyer in Galt. p. 214, n. 35; J. Schwietering, *Zur Geschichte vom Speer und Schwert im 12 Jahrhundert*; R. Glover, 'English warfare in 1066' in *EHR*, LXVII (1952), p. 14 and n. 3.

[2] Twelfth-century writers described the charge by a combination of verb and adverb. The verb most commonly used was *irruere*; others were *invadere*, *impetere*, *occurrere*. The adverbs were *acriter*, *acerrime*, *fortiter*, *vehementer*, *viriliter*, *violenter*, *constanter*, *strenue*, *impetuose*, *velocissime*.

[3] Before they charged the knights advanced slowly—*gradatim*, *paulatim*,

first assault, the knight continued the fight with his sword.[1] The onset of the medieval *acies* was not the same as that of a drilled cavalry squadron in modern times. The disciplined troops of recent generations have been trained to act as a unit; even after their original charge they could be controlled, reformed, and led to new tasks in the same action. The attack of the medieval horsemen, though it relied for its effect on the collective mass of the participants, was essentially an aggregate of many individual charges; it depended for its success on impact with an enemy who, in resisting, would be shattered by its weight. If the enemy, like the Turks, was able to remove himself from its path, then the Franks, their formation loosening as they advanced, were vulnerable to counter-attack. Nor, after their original charge, could they be any longer controlled by the commander. A squadron (*acies*) of knights was like a projectile in the hands of .the commander. When directed against the enemy it could strike him only once, and therefore to succeed must strike and shatter him

---

pedetemptim, gradu lento—towards the enemy. See Heermann, p. 118 and n. 1, to which may be added *Anon.* pp. 84, 212. The sentence quoted by Heermann from Baldric of Dol is to be found not, as he said, on p. 95 of *RHC. Hist. occ.* IV, but on p. 108.

The sources do not justify Delbrück's remarks (III, p. 293). He said that the Franks charged the enemy at a slow pace, 'Die Regel war, langsam anzureiten'. He supported this statement by quoting Heermann's inaccurate reference to Baldric. In Delbrück's work the quotation was also inapposite, since Baldric was referring, not to a charge, but to preparation for battle.

[1] One of the best descriptions of a charging knight in the sources of crusading history was given by Galt. pp. 81–2: 'Nostri vero virili audacia freti illorum et audaciam et ingenium postponentes, *adstrictis lateri clipeis, palpatis lanceis, pressis calcaribus*, ut decet milites, his *simul* omnibus in medios hostes se conferunt, ictibusque asperis militarie agentes quosdam prosternunt humi, vicissim effuso sanguine, quosdam compellunt ad tartara devehi letali vulnere. haec inter praeludia Robertus de Veteri Ponte, haud segniter agens, more solito probitati inhaerendo cum *inpetu strenui animi* et *velocitate equi sui ferocissimi*, plures illorum *gregatim* equitantes *inpetiit* et *percussit*, statimque in quodam *fracta lancea adstricto mucrone* alios *repercussit*, demum et ipse a pluribus repercussus, *equo suo telo multiplici perforato*, vi inevitabili ingruente occidit. Nec oblitus matris suae filii, licet crebris lancearum sagittarumque ictibus humi premeretur, audaciae tamen levitate vires resumendo surrexit et ense reverberans contra nititur, suisque visis ei succurrere properantibus perstans animosius clamavit: "adeste, sodales, adeste, subnixi militibus viribus!" nec mora: conveniunt eique *alterum equum attribuunt*, quo adscendente, *vibrato ense* sociis inquit, inlatum dolorem vindicta posse minui.'

The words in italic give precise details of the knights' fighting tactics.

uno impetu, in a single attack. The elusive tactics of the Turks set the Franks the problem of timing the charge, which was their most powerful tactical weapon, so that it succeeded in making contact with the main body of the enemy. The Frankish charge was renowned and feared throughout the middle East.[1]

To turn from the mounted to the unmounted troops, military historians have too often discussed the medieval *pedes* as if he were a trained soldier, and have somewhat obscured the wide meaning which the term possessed. Like the word *miles*, it included fighting men of very different degrees of military experience, skill, and equipment. So long as a man had no weapon he was *imbellis*, and one of the *vulgus inerme*; but as soon as he was armed, and was prepared, at the direction of the leader of the group with which he found himself, to kill its enemies, then he became a *pedes* in the military sense.[2] A man with no experience of warfare, so long as he had a bow, spear, or club, had some military value, while that of a sufficiently large group of such men could be considerable.[3] But there were also men to whom warfare was almost a profession, who campaigned on foot regularly, who were well armed and armoured, and whose experience had given them considerable skill at arms and in military matters generally. These too were called *pedites*.[4] Both extremes existed in the Latin Orient. At one end of the scale was the foot-soldier with the

---

[1] Anna, pp. 122–3: 'The irresistible first shock' (of the Franks). She explains that the first onslaught was invincible (p. 283); then they were vulnerable (p. 342); a Frank on horseback 'would make a hole through the walls of Babylon'. IQ, p. 176, 'famous onset'; p. 284; 'famous onslaught'; p. 292; 'famous charge'. The most sustained description of a Frankish charge is given in BD, pp. 258–9, in his account of Arsuf.

[2] Odo (p. 57) wished that on the Second Crusade the pope, who had regulated the arms and baggage of the knights, had ordered all the people on foot to carry arms: 'Sed eque utinam pedites instruxisset, retentisque debilibus, fortibus quibusque pro pera gladium et pro baculo arcum dedisset, quia semper debiles et inermes suis sunt onus, hostibus preda.'

[3] Even today, when the man armed with simple weapons has far less chance than in the Middle Ages of fighting successfully against first-class troops with first-class equipment, the general statement above holds good. It was fully demonstrated in the early days of the Home Guard in 1940.

[4] Their existence was sometimes indicated in the texts by such phrases as Fulcher, p. 447, 'habens secum (*sc.* rex Balduinus) trecentos milites lectissimos, et clientes advectitios quadringentos probissimos'; WT, p. 1122, 'Erant enim eis equites ad mille trecentos; peditum vero armatorum egregie quindecim millium summam dicebatur numerus excedere'.

equipment envisaged by Henry Plantagenet in his Assize of Arms; or described by the author of the *Itinerarium*[1] and Beha-ed-Din.[2] He wore an iron cap, with body protection of armour, leather, or quilted linen, perhaps carried a shield, and was armed with a spear and bow or crossbow. At the other was the pilgrim, who came on crusade in his ordinary garments, but bearing a bow or spear instead of the pilgrim's staff; or the Syrian Frank who was one of the *universus populus*, and who bore arms only on the rare occasions on which he was called out by the king of Jerusalem.

Some writers have regarded Latin Syria as the theatre of war in which it was necessary to create an efficient infantry force,[3] and have considered that the lessons learned in warfare against the Turks influenced contemporary practice in western Europe.[4] In any discussion of this subject there are two related questions to be considered: first, whether during the century there was any growth in the skill and equipment of the infantry in Latin Syria; second, whether leaders assigned them a more important role in operations, and made a more skilful use of them in their tactical plans.

With regard to the first of these questions, it is easy to conclude that the 'pedites satellites rigidissimi' described in both Eastern and Western sources,[5] and who foiled the most violent efforts of the enemy against the Latin rear at Arsuf, played a far more distinguished role in the Third Crusade than did their counter-parts in the First.[6] Yet it is possible to draw too strong a contrast, for in important respects the infantry of 1191 resembled those of 1098. Eyewitnesses have given an indelible impression of the discipline and steadiness of the unmounted men during the Third Crusade; but they did not all display these qualities,[7] and a runaway horse could be the occasion of sudden panic among the *pedites* at Acre[8] in 1190 no less than at Antioch[9] in 1097. Nor had

---

[1] *Itin.* p. 99.   [2] BD, p. 251.   [3] Köhler, III, pt. 3, p. 209.
[4] Delpech, II, p. 224, where the knights of the military Orders, 'ce petit noyau de vieilles barbes militaires', are described as schoolmasters who educated in warfare the knights who came on pilgrimage from Europe.
[5] *Itin.* p. 263; BD, pp. 199, 251.
[6] Comparison instituted by Delpech, II, p. 154.
[7] *Itin.* p. 263. At Arsuf many crossbowmen threw down their weapons and left the firing line.
[8] *Itin.* p. 70.   [9] RA, p. 243.

their equipment changed. The bows and crossbows so effective in the hands of the archers at Arsuf were carried[1] and were used[2] by pilgrims on the First Crusade. The spear was a normal infantry weapon throughout the century. Delbrück considered that during the twelfth century the footsoldiers never exceeded their performance at Dorylaeum.[3] His judgement rests mainly on an unconvincing sentence from Ralph of Caen[4] but other facts lead to the same conclusion. The supposed incompetence of the foot-soldiers at the beginning of the Crusades has been deduced from the small part they played in the battle of Dorylaeum.[5] When the battle began Bohemond took only the knights into battle and left all unmounted men in the camp.[6] Bohemond's dispositions are given by the Anonymous, who was always well informed on the deeds of that Norman prince.[7] When contact was made with the Turks he thought only of a pitched battle, and gave orders to make camp. Historians

---

[1] Fulcher, p. 329. Men who forsook the pilgrimage during the First Crusade 'arcubus suis venditis, et baculis peregrinationis resumptis, ad domos suas ignavi regressi sunt'. Anna Comnena (p. 255) had a very clear recollection of the crossbows carried by the Latins on the First Crusade.
[2] For the use of crossbows on the First Crusade, *Anon.* p. 38. For archery in battle, *Anon.* p. 212; *HEp.* 158.   [3] Delbrück, III, p. 429.
[4] Delbrück, *ibid.* and p. 421. The full sentence from RC, p. 622: 'Militaris fugae impetus pedestrem conculcat tarditatem, inque vicem densissima pedestrium hastarum sylva nunc fugam impedit, nunc exstinguit; fitque vel hosti miseranda clades, quum terga sagittis horrent, ilia lanceis, velut torrendorum veribus, affiguntur.' Delbrück's comment on this was (III, p. 421) 'Das Fussvolk gewährt den Rittern Schutz'. This is at least an understatement. Ralph intended to describe a tragedy arising from lamentable confusion; the fleeing knights were spitted on the lances of their own unmounted followers. The ultimate effect of the disaster perhaps was to check the Turks; but like other occurrences in the battle (cf. Fulcher, p. 335) the achievement was the result of accident rather than design, and the remark of Delbrück (p. 429) that 'mehr hat das Spiessvolk auch zu späteren Zeiten in unglücklich verlaufenden Gefechten nicht geleistet' is only a partial truth.
[5] The role of the foot in this battle is fundamental to the arguments of those historians who have described the history of the twelfth-century *pedites* in terms of progress; Delpech, II, pp. 154, 186; Heermann, p. 122; Köhler, III, pt. 3, p. 209.
[6] *Anon.* p. 44. Köhler's argument, III, pt. 3, p. 141, n. 5 that Fulcher also gave this information, is worthless. Because, said Köhler, Fulcher recorded that many unmounted Latins were killed in the camp, this confirmed the information of the Anonymous that all the *pedites* had stayed in the camp. Unconvincing reasoning of this kind is typical of the work both of Delpech and Köhler.   [7] Bréhier in *Anon.* p. ii.

have drawn attention to the fact that when the battle began the knights went to meet the enemy, while the foot were left on camp duties; this arrangement has been interpreted as the allotment of an inferior role to men unfitted for battle.[1] It has been overlooked, however, that Bohemond issued two sets of orders. He first commanded that the knights dismount and pitch camp; before this could be completed, the threats of Turkish attack demanded immediate resistance. Therefore the two essential tasks were divided: the *milites* were to attack the Turks and the *pedites* were to continue making camp.[2] It may be said that they were given the subordinate part; but it was one which, despite the proximity of the enemy, had first been given to the knights, and one which was essential to the plan of halting and giving battle. It by no means proved that the foot-soldiers were unfit for war.

Nor was the situation unique, for one similar arose during the siege of Antioch. During the first week in February 1098 it was known that a Muslim force was marching to relieve the beleaguered garrison.[3] Once more there were two military tasks to be performed: it was necessary to defeat the enemy field army, and to prevent the garrison by a sortie from either joining hands with the relieving force, or destroying the Latin camp. Therefore it was decided by the Latin leaders that the knights who still had fit horses should meet the approaching enemy, and that the rest of the army should remain in camp and hold themselves ready to deal with any attack from within the city.[4] On 9 February 1098 both divisions of the Franks were in action. The knights won a victory by the lake of Antioch; the foot-soldiers no less successfully repulsed a sortie by the garrison.[5] As at Dorylaeum the foot played a less important part than the knights, but it is equally true that on both occasions they were assigned, and they performed, an essential military task.

[1] Cf. Bréhier in *Anon.* p. 45, n. 7.

[2] *Anon.* p. 44. The whole passage reads: 'Sapiens vir Boamundus videns innumerabiles Turcos procul stridentes et clamantes demoniaca voce, protinus jussit omnes milites descendere et tentoria celeriter extendere. Priusquam tentoria fuissent extensa, rursus dixit omnibus militibus: Seniores et fortissimi milites Christi, ecce modo bellum angustum est undique circa nos. Igitur omnes eant viriliter obviam illis et pedites prudenter et citius extendant tentoria.'

[3] Grousset, I, p. 86; Chalandon, *Première Croisade*, p. 194.

[4] *Anon.* p. 82; RA, p. 246.   [5] *Anon.* p. 86; RA, p. 247.

If the eyewitness accounts of Dorylaeum do not necessarily prove the military incompetence of the dismounted men in 1097, any theory which envisages their subsequent progress is left standing on weakened foundations. Nor are other arguments advanced in its support any more convincing. Delpech and Heermann both depicted growth by reference to the occasions during the early twelfth century on which the Syrian infantry were mentioned in the sources for distinguished service;[1] but the multiplication of such examples does not necessarily imply progress.[2] Such actions did not grow more frequent with the passing of time. The theory of development presented by these writers depended almost entirely on the conventional interpretation of the unfitness of the foot-soldiers for war in 1097 and early 1098.

The idea of a progressively skilful infantry fails not only because this interpretation of Dorylaeum is unsatisfactory, but because their deeds in battle afford no evidence of professional expertise. They never revealed power in offence nor in manœuvre. Throughout the century their whole ability was in defence; by their mass, their spears, and their archery they could hold the Turkish horsemen at bay. All their feats would have been possible at any time in history to a body of resolute men armed with bow and spear. At Dorylaeum they formed a mass not by design but through confusion, but the Turks could not break it.[3] Their out-

[1] Heermann, pp. 122–3.
[2] An example of Delpech's argument may be taken from *Tactique*, II, pp. 195–9. His reconstruction of the battle of Hab is of little value, since he ignored the best contemporary source, Walter, and used only William of Tyre. It is known that the foot-soldiers did well at Hab, although their feat was no different from others accomplished by their predecessors, in that they repulsed a Turkish attack (Galt. p. 103). Delpech, however, connects their performance with an event described by WT, p. 566, *sub anno* 1124. In that year the army of Jerusalem was besieging Tyre. The garrison of Ascalon followed their normal practice on such occasions and raided towards Jerusalem. No knights were in the city, but some burgesses took up arms and went out against the raiders, and by their resolute bearing forced the Egyptians to withdraw. Once again Delpech used William of Tyre, although the event was first recorded by a contemporary, Fulcher, pp. 459–60.
Delpech connected the two events in this way (II, p. 197): the pedites did so well at Hab, and by this time had made such good progress, that in 1124 they were able at Jerusalem to take the field without *milites*. The inadequacy of such an argument is self-evident.
[3] Fulcher, p. 335, said of the Latins: 'nos quidem omnes in unum conglobati, tanquam oves clausae ovili, trepidi et pavefacti ab hostibus undique circumvallabamur, ut nullatenus aliquorsum procedere valeremus.' Yet

stretched spears caused casualties to their own knights, but their flight was checked and the day saved.[1] On 28 June 1098[2] and at Jaffa in 1102[3] they were to show the same ability to check mounted attacks, and throughout the twelfth century this continued to be their main function.

An answer is thus provided to the second question: whether the military leaders found new uses for the foot-soldiers and gave them a more important part to play in military operations. It is certain that they formed a part of nearly every army assembled in Latin Syria during the twelfth century,[4] but their formation, like their equipment, remained unchanged throughout the century. On the battlefield of 28 June 1098 they went before the knights.[5] By their mass and their weapons they covered the horsemen from enemy attack until these were ready to ride out and to deliver their all-important charge. At Ascalon in the following year,[6] at the Ager Sanguinis and at Hab in 1119, they were formed in front of the knights.[7] On those occasions when a Latin force by its solidity resisted Turkish attack, as in 1147,[8] 1170,[9] and 1182,[10] it may reasonably be conjectured that the formation resembled that subsequently adopted at Arsuf in 1191,[11] with the foot-soldiers formed 'quasi murus' between the knight and the enemy. Certainly in the battles of the last years of the kingdom, at Hattin[12] and at Acre,[13] the foot-soldiers were still assigned the role which they had performed three generations earlier at Antioch and Ascalon.

IV. MILITARY IDEAS

Consideration will be given in this section to the ideas in accordance with which the Latin commanders handled their forces in the field. In the modern state there is a corpus of accepted military

---

though they had been driven into this plight, it checked further Turkish progress. It is typical of Köhler that he sees in the phrase 'in unum conglobati' the result of a planned, well-executed manœuvre (III, pt. 2, pp. 257–8).

[1] See above, p. 117, n. 4.   [2] RA, p. 260; Heermann, p. 44.
[3] Fulcher, pp. 404–5; Heermann, p. 68.
[4] When commanders went to war *cum solis equitibus* this fact was mentioned as abnormal; WT, pp. 921, 1108.
[5] Below, p. 173.   [6] Below, p. 174.   [7] Below, pp. 179, 181.
[8] Below, pp. 158–9.   [9] Below, p. 127.   [10] Below, p. 152.
[11] Below, p. 164.   [12] Below, p. 196.   [13] Below, p. 187.

doctrine on which the training of the troops and the education of the leaders is based; in the Middle Ages there were works on military theory, but they were not put to the same practical use.

The best known work of this kind was the *Epitoma rei militaris* of Vegetius, parts of which were incorporated during the Middle Ages into the work of many scholars.[1] The application of its principles, however, required troops trained to the degree of skill and discipline which would enable them to adopt the prescribed formations, and to carry out the necessary movements in the face of the enemy. Such troops were available neither in Latin Syria nor in any other feudal state during the twelfth century, and the influence of Vegetius on medieval military methods has still to be convincingly demonstrated.[2] Delpech argued that the Roman theorist inspired the ideas of the Syrian Franks in war, but his views are based on reasoning so faulty that they are without value.[3]

The crusaders came into contact with one rich source of military ideas. In the East Roman empire warfare had been treated for centuries as a science, so that manuals, text-books, and theoretical treatises had been written covering all branches of the military art.[4] Two of the best were the work of emperors: the *Strategicon* was written by Maurice in or about the year 580, and the *Tactica* by Leo the Wise, who ruled from 886 to 912.[5] Such writers

[1] Delbrück, III, pp. 669–77.

[2] Erben, *Kriegsgeschichte*, pp. 58–65, considered that the influence of Vegetius has been much underestimated, and that the matter deserves thorough research.

[3] Delpech, II, pp. 127–46. This historian's method was to find in medieval texts military ideas and arrangements which appear in Vegetius. For him this was sufficient to prove the influence of this writer on medieval military practice. He even uses verbal similarity as evidence for his argument; e.g. (p. 135) the use of the phrase 'quasi murus' to describe infantry both by Vegetius and certain medieval writers. Delpech allowed no inventive faculty to the Middle Ages, nor even that of common sense. Because in the Middle Ages commanders chose a battlefield so that they could fight on higher ground than the enemy, or could fight with the sun at their back, 'c'est encore à Végèce que le Moyen-Age doit le conseil de choisir ainsi ses champs de bataille' (p. 140). On these and other equally childish arguments was based the final conclusion (p. 146): 'Le rôle de Végèce auprès du monde féodal dut donc avoir quelque analogie avec celui des officiers européens que les princes asiatiques appellent, de nos jours, à organiser leurs armées.' For the use still made of Delpech's work, see above, p. 8.

[4] Runciman, *Byzantine Civilization*, p. 137.

[5] Jähns, *Geschichte der Kriegswissenschaften*, I, 152–6, 160–71; Aussaresses,

discussed the organization and administration of the army, its chain of command, its subdivision into units, the tactical handling of those units in the field, and the strategical considerations to be observed by its leaders.[1] Nor were such matters discussed only in the realm of theory; they were applied to the hard facts of the empire's military problems. The characteristic military methods of the various peoples were carefully analysed, and tactics were devised to enable the Greeks to take full advantage of their weaknesses.[2]

Now there were occasions on which the crusaders enjoyed the benefit of Byzantine advice on military affairs; Alexius Comnenus for example, is said by his daughter to have aided in this way the leaders of the First Crusade.[3] There were as well campaigns in which Franks took the field with Byzantine forces.[4] It has therefore to be asked to what extent they were the pupils in warfare of Byzantium.

Although there is a lack of good evidence of this matter, it seems certain that there can have been little direct connexion between the military methods of the two peoples. The rational and consistent application of a system of tactics requires a professional standing force, fashioned by drill and discipline into an instrument which can readily respond to the will of the commander. This essential condition existed in Byzantium to a much greater degree than in Latin Syria or in any other feudal society. In East Rome the abstract idea of the state had been preserved. Its functions were clearly articulated and were embodied in departments of government staffed by salaried officials. Until the Saljuq Turks overran Asia Minor after 1071, the East Roman Empire was the most stable and best-governed state in the world and the army was a highly organized department of that state. It was permanent, professional, paid by the state, and organized into regular units.[5] It could therefore be trained and handled in

---

L'Armée byzantine à la fin du VIe siècle d'après le Strategicon de l'empereur Maurice; A. Dain, L'Extrait tactique tiré de Léon le Sage.

[1] Oman, Art of War, I, pp. 171–217; Lot, L'Art militaire, I, pp. 43–73.
[2] Oman, I, pp. 204–16.   [3] Anna, pp. 264, 267.
[4] In 1138, 1164, and 1169.
[5] On the political institutions of the East Roman empire, see L. Bréhier, Les Institutions de l'Empire byzantin (1949). More briefly, W. Ensslin in Byzantium (edited by Baynes and Moss), pp. 268–307 and Runciman,

accordance with a developed military science. Not so the armies in the feudal society of western Europe and Latin Syria, for they were temporary and amateur, based on the service owed by individuals as part of their obligation as tenants, sometimes supplemented by recruits drawn from other sources already discussed. Forces such as these would not be trained to the degree of corporate manœuvre demanded by Byzantine military science.

Within their limits, however, the Franks may have adopted certain Byzantine military ideas. There is some similarity between the tactical plans adopted by Bohemond in the battles around Antioch in 1097-8 and the methods devised by the Greeks as a counter to the mobile attack made by mounted archers;[1] it is known, too, that Alexius Comnenus, in his campaigns against the Turks, adopted the same close marching order which was so often employed by the Syrian Franks.[2] In these respects it is possible that the Latins learned from the Greeks; but without further evidence the matter cannot be regarded as proven. The similarity may equally well be due to reactions in the face of Turkish tactics which were common to both Latin and Greek commanders.

The Syrian Franks appear to have had no elaborate theories of warfare, either written or traditional; yet no general can lead even a small force into action without a plan, which will be the result of his ideas on war. In Syria some of these were merely the result of applying common sense to known conditions. To take a simple example, the Franks knew of the soldiers' temptation to take immediate advantage of an opportunity to acquire spoils even before the battle was over; therefore commanders sometimes took measures to ensure that no man should turn aside from an engagement in search of spoil.[3] It was likewise considered

---

Byzantine Civilization, pp. 81–107. On the army see Bréhier, *Institutions*, pp. 334–403; Ensslin, *Byzantium*, pp. 294–304; Runciman, *Byz. Civilization*, pp. 136–49.

[1] Below, pp. 170–4.   [2] Below, p. 156.

[3] RA, p. 259, for orders ascribed to Saint Andrew before battle of 28 June 1098. For Ascalon, 1099, AA, pp. 491–2. Daimbert, in *HEp*. p. 172, wrote that at that battle the defeat of the Egyptians would have been much heavier if the *spolia castrorum* had not detained many Franks. To leave the line of march in search of plunder is still a crime in the British Army under Section 6 of the Army Act.

unwise to accept battle with an enemy who enjoyed a great numerical superiority. Since the numbers of the Muslims were consistently overestimated by contemporaries, the existence of this common-sense principle is not always apparent in their writings. From their accounts it seems that the Franks would fight against any odds, however great. But on at least one occasion the most experienced leaders of the Latin army decided against battle on account of the great numerical superiority of the enemy.[1]

Further light is thrown on the comparatively simple ideas of the twelfth century by William of Tyre's use of a phrase which often appeared in classical writings and in those of Vegetius: it was 'disciplina militaris'. According to William certain military ideas and actions were 'juxta disciplinam militarem', and others 'contra'.[2] Some of them were no more than common-sense precautions; military science was said to require, for example, that a commander should be at all times alert and on his guard against surprise. When in 1157 Nur al-din ambushed Baldwin III and his knights near Lake Huleh in the upper Jordan valley, William recorded that no watch was kept in the Latin camp; 'ubi nocte illa longe aliter, quam disciplina militaris exigeret, et imprudenter se habens, non observata castrorum lege, requievit exercitus'.[3]

From nearly all medieval descriptions of military operations, it is clear that, to the Franks, an indispensable preliminary to any engagement was to subdivide the army into a number of smaller units and to marshal them in the field in a prearranged order.[4]

---

[1] WT, p. 1038. The occasion was the invasion of southern Palestine by Saladin in 1177. 'Egressus autem christianus exercitus, inspecta partis adversae multitudine infinita; qui sensus habebant magis exercitatos in talibus, tutius *esse dicebant in se subsistere, quam dubiis belli eventibus inconsulte se committere.*' The last thirteen words have been italicized because they are important evidence on Frankish ideas of battle as a method of warfare.

[2] WT, pp. 529, 725, 849, 1042, 1119.   [3] WT, p. 840.

[4] References to this process may be found in all the sources of crusading history. Some examples are: *Anon.* pp. 150, 212; Fulcher, pp. 392, 451; Galt. pp. 70, 73; WT, pp. 130, 268, 529, 925; *HEF*, pp. 34, 84. These references could be multiplied fifty-fold. The most commonly used descriptive phrase was *acies ordinare*. Alternative nouns to *acies* were: *turmae, agmina, catervae, ordines*. Other verbs: *disponere, componere, instruere, stabilire, dirigere*. The verb-noun phrase was sometimes accompanied by an adverb, which too was often a reflexion of contemporary military ideas: *decenter, competenter, ordinatim, ordinate, ordinatissime*, and *ut decet*.

Thus to begin the fight in a well-organized formation was also a feature of the 'disciplina militaris'.[1] Such measures were necessary, as they will always be in any military force, in the interests of control; no commander can issue orders to the whole body of his troops except through subordinate leaders. Furthermore, in Latin Syria, once the knights had charged, the commander, who himself fought with lance and sword in the battle, had little further control over them. In order to direct operations until the final charge, it was in his interests to keep them in their original battle order for as long as possible. Another inducement to follow this course was provided by the Turkish tactics. It has been seen that the Turks relied on archery and movement to loosen and unsettle the Latin formation before coming to close quarters in an attempt to finish the battle. The defence against such tactics therefore lay in maintaining formation and in presenting no weakness for the Turks to exploit. Thus the 'disciplina militaris' required the commander not only to organize squadrons and to dispose them in order, but also to maintain formation until the final decisive charge.

Ideas similar to those held by William of Tyre on 'disciplina militaris' were expressed by Fulcher when he gave the reasons for the defeats of Baldwin I at Ramla in 1102 and al-Sannabra in 1113. On the first occasion the king was blamed for not awaiting the arrival of all the forces at his disposal, for leading his men into action without having organized them in battle order, and for leaving behind his foot-soldiers.[2] Contemporary opinion censured him in much the same terms for the rash attack which led to his defeat eleven years later.[3] The events which led to the far more disastrous defeat in 1119 of Prince Roger and the army of Antioch began when he disregarded the advice of the patriarch to await the arrival of the forces of King Baldwin II and Count Pons

[1] WT, p. 725, '. . . contra rei militaris disciplinam ordines solverent . . .'; p. 896, '. . . dum incautius insequuntur, dissolutisque agminibus et contra disciplinam militarem passim discurrentibus evagantur. . . .'

[2] Fulcher, p. 400: 'Hoc siquidem immodestia regis magna fuit, qui gentem suam exspectare neglexit, nec ordinate, sicut oportet sapienter ire, ad bellum processit. Sed, absque peditibus, milites suos vix exspectans, acceleravit hostes appetere. . . .'

[3] Fulcher, p. 426: 'Unde omnes isti contristati sunt valde et immodestiam regis vituperaverunt, eo quod sine consilio eorum et auxilio inordinate et inconsulte adversus hostes illos sic cucurrisset.'

of Tripoli, and when he left the well-protected and supplied base
of Artah and took up a bare, exposed position at the Ager Sanguinis.[1] Thirty years later Raymond, another prince of Antioch,
likewise lost an army and his life. His fault also was to go out
against the enemy before all his available forces had collected,
and then to remain in a position which invited attack by the
enemy, rather than to take advantage of the shelter offered by one
of his own fortresses.[2] In 1187, immediately before the battle of
Hattin, Raymond of Tripoli counselled King Guy not to leave his
well-supplied base at Saffuriya;[3] and in some accounts he is said
to have advised him to give battle near the defended Frankish
towns on the coast.[4]

The sources therefore provide evidence of a number of simple
though clear contemporary ideas on the conduct of war. The
actions of military leaders could be influenced by the numerical
strength of the enemy; they knew the importance of collecting all
their own available troops before going out to meet him. In fighting a campaign they appreciated the unwisdom of leaving well-
supplied and protected bases without good cause, and they
valued the neighbourhood of their own fortresses in which they
might, and often did, find refuge in an emergency.[5] Above all,
their military doctrine taught them that an army should be
subdivided into smaller units, and that the formation adopted
should be maintained until the decisive charge was made.

The maintenance of their formation was a problem which
faced the Syrian Franks throughout the twelfth century, not only

[1] Galt. pp. 79–80.   [2] WT, p. 772.

[3] Libellus, p. 221; Eracles, p. 50, variant C.

[4] Eracles, p. 50; below, pp. 192–4.

[5] After the Egyptian victory at Ramla some of the defeated Franks took
refuge in a weak tower nearby; Fulcher, pp. 401–2. After Il Ghazi's victory at
the Ager Sanguinis, Reginald Mansoer with a few followers fled to the tower
at Sarmeda; Galt. p. 89.

In 1137, Fulk led a force to relieve Ba'rin, which was besieged by Zanki.
The Latin army was attacked and scattered as it approached the fortress,
within which the king and other survivors were able to find shelter; WT,
p. 644.

After Nur al-Din's successful ambush in 1157, Baldwin III fled from the
fight to the safety of Safad; WT, p. 842. In 1179 survivors fled from Marj
'Ayyun to the castle of Shaqif Arnun; WT, p. 1057. Two years before, when
Saladin had invaded Palestine from Egypt, the king and his army had taken
temporary shelter in Ascalon; WT, p. 1038.

to enable the commander to exercise control, but to counter those Turkish tactics which have been described in an earlier chapter. The importance attached by the Franks to preserving the solidity and cohesion of their battle or marching order may be seen in William of Tyre's use of the phrase *agmen* or *aciem dissolvere*. Loss of formation by organized squadrons was the prelude, or even the symptom, of defeat.[1] To resist the Turk it was essential to prevent him from separating the Franks one from the other.[2] In 1170 Amalric led a force to oppose Saladin's invasion of southern Palestine. The Muslims attempted to destroy the Franks, but these preserved themselves by the solidity of their array. 'Illi [*sc*. Turci] statim in nostros irruentes, tentabant, si unquam possent eos ab invicem separare; sed nostri, propitia divinitate, solidius inter se conglobati, et hostium sustinebant impetus, et iter maturatis gressibus conficiebant.'[3]

The need for the Franks to remain 'solidius inter se conglobati' was even more necessary when they fought on the march than on the normal battlefield. Any gaps in the column enabled the Turks to single out some part of the Latin force for attack. This was discovered at heavy cost by the pilgrims led across Asia Minor by Louis VII of France in 1147. At one point the leader of the vanguard, Geoffrey de Rancogne, disregarded his orders and went too far ahead of the main body. As a result the Turks were able to develop a strong attack on those who followed, to throw the whole line of march into confusion and to inflict great losses.[4] To prevent the recurrence of such a disaster the line of march was more thoroughly organized, with advance-, flank-, and rear-guards, in which archers on foot were given a prominent part. Thereafter, 'fiebat juxta preceptum processio'.[5]

In 1191 the Turks gained a similar success. On the day on

---

[1] WT, p. 748; when the Turks inflicted a defeat on the French in Asia Minor in 1147, 'nostras violenter acies dissolvunt.' WT, p. 838; when the Hospitallers were beaten by Nur al-Din in 1157, '[Turci] agmen dissolvunt'. WT, p. 896; the Franks were defeated at Harim in 1164, 'agminibus dissolutis'. WT, p. 725, in their march to Bosra in 1147, the Franks under Baldwin III took special defensive measures 'ne si contra rei militaris disciplinam ordines solverent'.

[2] During the march across Asia Minor during the Second Crusade, the Turks on one occasion suffered heavy losses because 'divisi sunt alter ab altero'. Odo, p. 69.

[3] WT, p. 976.   [4] Odo, pp. 67–70; WT, pp. 747–8.   [5] Odo, p. 72.

which King Richard began his southward march from Acre, the column, for which advance- and rear-guards had been appointed, was attacked by part of Saladin's army. The line of march was widely spaced, and the Muslims were repulsed only with difficulty. The lesson was learnt, and the Christian army continued its progress in more solid order.[1] That a force should be 'seré e rengié' was the highest praise which Ambroise could bestow upon it. On two occasions he recorded with approval a battle order so solid that it was impossible to throw a plum[2] or an apple[3] into the ranks without hitting a man or horse.

The maintenance of close order in face of enemy provocation was an achievement for which historians have not given twelfth-century commanders in Syria sufficient credit. To endure attack without striking back at the enemy demands severe restraint of normal human instincts, and in all ages soldiers have borne such a situation only with difficulty. To none was it more intolerable than the medieval knight, who in war was an individualist jealous of his personal prowess and honour. It is possible to see in the sources the difficulties experienced by commanders in Syria throughout the century in checking the ardour of their knights and compelling them to remain in the ranks in the face of enemy attack. Ralph of Caen, whose account of the battle of Dorylaeum was based on information received from Tancred himself, told of Bohemond's efforts to restrain the ardour of Tancred and other young men of spirit.[4] Nearly a century later King Richard faced the same problem on the day of Arsuf. The Knights of St John in the rear-guard, forbidden to strike back against heavy enemy attacks, were stung by thoughts of the possible infamy to which their enforced inactivity exposed them,[5] and by their inability to

[1] *Est.* 5829: 'plus seree et mielz rengiee'.
[2] *Est.* 3975–86, describing the array on Saint Martin's Day, 1190.
[3] *Est.* 6161–2, describing the Latin order at Arsuf:
    'Issi serré que d'une pome
    Ne ferissiez fors beste ou home.'
[4] RC, p. 623: 'Boamundo enim invito, quin prohibente, res coepta vix comites aliquot elicere impetravit; ideo autem prohibente quod exercitus hostilis diffusus nostrum quadam theatrali specie circumsepserat, ex omni parte necem significans inclusis. Quamobrem ducum Christianorum providentia aestuantibus juvenum animis ad congressum egressum negabat, ne forte paucorum temeritas rei ordinem turbaret universum.'
[5] *Itin.* pp. 266–8; *Est.* 6378–402.

prevent the Turkish archers from taking a heavy toll of their horses. Richard held them in check as long as he could, but finally the strain was too great, and the knights of the rear-guard launched their charge before the king had given his signal.[1]

The same difficulty arose in the march to Bosra undertaken by King Baldwin III in the spring of 1147. Both on the outward and homeward journeys the Latin column was pressed by the enemy, and the normal measures were taken to ensure a solid formation. Strict orders were given that no man was to leave the ranks under pain of severe punishment.[2] One Turkish horseman in the Latin army was unable to endure further attacks. He rode out, killed an adversary, and so dismayed the enemy and heartened the Franks that excuses were found for his breach of orders.[3]

In framing their statutes the Templars recognized the existence of this problem. The conduct of the knights when marshalled in their squadrons was carefully regulated, and to leave the ranks without permission was strictly forbidden.[4] As the only exceptions to this rule, the knight might test his horse and harness by a short gallop, or rescue a Christian in danger of imminent death at the hands of a Muslim, without special leave.[5] Otherwise any breach of the standing order brought him severe punishment,[6] and the very existence of such penalties proves to some extent the difficulty of enforcing the rule. In 1115 Prince Roger of Antioch compelled his troops to resist Turkish provocation by mounting a fast horse, and by riding through the camp with a

---

[1] *Itin.* p. 268; *Est.* 6421 *et. seq.*

[2] WT, p. 725: 'Nostri autem proposita lege ad eos erumpere non auderent, ne si, contra rei militaris disciplinam ordines solverent, duriorem in se tanquam locorum desertores experirentur sententiam.'

[3] WT, *ibid.* The sally by a single knight unable to restrain his desire to strike back at the enemy and eager for personal distinction was probably more frequent than the sources record. For an instance see Usamah, p. 98. This occurred in the campaign of 1111, when the Frankish army as a whole carefully avoided offensive action. See also Derenbourg, *Vie d'Ousâma*, pp. 89–93.

[4] *Règle*, no. 162: 'Ne nul frere ne doit poindre ne desranger sans congié.'

[5] *Règle*, nos. 162, 163.

[6] It was one of the serious offences for which a Templar could be deprived of his habit; *Règle*, no. 243. The same rule obtained among the knights of St John; *Itin.* pp. 371–2. But on this occasion, as in the example from WT, quoted above, the offender was excused because there was good reason for his action, and his sortie was successful. See also *Règle*, nos. 613–15.

drawn sword threatening death to any man who dared to leave the camp.[1]

A measure which contributed to the main object of achieving and preserving the cohesion of the army was the close co-operation of horse- and foot-soldiers. This factor has been singled out for special emphasis by military historians. It has been held, first, that the liaison of the two arms on the battlefield was essential to the success of the Franks in war,[2] and second, that when this was understood by the Muslims they concentrated their efforts on separating the Latin knights and infantry, and by their success in doing so won many notable victories.[3]

In some respects knights and foot were complementary to each other. The foot, on both the line of march and the battle-field, were usually placed between the enemy and the knights, who, until the moment came to make their decisive charge, were thus protected by a living barrier armed with spears and bows. On the other hand the foot themselves were generally incapable of successful offensive action, and could not on their own resist attacks by a mounted enemy for an indefinite period. For relief from Muslim pressure they looked to the knights, who were also necessary to achieve final victory in battle. In the twelfth century this idea of mutual aid between horse- and foot-soldiers was well understood, and found expression in contemporary writing.[4]

[1] It is to be supposed that he did not express himself quite in the formal manner reported by his chancellor; Galt. p. 69: 'Fide Dei, qua vivimus, si quis egredi iam praesumpserit, meo peribit gladio.'

[2] Delpech, I, p. 359; II, pp. 186–7; Oman, I, pp. 296, 320.

[3] Delpech, *ut supra*; Köhler, III, pt. 3, pp. 138, 213, 215; accepted by M. W. Baldwin, *Raymond III of Tripolis*, p. 99.

[4] Fulcher in his account of the two battles fought by Baldwin I near Ramla and Jaffa in 1102, speaks first of the error made by the king in giving battle without his *pedites*, and later of *pedites* who lacked protection from the knights: 'Sed, absque peditibus . . . acceleravit hostes appetere' (p. 400); and 'pedites nostros absque protectione militum videbant' (p. 405). The idea of mutual help between horse and foot implied in these two sentences was more directly expressed in Fulcher's account of the battle of Marj es-Suffar in 1126: 'Ordinatae sunt in parte nostra tam militum quam peditum acies duodecim, ut ab alterutra corroboraretur caterva, si necessitas admoneret' (p. 477). For the precise meaning of this sentence, see Heermann, p. 99; Oman, I, p. 303, n. 1. See also Galt. p. 103: battle of Hab, 1119, 'tribus aciebus antepositis, manus pedestris, ut has protegat et ab his protegatur, retro sistitur'.

Odo, p. 72: 'Ultimi quoque milites et pedites hostibus fere mixti transierunt sine dampno, mutua probitate defensi.'

Modern historians have gone further than the sources on which they rely, and have overemphasized this to the exclusion of other important factors. This is particularly true of Delpech, and other historians have accepted his ideas on the subject. In his comments on the defeat of Baldwin I at Ramla in 1102, he selected as the most important reason the fact that the king went into battle without his foot-soldiers.[1] According to contemporary opinion, expressed by Fulcher, the king was beaten not only on this account, but also because he attacked withôut awaiting all his available troops, and because he did not set his force in battle order.[2] None of these factors was stated to be more important than the other, and Delpech had no good reason for emphasizing the one at the expense of the rest. There are better grounds for asserting that the true cause of defeat was the rash frame of mind in which the king approached the problem.

Delpech considered further that after 1145 the Muslims exerted themselves to separate the Latin horse and foot.[3] He brought together an impressive list of victories which, in his view, were gained by the Muslims because they succeeded in this tactical aim. The researches of Delpech, however, were not objective. He read the sources looking for this development, and it appears that he was determined to find it at all costs. His work on the battle of al-Babein provides a fair sample of his reasoning.[4] It was a battle fought during Amalric's third Egyptian campaign in 1167. The king was opposed in that country by an army sent from Syria by Nur al-Din and under the leadership of Shirkuh.[5] If either of these forces could destroy the other, then the victorious leader

---

Libellus, p. 213: battle of 1 May 1187, '... milites et pedites in duas partes diviserunt, ut nec isti illis, nec illi istis mutuo adjutorio adjuvarent.'

Libellus, p. 224: battle of Hattin, 1187, 'Cum autem ordinati essent, et per acies distincti, preceperunt peditibus ut sagittando munirent exercitum, quatinus milites levius hostibus obstarent, ut milites muniti per pedites a sagittariis hostibus, et pedites per lanceas militum ab incursu hostium essent adiuti; et ita utrique mutuo adiutorio defensi salutem obtinerent'.

Libellus, p. 225: battle of Hattin, 'Rex autem et ceteri, ut viderunt quod ... ipsi sine servientibus contra sagittas Turcorum non possent subsistere...'.

[1] Delpech, II, pp. 187–90.   [2] Fulcher, p. 400; above, p. 125.

[3] Delpech, II, p. 187: 'Telle fut la grande tactique, on pourrait dire l'unique tactique des Nour-Eddin, des Schirkouh, des Saladin, des Bibars.'

[4] II, pp. 209–13.

[5] Grousset, II, pp. 480–504; *RGKJ*, pp. 322–30; Schlumberger, *Campagnes du roi Amaury*, pp. 107–68.

was likely to become master of Egypt. Since Amalric was on this occasion the ally and nominal protector of the Fatimid government, it was in his interest to exploit his advantage by bringing Shirkuh to battle; the Turkish leader, on the other hand, sought to avoid it.

For some weeks Shirkuh was able to keep the Nile between himself and the Franks. When, with some difficulty, Amalric succeeded in crossing the river, the Turks rapidly withdrew into upper Egypt. Amalric at once pursued, and was so eager to overtake them that he went ahead with his horsemen and left his foot to follow at the best pace they could.[1] They had still not overtaken him when Shirkuh turned to give battle at al-Babein. In this battle the Franks did not destroy Shirkuh's army. Delpech not only attributed this result to his lack of foot-soldiers,[2] but gave his readers the impression that Shirkuh had by design separated Frankish horse and foot. In the heading of the chapter in which he discussed the battle Delpech wrote: 'Bataille de Babeïn (1167); les Musulmans séparent les deux armes des Chrétiens pour les battre isolément.'[3] In fact the separation of Amalric's horse and foot was not, as Delpech stated, brought about by the Muslims; it was arranged by Amalric of his own free choice. Nor did the Muslims beat the two arms separately; they never came into contact with the Latin foot at all. What undoubtedly did happen in the battles was that Shirkuh succeeded in breaking the battle order of the Franks by inducing a part of their army to leave the field in pursuit of Saladin, who had retreated in accordance with a plan made before the battle. Delpech appears to have been so limited by his prejudice, that he could think only in terms of the separation of horse and foot.

At Marj 'Ayyun in 1179 the army of Baldwin IV advanced against detachments of Saladin's force so rapidly that the knights outstripped all but the most active of the foot-soldiers.[4] This fact alone was for Delpech a sufficient explanation of the ensuing Latin defeat.[5] In fact, the battle appears to have fallen into two parts. The first attack of the Franks, despite the separation of

---

[1] WT, p. 921: 'relictis pedestribus auxiliis, dominus rex cum solis equitibus ad iter accingitur'.

[2] Delpech, II, p. 212. [3] II, p. 185. [4] WT, p. 1055; below, p. 186.

[5] Delpech, II, p. 216.

horse and foot, achieved an easy success, because it was delivered against Muslim raiding parties. As a result the Franks relaxed their vigilance and their formation. When Saladin appeared with the main body of his army, they were unprepared for further combat, and were heavily defeated.[1]

In his analysis of military events in Latin Syria, Delpech exerted himself to show the separation of *milites* and *pedites* as the sole or principal cause of Christian defeats; in fact the separation was more often the symptom of that cause. At Ramla in 1102,[2] as at Cresson in 1187,[3] it was a symptom of the rash imprudence displayed by the Latin commander; at Huleh[4] and Harim, of his carelessness and lack of normal precaution when in the neighbourhood of the enemy; at Hattin, of the collapse of the foot-soldiers' morale after their ordeal during the previous night.[5] The defeat of the Franks was never simply the result of a mechanical defect in their battle formation; nor is there any well-authenticated instance of such a defect being achieved by the military skill of the Muslims. Defeat was always the result of some failure in leadership or morale which sometimes revealed itself in the untimely[6] separation of knights and foot-soldiers. The military ideas of the age demanded that before an engagement the commander drew up his force in orderly array; and since the Turks depended for tactical success in finding or creating a weakness in that formation, it was a further necessity that the Franks should maintain it until the final charge was delivered by the knights. The ruling idea was to preserve the cohesion and solidity of the whole force; the close co-operation of horse and foot was an important contributory factor to that end.

It has been argued in an earlier chapter that reference to the outstanding events in the history of warfare in Latin Syria is sufficient to show that military effort was limited to the immediate object of the campaign; it was not devoted to the complete overthrow of the enemy.[7] The existence of this conception of limited warfare as part of the contemporary outlook on war was

---

[1] WT, pp. 1055-6; Grousset, II, pp. 674-6; *RGKJ*, pp. 384-5.
[2] Above, p. 125.   [3] Below, p. 197.
[4] Above, p. 124; Delpech, II, pp. 206-7.   [5] Below, p. 197.
[6] It is a relevant fact that the Franks gained their victories by their renowned charge, that is, by a timely separation of the two arms.
[7] Above, pp. 22-5.

nowhere better demonstrated than in 1164, when Nur al-Din attacked Harim in the principality of Antioch.[1] The northern Franks assisted by Calaman, the Byzantine governor of Cilicia, and by Thoros, the greatest of the independent Armenian princes, formed a powerful coalition against him.[2] On their approach, Nur al-Din raised the siege. Muslim historians assert that his intention was to draw the Franks after him in pursuit, but his action may simply have been in accordance with twelfth-century practice. He may not have wished to risk a battle in order to further his plan of invasion. Therefore he withdrew, Harim was relieved, and the object of the invaders was achieved.

Faulty leadership, however, committed the Franks to a pursuit of Nur al-Din's force. This movement was carried out rapidly and carelessly. The Frankish column split apart and lost formation, so that the Muslims were able to turn and defeat the detachments into which the Christian army had become divided. As a result of this victory Nur al-Din captured Harim, and, later in the same year, Banyas. The Arab historians have said that Nur al-Din won by virtue of an elaborate plan involving two feigned retreats and an ambush.[3] Some modern historians have followed these accounts, and have presented the whole episode as yet another action in which Nur al-Din's superior guile enabled him to separate the Christian horse- and foot-soldiers, and so gave him the victory.[4]

Such an account is in accordance with the evidence of Arab historians writing many years after the event, but it does not reflect the comments made by King Amalric himself only five months after the battle. The Arab writers, and the modern historians who have followed them, overlooked the fact that Nur al-Din's plans would have meant nothing if the Franks had not pursued him; and the military ideas of the day condemned that pursuit and considered that the Latin princes had achieved their military task, when they had raised the siege of Harim.

In a letter to Louis VII of France Amalric wrote:[5]

[1] Grousset, II, pp. 459–64; *RGKJ*, pp. 317–19. On Harim see Rey, *Colonies*, p. 341; Dussaud, *Topographie*, pp. 171–2; Cahen, *Syrie du Nord*, p. 135.
[2] WT, p. 896; IA, p. 538; *AM*, p. 219, 221; KD in *ROL*, III, p. 539.
[3] IA, p. 539; *AM*, p. 222.
[4] Delpech, II, 207–8; Köhler, III, pt. 3, pp. 211–13.
[5] Letter dated 14 January 1165. The battle had been fought on the pre-

... factum est ut Comes Tripolitanus et Princeps Antiochenus cum multo exercitu ad liberandum castellum prope Antiochiam situm, nomine Haring, quod Noradinus cum innumera multitudine obsederat, irent, et, auxilio divino, hostibus eorum adventui cedentibus, liberarent. Accidit autem ut, dum praefati Princeps scilicet et Comes, non contenti tanto Dei beneficio, superbe hostes ad loca naturaliter munitissima insequerentur, ipsos ab hostibus capi, et omnem eorum exercitum partim capi, partim occidi.

William of Tyre judged the events of this campaign by the same ideas as those expressed by his king.[1]

That such ideas could also be held during the twelfth century by the Muslim enemies of the Franks is shown in the accounts given by Ibn al-Athir and Kemal ed-Din of the relief of Aleppo by Aq-Sunqur Bursuqi of Mosul. On 8 October 1124, Baldwin II laid siege to the city.[2] By the following January the plight of the inhabitants was desperate, and they were saved only by the army led into Syria by Bursuqi. When the news reached Baldwin he at once withdrew his army from the siege. The Arab historians related that there were many Muslims who wished to pursue the Franks; but Bursuqi knew that his immediate military objective, the relief of Aleppo, was accomplished. The Franks had left Muslim territory, and for the present could be left in peace.[3]

The idea of limited warfare, and of achieving a military objective with an economy of effort, commended itself to the Franks. They had insufficient men and means to raise a numerous army; their dominion in Syria was based on the fortified towns and castles; by a defeat in the field they risked losing both army and

---

ceding 10 August; *Reg.* no. 411. Full text is in Bouquet, *Recueil des historiens des Gaules*, vol. XVI, p. 79, no. 243.

[1] In a single sentence, WT (p. 896) explains the error made and gives the military causes for defeat: 'Sane Noradinus, et qui cum eo erant Parthorum principes, communicato consilio, tutius opinantes, obsidione sponte soluta, discedere, quam cum hostibus pene jam instantibus incaute congredi, compositis sarcinis, recedere moliebantur; nostri vero nihilominus eis instantes, dato successu et prosperi abutentes, dum eis non sufficit, quod oppidanos obsidione tantorum principum expedierant, dum incautius insequuntur, dissolutisque agminibus et contra disciplinam militarem passim discurrentibus evagantur, recurrentibus subito animumque et vires resumentibus Turcis, quibusdam locorum palustrium angustiis comprehensi, primo franguntur impetu.'

[2] Grousset, I, p. 627; *RGKJ*, pp. 172–5; Cahen, *Syrie du Nord*, p. 300.

[3] IA, p. 361; KD, p. 650.

strong places. It was not therefore in their interest to fight unnecessary battles.

An additional consideration was that success in a defensive campaign could be achieved as fully without battle as by the use of that method. The defeat of the invader meant the end of the campaign, but with the creation of a strong Muslim state in western Asia by Zanki, Nur al-Din, and Saladin, such a victory achieved little more. These leaders disposed of reserves of strength which enabled them to put fresh forces into the field with a minimum of delay.[1] Successful battle, with all its risks, had little more than an immediate and temporary effect against a determined enemy, and the gamble appears even less justified when it is remembered that this same effect could be achieved without it. Throughout the century the large Muslim armies required for successful invasion dispersed to their homes in the autumn. So long as they could be prevented from forming a successful siege during the campaigning season, and this could be done by keeping an army in their neighbourhood to cut off supplies and to threaten siege operations, their invasion had no permanent results. The essential objects of a defensive campaign could therefore be achieved without battle, and by waiting for the enemy forces to melt away of their own accord. There is no doubt that contemporary observers were conscious of these factors which so strongly influenced military activity.[2]

[1] Nur al-Din's defeat at al-Buqaia in 1163 only provoked in him thoughts of revenge; *AM*, pp. 209–10. In the very next year he was able to win a far more important victory over the Franks at Harim. In 1177 Saladin was heavily defeated by Baldwin IV at Mont Gisard, but fully revenged himself in 1179.

[2] That Muslim armies in fact dispersed of their own accord without being forced to do so by enemy action was shown in the preceding chapter. For evidence that contemporaries understood that this reduced the military effort required from a defending ruler see:

(a) IA, p. 296. In his account of the 1115 campaign IA stated that the Syrian allies, i.e. the rulers of the Latin states, Tughtagin of Damascus and Lulu of Aleppo, would avoid coming to grips with the enemy for two reasons: the sultan's army, led by Bursuq b. Bursuq, was too large (cf. above, p. 124); and as winter approached it would disperse of its own accord. The translation reads:

'Il fut convenu entre les confédérés qu'on éviterait de se trouver en présence de l'armée du sulthan, à cause du grand nombre de ses guerriers. L'armée musulmane, se dirent-ils, dès que l'hiver approchera, se dispersera d'elle-même.'

Finally, it was understood in Latin Syria that the outcome of battle was always determined partly by chance. It could not be otherwise. Before an engagement the commander could use his art to ensure that ground, weather, numbers, supplies, and communications favoured his own men; he could determine the formation in which they could best begin the battle, and could plan the time, order, and direction of their attack. But once he had launched them at the enemy they were beyond his control, the more so as he himself was usually playing a distinguished personal part in the action. Most engagements were soldiers' battles which finally depended on factors other than the will of the commander. In William of Tyre's History, military events were frequently described as 'dubii' and 'ancipites'.[1] Such expressions may have been to some extent conventional, but they corresponded to known conditions, and it is unlikely that they had lost all literal meaning.

(b) IA, p. 501; KD in *ROL*, III, p. 529. Both historians tell the story of a Frankish *castellanus* at Harim. When in 1156 or 1157 Nur al-Din besieged the place, the Frank sent a message, presumably to Antioch, that he was well able to sustain the siege, and that it was unnecessary to send an army to relieve him. He is said to have pointed out that if such an army was defeated by Nur al-Din, the Muslim ruler would take Harim and other places. Whether these facts took place or not, the anecdote is good evidence of contemporary ideas on military affairs.

(c) *Ernoul*, p. 159. Raymond of Tripoli's advice to Guy on 2 July 1187 that he should not attempt to relieve Tiberias was based on this same idea: the Muslims would certainly take Tiberias and destroy it, but they would not retain it, since they would disperse in the normal way. Raymond's counsel was that the temporary loss of Tiberias was better than the loss of the army and possibly of the kingdom:

'Et si sai bien que se li Sarrasin le prendent qu'il ne le tenront pas, ains l'abateront, puis si s'en iront. . . . t s'il prendent me feme et mes hommes et mon avoir, et il abatent me cité, jou les raverai quant je porrai, et refremerai me cité quant je porai. . . .'

[1] E.g. WT, p. 840, '[Noradinus] nolens se dubiis bellorum submittere casibus'; p. 845, '[Noradinus] tamen bellorum declinans insidias et casus praeliorum ancipites. . . .' Similar expressions are to be found on pp. 584, 926, 1038, 1041. AA, p. 682.

CHAPTER VI

THE LATIN FIELD ARMY IN ACTION

I. THE BACKGROUND OF WARFARE

O F all men', said Usamah, 'the Franks are the most cautious in warfare.'[1] At first sight this is a surprising judgement on a people renowned for their reckless fury in battle, yet the words were written by one who had often fought against the Franks in Syria, and who had reflected much on his experiences. The matters discussed in the foregoing chapters do something to explain his dictum. In Syria the Franks encountered military problems, both strategic and tactical, which imposed caution and restraint.

They fought only for limited objectives. Settled as they were on the fringe of Muslim Asia, they could never hope to overwhelm the whole strength of Islam. Originally they came to conquer certain territories which had for them unique religious associations, and they stayed to defend these conquests against counter-attack. Conquests and settlement involved domination of the land and its inhabitants, and to be continuously effective such domination needed to be based on castles and walled towns. The acquisition or successful defence of strong places was the highest prize of warfare, beside which success in battle was of secondary importance. Victory in the field, as the events of the First Crusade and the early years of the settlement showed, could help an invader, but mainly because destruction of the opposing army left him free to develop an uninterrupted attack on the fortresses. To the defender, battle was less important. His first object was to keep his army in being, for its mere existence was a standing hindrance and threat to the operations of the invader. After the first generation of conquest, the Syrian Franks frequently pursued this kind of defensive warfare.

They had other reasons for caution. They knew that the outcome of any battle must be doubtful, and that the consequences

[1] Usamah, p. 42.

of defeat could be immense. Large numbers of knights, of whom there were never enough in Syria, might be killed or captured. The all-important fortresses were exposed to a double threat: there was nothing to prevent the victorious enemy turning his whole resources against them; and they were left with inadequate garrisons, since these had been depleted to provide the field army. In these circumstances, too, it became clear that many Syrian Christians and Muslims were either indifferent to the fate of their Latin overlords, or welcomed their discomfiture. In contrast, the rewards of victory were hardly a sufficient inducement to undertake such risks. During the first generation of conquest, until Zanki appeared at Aleppo in 1127 to begin the unification of Muslim Syria, success in battle was essential to establish and maintain the Latin states. Thereafter its profits diminished. It could not win permanent relief from Muslim pressure, for leaders like Zanki, Nur al-Din, and Saladin had sufficient resources to return to the attack. Victory in battle terminated the campaign and secured the withdrawal of the invader. But these ends were achieved in the normal course of events by the approach of winter and the desire of the Muslim troops to return to their homes, a desire which was all the stronger if the existence of a Latin army limited their opportunity to plunder and prevented them from achieving any striking success. In much crusading warfare the rewards of victory in battle could be won by other means which did not involve the penalties of defeat.

Once in contact with the enemy, the Franks still needed to show careful restraint. In order to avoid battle with their usual and most respected enemy, the Turks, they had not merely to refrain from taking offensive action: they had also to withstand various forms of provocation, which have already been discussed. In the face of archery, of feigned retreat, of attacks on flank and rear as quickly mounted and as quickly broken off, the Franks had to curb their longing to strike back, and, whether on the march or formed up on the battlefield, so to dispose their forces that they could withstand encirclement and provocation until they could effectively deliver their own principal weapon, the charge of the mounted troops.

The dictum of Usamah was therefore fully justified. Throughout the century the Franks were compelled to exercise caution not only in deciding whether or not they would give battle, but also in the battle itself. Military methods both on campaign and in combat resulted from factors which have been discussed in foregoing chapters. There these factors have been isolated and considered singly, but military events were fashioned by the interplay of several. In order to demonstrate this process the rest of this chapter is devoted to the description, first, of certain campaigns in which the Franks, although refusing battle, successfully repelled invasion; second, of battles fought on the march, a form of engagement then peculiar to Latin Syria; third, of pitched battles.

II. CAMPAIGNS WITHOUT BATTLE

The organization of the Muslim counter-attack against the Latin states made in the year 1111 [1] was ordered by the sultan. [2] In command he appointed Mawdud b. Altuntash, to whom the government of Mosul had been assigned, and ordered other amirs who held *iqta's* in Mesopotamia to join Mawdud with their military contingents. [3] The progress of this composite force into Syria demonstrated both the extent to which Frankish authority shrank within the walled places during time of invasion, and the inability of fortresses to check the advance of an enemy force which was prepared to pass them by. Mawdud marched through the heart of the Frankish county of Edessa, attacked its capital and Tell Bashir, and finally came to Aleppo. [4]

The events which followed abundantly revealed the division of Islam which was largely responsible for the military successes of the Franks during the first generation of the Latin occupation.

---

[1] Usamah (pp. 97–8) was an eyewitness of events at Shaizar. For accounts by contemporaries who were in Syria, see Fulcher, pp. 423–4; IQ, pp. 114–19; ME, pp. 96–7. For a contemporary who was not in Syria, see AA, pp. 681–4, who was well informed only on the siege of Tell Bashir. For Syrians who were not contemporaries, see WT, pp. 480–1; IA, pp. 279–83; *AM*, pp. 33–4; KD, pp. 599–601. For modern accounts, see *RGKJ*, pp. 89–92; Stevenson, *Crusaders in the East*, pp. 91–3; Grousset, I, pp. 460–72; Cahen, *Syrie du Nord*, pp. 261–3; Derenbourg, *Vie d'Ousâma*, pp. 89–94.

[2] IQ, p. 111; IA, p. 280; KD, p. 599.

[3] These included Sukman al-Qutbi (of Armenia and the Diyar Bakr); Bursuq b. Bursuq of Hamadhan, Ahmadil; IQ, p. 114; IA, p. 280.

[4] IQ, p. 115; IA, pp. 281–2; Fulcher, p. 423; ME, p. 96; WT, p. 481.

The rulers of Muslim Syria saw in these expeditions from Mesopotamia not only an attack on the Franks but an attempt by the
sultan to re-establish his direct control over themselves.[1] Therefore, despite the fact that the great army of 1111 had been organized partly as the result of disturbances in Baghdad instituted by
certain citizens of an Aleppo threatened by Tancred,[2] and despite
the favour shown by popular opinion in Aleppo to the army of
Mawdud encamped without its gates, Rudwan refused to admit
to his city the allies whom he feared.[3] At Aleppo, Mawdud was
joined by Tughtagin of Damascus, but this atabeg too feared the
sultan's army, and all the Arab historians recorded the strained
relations between him and the Mesopotamian amirs.[4] At this
point too Mawdud's army exhibited the most crippling weakness
of all such composite forces: it began to disperse of its own accord.
From the first Bursuq and Sukman al-Qutbi had been ill and had
'disagreed with each other's plans'.[5] Sukman grew worse; with
his men he began his homeward journey, but died before he
reached the Euphrates.[6] As a result of this a large part of Mawdud's forces dispersed, in the words of Ibn al-Qalanisi, 'like the
tribes of Saba'.[7] Ahmadil was anxious to receive Sukman's lands
as an *iqta'* from the Sultan, and withdrew to press his claims.
Bursuq, too, a sick man borne in a litter, returned home.[8] Only
the *'askars* of Mawdud and Tughtagin remained, and these two
leaders, responding to a request for help from the Munqidhs of
Shaizar, marched to that town.[9] By contrast the Franks had
meanwhile demonstrated their military strength. Tancred had
acted fully in accordance with common-sense contemporary
ideas: he had immediately summoned his host to oppose the
invasion, but had not exposed it to attack until the other
Latin rulers had come to his assistance. He took up an excellent
position at Rugia, by the Jisr esh-Shoghr and the castles in its

---

[1] KD, p. 608.   [2] IQ, p. 111; IA, p. 279.   [3] IQ, p. 115; KD, p. 600.
[4] IQ, pp. 116–17; IA, p. 282; *AM*, p. 33; KD, pp. 600–1.
[5] IQ, p. 115; IA, p. 282.   [6] IQ, p. 116; IA, p. 282.
[7] IQ, p. 117.   [8] IQ, p. 117; IA, p. 282.
[9] The Munqidh brothers who ruled in Shaizar were subject to constant
attacks by Tancred, who had begun to build a castle near the town at
Tell b. Ma'shar; Derenbourg, *Vie d'Ousâma*, p. 91; IQ, p. 114; KD,
p. 599.

neighbourhood,[1] and awaited the arrival of King Baldwin, Bertrand of Tripoli, and Baldwin of Edessa. Once united, the Franks marched to Afamiya, and thence to make contact with the Muslims encamped at Shaizar.[2]

The methods there adopted by either side are clearly shown by the sources in outline, though not in detail. The Muslims vigorously employed their normal harassing tactics, which were directed to the objects of cutting off supplies from the Franks, and of preventing their watering their horses in the Orontes.[3] The Franks, on the other hand, withstood all provocation of archery and constantly renewed attacks and declined to give battle.[4] It seems that on occasions they were hard pressed by the Turks, and that then they fought to relieve the pressure,[5] but that there was a pitched battle of the kind recorded by Albert of Aix was not supported by better witnesses.[6]

In these circumstances the campaign ended. As a result of the Turkish activity supplies became scarce in the Latin camp, and they withdrew, still harassed by the enemy, to their own territory by way of Afamiya. To the end they maintained their close order and, with individual exceptions,[7] avoided offensive action which might loosen their formation.[8] As the campaigning season was far advanced and they had been given no opportunity to acquire conquest or spoils, the Muslim allies returned each to his own home.

In 1111 the Muslims had attempted to conquer some part of the Latin states. That they entirely failed was due to the passive strength of walled places like Edessa and Tell Bashir, to the dispersal of a large part of the Muslim army even before contact had

[1] The princes of Antioch had access to their territories across the Orontes by way of two bridges: the Jisr al-Hadid, which carried the main road to Aleppo, and the Jisr esh-Shoghr, across which the road led south-east to Kafrtab, Ma'arrat al-Nu'man, Afamiya, and so to Shaizar, Hama, and Hims. See Dussaud, *Topographie*, pp. 165–78.

[2] All this is in Fulcher, p. 423, and therefore reported by WT, p. 481. See also IQ, p. 118.

[3] IA, p. 283; KD, p. 601.

[4] IA, p. 283; ME, p. 97; Fulcher, p. 424: 'Milites nostri . . . vitantes damnum noluerunt eos impetere.'

[5] IQ, p. 119.

[6] AA (p. 684) was not well informed on these events, and Grousset (I, 470) appears to give undue prominence to his assertion that a battle was fought.

[7] Usamah, p. 98.   [8] Fulcher, p. 424.

been made with the Franks, and the resolute refusal of the Franks themselves to risk their army in the battle to which the Muslims attempted to provoke them.

After the assassination of Mawdud, and the failure of aq-Sunqur Bursuqi as leader of the attack on Edessa in 1114, the sultan appointed Bursuq b. Bursuq, ruler of Hamadhan, to command the counter-crusade against Latin Syria in the following year.[1] But Syrian Muslims as well as Franks felt themselves threatened by this great expedition; and where in 1111 the rulers of Muslim Syria had refused co-operation or given lukewarm support to the invader, in 1115 they allied with the Franks against Bursuq's army.[2]

The preparations of Roger of Antioch to meet this invasion were fully described by his chancellor, who took a personal part in these events. He has left a clear and detailed picture of the manner in which a Latin ruler discharged his military responsibilities.[3] The great earthquake on 29 November 1114[4] had caused serious damage in northern Syria, and in the spring of the following year Roger was personally directing the work of restoring the castles of his principality, and especially those which stood nearest enemy territory. At the same time he summoned his army to the Jisr al-Hadid, sent agents into Mesopotamia to gather information on enemy movement, and conferred with Ralph de Acon on the measures necessary to put the city of Antioch in a state of defence.[5] When this had been done, he sent equipment and supplies to the army, and himself joined them at Jisr

[1] For the campaign of 1115 the best source is the work of Roger's chancellor, Walter, a participant and eyewitness of the events he describes. Fulcher was in Syria in 1115, but did not leave Jerusalem. William of Tyre used the accounts of both these writers in his own work. Of Muslim contemporaries, IQ gave no information, and Usamah did little more than give a detailed description of Bursuq's siege of Kafr Tab; see Galt. pp. 65–76; Fulcher, pp. 429–31; AA, pp. 701–2; WT, pp. 493–8; IA, pp. 295–8; KD, pp. 608–10; ME, pp. 114–16; *RGKJ*, pp. 107–12; Stevenson, *Crusaders in the East*, pp. 97–100; Grousset, I, pp. 495–510; Cahen, *Syrie du Nord*, pp. 271–5; Derenbourg, *Vie d'Ousâma*, pp. 98–107; Runciman, II, pp. 130–3.

[2] The conscience of IQ, a pious Muslim, could apparently not reconcile itself to Tughtagin's action. He gave no account of this campaign, but told at some length of Tughtagin's reconciliation with the court of Baghdad in the following year. Walter the chancellor did not relish the alliance, but recorded it; Galt. p. 67; Fulcher, p. 429; IA, p. 296; KD, p. 608; ME, p. 115.

[3] Galt. pp. 65–70.   [4] Galt. p. 63; ME, pp. 110–12.   [5] Galt. p. 65.

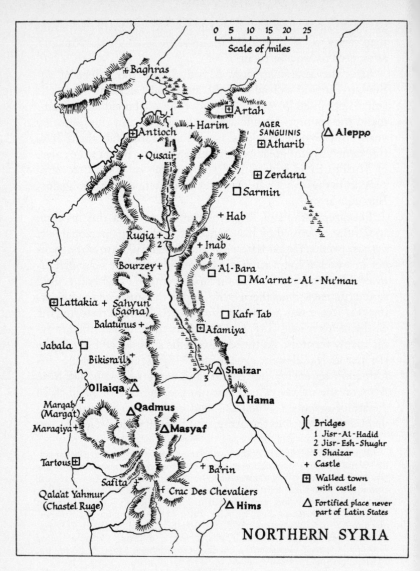

Scale of miles

0 5 10 15 20 25

+ Baghras

1

+ Artah

+ Harim

AGER
SANGUINIS

△ Aleppo

Antioch

Atharib

+ Qusair

Zerdana

Sarmin

+ Hab

Rugia +

2

+ Inab

Bourzey +

Al-Bara

Ma'arrat - Al - Nu'man

Lattakia +

Sahyun
(Saona)

Kafr Tab

Balatunus +

Afamiya

Jabala

Bikisra'il +

3

△ Shaizar

Ollaiqa △

△ Hama

Marqab
(Margat)

Qadmus △

Maraqiya +

△ Masyaf

Tartous

){ Bridges
1 Jisr-Al-Hadid
2 Jisr-Esh-Shughr
3 Shaizar

+ Ba'rin

+ Castle

Safita +

+ Crac Des Chevaliers

⊞ Walled town
with castle

Qala'at Yahmur
(Chastel Ruge)

△ Hims

△ Fortified place never
part of Latin States

NORTHERN SYRIA

MAP I

[144]

al-Hadid.[1] There he received the reports of the agents he had earlier despatched *ad Parthorum partes*, and on hearing that the sultan had decided to invade Syria, he took advice on the best course to pursue. As a result the army took the main Antioch-Aleppo road as far as Atharib,[2] where Roger came to an understanding with Tughtagin, Il Ghazi, and the ruler of Aleppo, for common resistance to the sultan's army.[3]

According to Ibn al Athir the allies decided to take advantage of the likely dissolution, on the approach of winter, of Bursuq's composite army, and to avoid exposing themselves to his attack.[4] Therefore they concentrated their forces at Afamiya, a place well fitted to serve as a base for the army. It was well supplied and protected, was reasonably near both Hims and Shaizar, of which the rulers were potential allies of the invaders, and was a place from which an army could march to meet attacks against either Aleppo, Antioch, or Damascus. In fact Bursuq lost no time in joining his Syrian allies. He took Hama by assault, bestowed it on Kirkhan of Hims, and then led his army to Shaizar.[5] His men at once made contact with Roger and his allies, who had for two months been awaiting the invasion at Afamiya. The invaders attempted to lure the Franks into premature attacks, both by harassing their camp, and by a diversion against the Latin town of Kafr Tab.[6] The general position of the two armies at this stage resembled that during the campaign four years earlier, which has already been described.

Roger had been no less provident than Tancred in organizing

---

[1] Galt. p. 66: 'deinde praemissis armis aliisque belli et victus necessariis. . . in expeditionem profectus est.'

[2] Galt. p. 66. For Atharib, see Rey, *Colonies*, p. 330; Dussaud, *Topographie*, p. 219; Cahen, *Syrie du Nord*, p. 154.

[3] Galt. pp. 66–7. Walter's feelings regarding this pact were probably shared by many other Christians, and, as IQ's silence on these events shows, certainly by many Muslims. Walter had the literary problem of recording the pact while at the same time expressing suitably anti-Muslim sentiments. His account on pp. 66–7 is therefore uneasy and involved. See also Grousset, I, pp. 499–500.

[4] IA, pp. 296–7; Derenbourg, *Vie d'Ousâma*, p. 100.

[5] Galt. p. 68. IA (p. 296) stated that because Bursuq gave all his Syrian conquests to his ally Kirkhan, the other amirs who had brought contingents to the army were offended, and their interest in the campaign decreased. At a later stage the disposal of Buza'a caused jealousy and division in the army; IA, p. 297; KD, p. 609.

[6] IA, p. 297.

maximum resistance. As soon as he knew that Bursuq had entered
Syria, but not before, he had requested the aid of both King
Baldwin and Pons of Tripoli.[1] Baldwin showed that promptness
to meet invasion which was to distinguish the kings of Jerusalem
throughout the century. On the same day that he received Roger's
message he sent to warn Pons that he should prepare to accom-
pany him to join Roger, and sent the strictest instructions to
Roger that no attack should be made on the enemy before the
arrival of the armies of Jerusalem and Tripoli.[2] Walter has recorded Roger's vigorous execution of these instructions. When
Bursuq's men began harassing his camp, he issued an order that
no man should accept the enemy's challenge under pain of losing
his eyes.[3] When enemy pressure increased, he rode through the
camp with a drawn sword and forbade any counter-attack by his
men.[4]

The difficulties encountered by Latin commanders in enforcing on their knights caution in the face of the enemy have already
been discussed.[5] Such a policy is always unpopular with men
who are being attacked by the enemy and restrained from striking
back, and also with those who in war honour only courage and
brute force, and who despise all forms of cunning and ingenuity.
There were men in Roger's army who thought that his actions
were dictated by fear, although there were others who understood that he was awaiting a suitable opportunity to attack the
Turks after the arrival of the king.[6] A similar division of opinion

[1] Galt. p. 67.   [2] Galt. pp. 67–8.

[3] Galt. p. 68: 'princeps vero, Christianitatis sacramento et fraterna regis
dilectione coniuratus, tam praeludium quam et belli aditum, erutione
oculorum interposita, generaliter omnibus suis abdicat.'

[4] Above, p. 129.   [5] Above, p. 128.

[6] It was normal for a medieval knight to hold to the straightforward
military virtues of bravery and violence, and to despise all cleverness and
cunning. Oman appears to have been a victim to the same prejudices. Writing
of Byzantine strategy in his *Art of War*, I, p. 202, he stated 'they had a strong
predilection for stratagems, ambushes and simulated retreats. For the officer
who fought without having first secured all the advantages for his own side
they had the greatest contempt. *Nor must we blame them too much for such
views. . .*'; and *ibid.* 'the East Romans *felt no proper sense of shame* for some of
their over-ingenious stratagems in war'. (My italic.)

Walter described the controversy of 1115 in these terms (Galt. p. 69):
'quidam etiam nostrorum id facti timiditati reputant, nonnulli autem capacior-
is ingenii hoc fieri de principis industria coniiciunt, ut, explorato congrui
temporis articulo, non admonitione hostium nec praesumptione virium, sed

on military policy was to arise during the campaigns of 1183 and 1187.[1]

Even before Baldwin and Pons arrived at Roger's camp, Bursuq, who knew of their approach, marched away from Shaizar towards the east. It appeared that yet again an invasion of Syria had been successfully resisted. The Latins and their allies attacked and burned the lower town of Shaizar, and as the invader still did not reappear, each Syrian ruler led his contingent back to their homes.[2] Throughout the campaign Roger had organized his reconnaissance so carefully that it is surprising to find the Franks ignorant of Bursuq's movements. No sooner had they dispersed than the invaders reappeared to capture Kafr Tab, and made plans to attack Zerdana. Roger once more summoned his army, and left Antioch to cross the Orontes by the Jisr esh-Shoghr, and, like Tancred in 1111, to make Rugia his base for further movements against the enemy.[3] On 14 September he received information that the Muslims, unprepared for battle, were beginning to encamp at a water point in the valley of Sarmin.[4] Despite the fact that he was on the defensive, Roger took advantage of this opportunity to surprise the enemy, and on the same day attacked and defeated him at his camping ground.[5] This victory ended the campaign.

The military events of 1115 showed how great was the burden of military obligation on the feudal tenants. The army of Antioch was summoned in the spring. It remained long enough at Jisr al-Hadid for Roger to organize the strengthening of Antioch's defences and to make final preparations for the expected campaign.

---

sui regisque in proximo advenientis dispositione provida ingenioque experienti eos inpetere praevaleant. Saepius enim, ut expertum est, praevalet in bello cum audacia et ingenio pugnatorum paucitas, quam infrunita et vacillans armatorum multitudo.'

[1] Below, pp. 155, 194.
[2] Galt. pp. 69–70; Fulcher, p. 429; AA, p. 701; WT, p. 494; ME, pp. 115–16.
[3] All this in Galt. pp. 70–1.
[4] Galt. p. 72; Fulcher, p. 430; Hagenmeyer in Galt. pp. 182–3; Dussaud, *Topographie*, pp. 174, 221–2; Grousset, I, pp. 506–7.
[5] From all accounts it is clear that Roger achieved complete surprise. When the attack was made the Muslims were still making camp, and the troops were still arriving at the camping ground: Galt. p. 72; IA, pp. 297–8; KD, pp. 609–10; ME, p. 116.

It then marched to Atharib, and later to Afamiya, where it was
encamped for two months before Bursuq's force appeared.[1]
There followed an attack on Shaizar, the return march to the
territory of Antioch, and then the dismissal of the tenants and
troops to their homes. Within a few days they were summoned for
further service in order to meet Bursuq's renewed attack. In the
light of such conditions it is easy to understand the premature
dispersal of the Latin army at the time of Bursuq's first departure from Shaizar.

Military service was equally burdensome during Saladin's
attacks on the kingdom later in the century.[2] In 1180 Saladin had
concluded a truce both with Baldwin IV of Jerusalem and with
Raymond of Tripoli. Two years later he was provoked to resume
hostilities with Baldwin on account of a typical act of brigan-
dage committed by Renaud de Châtillon, then lord of Karak. On
11 May 1182 Saladin left Egypt with an army and marched towards Damascus by way of Aila, and the desert route.[3] The
Franks had information on these movements, and knew that
Saladin was passing through the lands normally controlled from
the Transjordan strongholds of Karak and Shawbak. The king
took the advice of his magnates on the solution of the problems
created by Saladin's march. One party favoured taking the army
across Jordan and protecting the territory through which Saladin
must pass; Raymond of Tripoli urged that such a course must
denude the kingdom of troops.[4]

Raymond's advice was ignored, and Grousset has strongly censured the decision to march beyond Jordan.[5] He does not appear
to have allowed, however, for the difficulty created by the clash of
feudal custom and military expediency. If the fief of any vassal
were attacked by the Muslims, the lord was bound to make every

[1] Galt. p. 67: 'Siquidem ante Apamiam castrametati per duos menses
morati sunt.'
[2] At this time WT was in Syria, chancellor of the kingdom, and archbishop
of Tyre. His record of the events of this year is the most valuable source available (WT, pp. 1087–101). Other well-informed contemporaries who were
not eyewitnesses were BD (p. 68), IA (pp. 651–3), AS (pp. 217–22) who
quoted contemporary records. There is a brief reference in KD in *ROL*,
IV, pp. 159–60. See also *RGKJ*, pp. 396–400; Stevenson, *Crusaders in the
East*, pp. 225–7; Lane-Poole, *Saladin*, pp. 167–9; Grousset, II, pp. 701–12.
[3] *RGKJ*, pp. 394–6; Grousset, II, p. 704.
[4] WT, p. 1088.   [5] II, p. 704.

effort to protect and, if necessary, to recover it. If he failed to do so the vassal was absolved from all service.[1] It was known that Saladin, as he passed through the Transjordan fief, might destroy the crops which were already white for the harvest, or take one of the strongholds on which Latin control of the lordship depended.[2] Baldwin accordingly led his army to Petra, ready to oppose any move by Saladin, whose line of progress was determined by the water points along the Darb al-Hajj.[3] If the Latins could have denied him the use of this water, they could have forced him out into the desert, thus protecting the cultivated lands near esh-Shawbak and Karak; but this they failed to achieve.[4]

During these events Saladin made use of two characteristic methods of warfare which he was to employ in all his later campaigns against the Franks. First, knowing that they required their whole military strength to face his main army, he took every opportunity to damage their territory by secondary attacks launched elsewhere, and which the Franks had not the resources to oppose.[5] Second, if he could not achieve his main objects in warfare, which were the conquest of Latin territory through the destruction of their army and the capture of the strong places, then he laid waste the cultivated country-side.[6] It has already

[1] *Livre au Roi*, pp. 625–6; Dodu, *Institutions*, pp. 191–2; La Monte, *Feudal Monarchy*, pp. 151–2. A similar situation had arisen in the principality of Antioch in 1119. Roger left the safety and abundance of his base at Artah in order to protect the lands of his vassals which were threatened by the enemy. This move from Artah to the Ager Sanguinis was a prime cause for his subsequent defeat and death. See Galt. pp. 79–80. It should be remarked that Grousset (II, p. 740) praised similar arrangements in 1184, when an army was taken to relieve Karak, and Saladin was able to ravage the unprotected kingdom. On this second occasion the plan was the work of Raymond of Tripoli, a hero of Grousset, who was inclined to allow his strong prejudice concerning the characters of whom he wrote to cloud his judgement of their actions.

[2] WT, p. 1088: 'Adjecit etiam, ut, in veniendo, regionem nostram quae est trans Jordanem pro posse damnificaret, aut fruges succendendo, quae jam albae erant ad messem, aut unum vel plura de praesidiis nostris, quae in ea erant provincia, violenter expugnando.'

[3] Grousset, II, pp. 704–5; C. P. Grant, *Syrian Desert*, pp. 223–4.

[4] WT, pp. 1091–2.

[5] He invaded the kingdom in 1177 because Baldwin had sent 100 knights and 2000 foot-soldiers to Antioch to help the count of Flanders besiege Harim; WT, p. 1037.

[6] In 1179 Saladin had established his main army near Banyas and had sent detachments to lay waste the country towards Sidon and Bairut. Similar destruction was a feature of the campaigns of 1182, 1183, 1184, and 1187.

been emphasized that the Franks regarded such activity as a prime cause of their own poverty and consequent inability to organize sufficient military resistance.[1] This policy of destructive raids so consistently followed by Saladin indicated that he too knew how gravely he could embarrass the Franks by such means. In this campaign of 1182 Saladin employed both methods. When Baldwin led his army to meet him in Transjordan, he left the kingdom without any other body of troops. When therefore Farrukh Shah, Saladin's nephew, to whom he had given authority in Damascus, invaded Galilee in company with the amirs of Bosra, Ba'albek, and Hims, they found the inhabitants defenceless. They plundered Dabburiya and many other places close by, and on their return towards Damascus recaptured from the Franks the castle of Habis Jaldak in the Sawad.[2]

Meanwhile Saladin had successfully established himself at the water point of Jerba, and from that place was able to ravage the cultivated neighbourhood of Shawbak.[3] There were Franks, and William of Tyre was among them, who thought that the army should have been used to occupy the water points of the Darb al-Hajj and so to drive Saladin out into the desert. There may have been a plan to do this, but it was never carried out and Saladin's march was not interrupted.[4] Yet, despite the criticism stated by William, the Franks, at the expense of temporary damage, had preserved their strongholds without exposing their army to possible destruction. These were the essential military achievements.

Following his arrival at Damascus, Saladin invaded the kingdom of Jerusalem without delay.[5] He camped at al-Quhwana at the southern end of Lake Tiberias,[6] and despatched detachments to harry the country-side,[7] one of which failed in an attack on Baisan in the Jordan valley.[8] He then crossed Jordan, and ascended the heights overlooking the course of the river between Lake

---

[1] Above, p. 100 and references.

[2] For this expedition see WT, pp. 1089–91; IA, pp. 651–2; AS, pp. 217–18.

[3] WT, p. 1091; IA, p. 651; AS, p. 217.   [4] WT, p. 1092.

[5] According to AS, p. 217, he arrived at Damascus on 22 June. AS (p. 219) states that he left the city on 11 July. See Stevenson, *Crusaders in the East*, p. 225, n. 3 and p. 226, n. 3.

[6] WT, p. 1093; IA, p. 652.

[7] IA (p. 652) says that the districts raided were the Jordan valley, Lejjan, Jenin, the district of Acre.

[8] WT, p. 1093; IA, p. 652

Tiberias and Baisan, and on which stood the new castle of Belvoir.[1]

The Franks opposed this invasion by methods which were typical of their normal military practice. Before it was launched the field army, on its return from Transjordan, had immediately been reassembled at Saffuriya. As usual, the base was skilfully chosen. It was abundantly provided with water, had good communication with Acre and the coastal plain, and enabled the Franks rapidly to make contact with an invader who crossed Jordan either north or south of Lake Tiberias.[2] Information of Saladin's movements was gained by quick reconnaissance,[3] and it was decided to make immediate contact with the enemy.[4] This was a normal decision, as was that to strengthen the Latin army by the addition of all immediately available troops, most of which were stationed in neighbouring castles.[5] The Franks marched

[1] WT, pp. 1093-4. The castle was and is known to the Arabs as Kawkab al-Hawa; Röhricht in *ZDPV*, x, p. 291.

[2] WT, p. 1092. In the two decades before 1187 Saffuriya was the normal base for a defensive campaign in northern Palestine; WT, pp. 987-8; JV, p. 1078; Abel, *Géographie de la Palestine*, I, pp. 140, 445.   [3] WT, p. 1093.

[4] WT, p. 1093. It is instructive to compare William's words with a recently published translation. William wrote:

'Quod ubi nostris per exploratores cognitum est, ad urbem praedictam sub omni celeritate exercitum dirigunt, ut militares copias, quae ad ejus loci et finitimorum municipiorum, Saphet videlicet et Belveir, tuitionem deputatae erant, secum assumerent, hostem protinus insecuturi.'

This has been translated by Emily Babcock and A. C. Krey in their *A History of Deeds done beyond the Sea*, II, p. 473:

'Scouts *soon* reported this fact to our leaders. *An immediate attack* was decided upon, and the forces were hastily despatched to Tiberias to unite with *the contingent that had been sent there* to protect that city and the fortified places in the vicinity, namely Saphet and Beauvoir.'

The cumulative effect of the liberties which the translators have taken with this passage (in italic) is to give a false picture of the military situation. It should be noticed:

(a) William said nothing about a decision to make an attack. The decision was to march to Tiberias 'hostem protinus insecuturi', that is, immediately to follow the enemy and therefore to make contact with him, but not to attack him. Avoidance of premature attack was a prime characteristic of Frankish warfare.

(b) The translators show the Latin army hastening to Tiberias in order to join 'with the contingent that had been sent there', that is, presumably, a contingent earlier detached from the main body. There is nothing in the text recording such a detachment; the meaning clearly is that they were to join forces with the garrisons normally stationed in those places.

[5] One of the castles from which troops were withdrawn was Belvoir, a place which Saladin was to threaten in this campaign.

to Tiberias, thence southward, along the Jordan valley, before
ascending the heights in the neighbourhood of Kawkab al-Hawa.
After a watchful night, they found themselves confronted by the
enemy.[1] A normal tactical situation developed: the Muslims attempted to force an engagement; the Franks relied on preserving
their formation, and refused to be drawn into a general engagement. They were assailed by the Turkish mounted archers, and it
is likely that from time to time the Turks came to close quarters.[2]
When they did so the Latin knights fought back, and this has
caused some writers to refer to the action as a battle.[3] It is more
probable that although there were short episodes in which there
was hard fighting, there was no pitched engagement. Denied
tactical success, Saladin withdrew to Damascus; but the military
duties of the king of Jerusalem's feudal tenants and mercenaries
were not yet complete. Saladin had planned an attack on Bairut
in conjunction with the Egyptian fleet, and when his watchers in
the Lebanon sighted the ships, Saladin quickly crossed that
range by the Munaitira pass and attacked the town. Once more
the Franks marched from Saffuriya. On this occasion they went
to Tyre, where the king organized all available ships, in order to
relieve Bairut by both land and sea. When he learnt of this
activity Saladin raised the siege and withdrew from Latin territory. This attack too was accompanied by a diversion in southern
Palestine by Egyptian troops, and by the usual devastation of the
Syrian country-side.

After a year's campaigning which added many cities of Mesopotamia, and the Syrian city of Aleppo, to his empire, Saladin
returned to Damascus on 24 August 1183. A month later he renewed his attack upon the Franks, and entered the kingdom by
the same route as in 1182.[4] He crossed Jordan south of Lake

[1] WT, p. 1094.
[2] IA, p. 653. See also a letter of Saladin to the caliph preserved by al-
Fadhil and quoted in AS, pp. 218–22. It refers to the difficulty of tempting
the Franks to combat, and although they were eventually made to fight, they
did so 'not of their own will, but were compelled by necessity' (p. 221).
[3] Notably Stevenson, *op. cit.* p. 227.
[4] For contemporary accounts of this campaign, see WT, pp. 1118–24;
Ernoul, pp. 98–103; BD, pp. 74–6; IA, pp. 663–4; AS, pp. 242–8. See also
RGKJ, pp. 403–6; Stevenson, *op. cit.* pp. 232–3; Lane-Poole, *Saladin*, pp.
177–9; Grousset, II, pp. 723–30; M. W. Baldwin, *Raymond III of Tripolis*,
pp. 49–53; Runciman, II, pp. 437–9.

Tiberias and led his army towards the heart of the kingdom by
way of the Nahr Jalud. After sacking Baisan, deserted by its inhabitants and its garrison, he encamped at some springs near
the head of the valley, and about eight miles east of al-Fule.[1]
Throughout the campaign Saladin followed his usual policy of
using detachments to inflict maximum damage on the Frankish
country-side. Some of the feats of his raiders have been recorded:
they destroyed the villages of Jenin and 'Afrabala; they attacked
the monastery on Mount Thabor; they looked down on Nazareth
from the surrounding hilltops;[2] they intercepted and destroyed
a contingent from Karak in Transjordan as it marched to join the
Latin army at Saffuriya;[3] after the two armies had made contact,
they cut off supplies from the Christian camp, and so caused a
grave shortage there.[4]

Once more the Franks had expected an attack and, when news
of the invasion was received, the army was already assembled at
Saffuriya under the command of Guy de Lusignan. Once Saladin's avenue of ingress was known, Guy led his army to al-Fule
by way of Nazareth. It was in the neighbourhood of this small
castle that the Franks were attacked by Saladin's force. The
sources do not allow the exact movements of the two forces to be
reconstructed, and historians have given slightly differing accounts of this episode. By placing reliance on the probably best
informed sources, William of Tyre and Beha ed-Din, it is certain
that the Franks' first objective was to establish themselves in a
position with available water at the head of the valley.[5] Since
Saladin had already occupied the water at 'Ain Jalud and probably therefore that at 'Ain Tuba'un, it was necessary for Guy to
challenge him for these places. It is apparent that once more the
Franks carefully formed their column and marched resolutely towards the water.[6] The Muslims harassed them with archery and

[1] WT, pp. 1118–19; *Ernoul*, p. 98; AS, pp. 244–5; BD, p. 74.
[2] All the foregoing is in WT, pp. 1119–20; AS, p. 246; BD, p. 76.
[3] BD, p. 74; AS, p. 245.
[4] WT, p. 1121; 'Unde subito fames exorta est in exercitu.'
[5] WT, p. 1119: 'ordinatis aciebus et juxta militarem disciplinam modo
competenti dispositis, versus fontem Tubaniae, ubi saepe dictus Salahadinus
cum ingenti egregiorum et selectorum militum manu secus aquas se loco-
verat, cuneos dirigunt, quasi propositum habentes, hostibus expulsis, aqua-
rum sibi vindicare commoditatem.'
[6] *Ernoul*, p. 99; AS, p. 247; BD, p. 75, 'The Franks kept their ranks close,

constantly renewed attacks; these were on occasions pressed home to an extent which provoked the Franks to counter-attacks to clear their lines.[1] As in 1111 and 1182 the Franks executed a fighting march which never quite became a pitched battle.

The two principal sources also make it clear that Saladin yielded the springs and moved his army further downstream.[2] In these new positions the armies watched each other for eight days. The Muslims continued to harass and to provoke the Christians[3] and to intercept supply columns attempting to reach the Latin camp. The Franks maintained a passive solidity which afforded the Muslims no chance of a tactical success. Saladin then attempted to induce the Franks to leave their position by himself marching towards Mount Thabor.[4] Guy did not follow him, but at once fell back towards al-Fule. The Muslims again hurried to attack but once more Latin solidity limited their action to archery and light, repeated assaults. Since he could achieve nothing and his own supplies were deficient, Saladin ended the campaign.[5] The Franks returned to Saffuriya.[6]

The episode showed that the defensive policy of the Franks required the establishment of the army in a well-supplied base. Saladin's marauding bands caused an acute crisis in the Latin camp due to lack of food.[7] The leaders organized the transport of supplies from neighbouring districts, although to bring them to the camp through a country-side infested by Saladin's troops was not easy. Conditions in the camp became easier when fish were discovered in the waters at Tuba'un in sufficient quantities to feed the whole army until the arrival of supply columns ended the threat of famine.[8]

---

and their infantry protected their knights, and they neither charged nor stopped, but continued their march to the spring—and there camped.'

[1] *Ernoul*, p. 99.

[2] WT, p. 1119: 'Subito Salahadinus castra solvens, ex insperato fontem deserit, inferiusque versus Bethsan . . . castrametatus est.' *Ernoul*, p. 99; BD, 75.

[3] BD, p. 75; AS, p. 245.   [4] BD, p. 75; IA, p. 663.

[5] BD, p. 75.   [6] *Ernoul*, p. 102.

[7] WT, p. 1121. The situation was aggravated because the Syrian Franks had brought food only for three days, while the Italian sailors and pilgrims who had joined the army had brought no food at all. See also *Ernoul*, pp. 99–100.

[8] WT, pp. 1121–2; *Ernoul*, p. 100.

During and after the campaign there was controversy among the Franks regarding the strategy of their leaders.[1] William of Tyre faithfully reported opinions which were voiced on both sides of the argument. He himself thought that, because the Latin army was the largest gathered within living memory,[2] and because Saladin was encamped on Christian territory which he devastated with impunity over a wide area, Guy should have initiated an attack on the Muslims. Others of a like mind thought that the native barons were responsible for the inactivity; jealous of Guy, they wished to deny him the credit of victory. Supporters of the military policy of 1183 rejoined that the Muslims were established on broken ground which rendered any attack against them an over-hazardous operation; in addition any such move would have invited a counter-attack from the bands posted by Saladin on all sides of the Latin camp for such a purpose.

Of modern historians who have discussed these arguments Baldwin has attached most importance to the personal jealousy felt by the native magnates towards Guy, who 'within two or three years of his arrival in the Holy Land . . . had not only married the king's sister and become a possible successor to the throne, but . . . had actually been appointed *bailli*'.[3] He was therefore strongly inclined to regard military policy during the campaign as the result of an attempt by the Syrian baronial party to discredit Guy. Grousset, on the other hand, approved the defensive strategy as the wisest which could have been pursued and which, if it had been repeated four years later, would have prevented the crowning disaster of Hattin.[4]

It is suggested that if the campaign is viewed against the whole background of military events in Latin Syria during the twelfth century, then it is clear there is nothing unusual or unexpected either in the defensive policy of 1183 or in the criticism it provoked. It has been shown already that to remain in the neighbourhood of the enemy while denying him any opportunity of major tactical success was the traditional role of a Latin army when facing a large-scale invasion. But never in history has such a policy

---

[1] For the following paragraph see WT, pp. 1122–3.

[2] WT, p. 1122. There were 1300 horsemen, and the armed men on foot were said to exceed 15,000.

[3] Baldwin, *Raymond III of Tripolis*, p. 51.   [4] Grousset, II, pp. 730.

been popular with the rank and file. Even Roger of Antioch, a bold and successful commander enjoying full authority over his army, had incurred such criticism in 1115;[1] small wonder therefore that Guy, whose authority was weak and enemies numerous, should have been blamed for adopting a similar course in 1183.

III. FIGHTING ON THE MARCH

It has been shown that the lightness and mobility of the Turks enabled them to attack a marching column.[2] So long as the Franks maintained their formation and showed no weak spot the Turks usually harassed them from bowshot range, or made momentary attacks which were quickly broken off; in such circumstances the Franks found it possible on many occasions to continue their march 'per hostes medios',[3] 'per medias hostium acies',[4] 'inter Turcos',[5] 'inter condensissimas Turcorum acies'.[5] The tactical objective of the Turks on such occasions was to halt the enemy column or to break into it; the Franks strove by discipline and control to remain 'solidius inter se conglobati'[6] and to continue their march in compact column. The Latin field army often found itself engaged in an action of this kind, when it was compelled 'viam aperire ferro'[7] through a harassing enemy. Neither this fact nor that the major battles of Hattin and Arsuf were engagements of this kind conducted on a large scale have been made clear in the standard works on medieval warfare.

From the earliest days of the Latin settlement, their leaders paid special attention to the formation of an army on the march. In August 1099, when the crusaders were approaching the battlefield of Ascalon, their force was divided into nine squadrons organized in three ranks of three squadrons, a square formation in which attack could be met equally well from whatever direction it developed.[8] The careful researches of Heermann established that a similar formation was organized by Baldwin II before the

---

[1] Above, p. 146.   [2] Above, p. 80.   [3] WT, p. 927.   [4] WT, p. 719.
[5] *HEF*, p. 80.   [6] WT, p. 976.   [7] WT, pp. 719, 977.
[8] RA, p. 303: 'Armati in novem turmis incedebant. Erant autem tres a tergo, tres a fronte, tres in medio sic ordinatae, ut, undecunque bellum se emergeret, in tribus ordinibus illis occurreretur, turma media manente cunctis ad praesidium.' Heermann, pp. 50–1; Köhler, III, pt. 3, p. 177; Oman, I, p. 289; Delbrück, III, pp. 317–18.

battle fought against Il Ghazi on 14 August 1119. The Franks fought in a square formation of three ranks of three squadrons, of which the centre were the *pedites*.[1]

It is possible that historians have overemphasized the importance of these two examples, because the square formation was not always adopted on the march. It demanded a broad front and was therefore practicable only in open country; a formation suited to the coastal plain near Ascalon was not possible in the hilly or broken ground common elsewhere in Syria. The Latin formation was normally a column, sometimes with flank-guards, sometimes all keeping to a road or track; its object was not only to guard against surprise, but to maintain its rate of progress even if the Turks harassed and opposed it.

This could not be achieved without a high degree of organization, discipline, and control. This was well demonstrated in the march across Asia Minor, in the winter of 1147/8, of that part of the Second Crusade led by Louis VII of France.[2] From the time he left Ephesus and marched along the course of the Maeander, the French were opposed by the Turks who took advantage of natural obstacles impeding the crusading march.[3] Louis recognized the necessity of an advance- and rear-guard, and these were appointed daily.[4] Simple organization of this kind was not enough. During the passage of a defile, disobedience to orders by the leader of the advance-guard caused his force to be separated from the main body. The Turks took advantage of the division of the Christian column in difficult ground, and were able to inflict heavy losses. This incident caused the French leaders to reorganize completely their line of march, and Odo gave an exact account of the new arrangements.[5] There were strict orders against

---

[1] Heermann, pp. 89–91, using the evidence of Galt. p. 103; see also Hagenmeyer in Galt. pp. 278–9.

[2] Odo, pp. 65–73; WT, pp. 744–50. William was informed by eyewitnesses, and was accepted by Kugler, *Studien zur Geschichte des zweiten Kreuzzugs*, pp. 21–34, as an original source. See also Grousset, II, pp. 240–4.

[3] Odo, p. 65; WT, pp. 746–7.   [4] WT, p. 747.

[5] Odo, pp. 71–2: 'Jubentur pati usque ad preceptum qui nos vexant, quia cito refugiunt, inimicos, et, cum jussi restiterint, ilico regredi premonent revocatos. Cognita lege docentur et gradum, ne qui de primo est vadat ad ultimum, vel ne se confundant custodes laterum. Illi vero quos natura fecerat pedites vel fortuna (multi enim nobiles, rebus perditis vel expensis, more insolito ibant in turba) ordinati sunt extremi omnium ut habentes arcus resisterent sagittis hostium.'

untimely sorties from the column. Enemy provocation was to be suffered 'usque ad preceptum' and when the Latin charge was ordered the knights were to return as soon as recalled. Advance-, flank-, and rear-guards were appointed, and each man was to keep his place in the column, and to avoid spreading confusion by attempting to give help at some point other than that at which he had been posted. The task of strengthening threatened sectors (which was the normal function of the reserve in the Middle Ages)[1] was allotted to a strong contingent led by the king himself.[2] With the introduction of organization, discipline, and control, the advance continued with greater success.

Shortly before these events the young King Baldwin III had encountered similar problems in Syria. In 1147 Altuntash, an amir who possessed Bosra and Salkhad, was out of favour with Mu'in al-Din Unur, the effective ruler of Damascus. Accordingly he offered these two places to the Franks.[3] The acceptance of the offer made by Altuntash involved a march to take possession of Bosra; the consequent military problem was to do so in face of resistance by the troops of Damascus who were assisted by those of Nur al-Din.[4] Early in the Frankish march the Turks appeared in surprising strength. The Franks were ready to give battle, but the wisest among them advised that camp be pitched. All night careful watch was kept, and next day counsel was taken to decide on the military action to be adopted. The chosen course was to continue the march, and they decided to fight their way to their destination.[5]

---

[1] Delbrück, III, pp. 307–8.   [2] Odo, p. 72.

[3] For the most original account of these events, see WT, pp. 715–28; IQ, pp. 276–9. See also AS, pp. 52–3; *RGKJ*, pp. 238–41; Grousset, II, pp. 211–25; Delpech, II, pp. 202–5; Runciman, II, pp. 241–3.

[4] IQ, p. 277.

[5] WT, p. 719. William's account of these events contains a summary of the tactical measures necessary to achieve the object decided upon:
'mane facto, communicato consilio, nostri procedendum esse decernunt; nam redire, cum ignominia plenum, tum pene videbatur impossibile. Verum hostes circumpositi utrumque impedire videntur. Tandem nostri animosius insistentes, per medias hostium acies, viam ferro aperiunt, et ad destinatum unanimiter locum contendunt; sed loricis, cassidibus, simul et clipeis onusti, lento incedebant gradu; hostium etiam circumposita multitudine praepediebantur. At vero equites, licet expedientius possent incedere, peditum tamen oportebat in incessu conformes fieri manipulis ne dissolveretur agmen et irruendi super cuneos hostibus daretur occasio.'

The features of the march were described by both William of Tyre and Ibn al-Qalanisi. In order to preserve the solid formation of their column the mounted knights kept their pace down to that of the foot-soldiers. Four days were required to reach Bosra. During that time the Latins suffered from thirst, as well as from the archery and harassing attacks of the Muslims, to which they themselves replied with arrows. On arrival at Bosra they found running water and enjoyed both refreshment and the knowledge that their exertions had succeeded.[1] Then came the news that the wife of Altuntash had admitted troops from Damascus into the citadel, and that the only course remaining was now to retreat.[2] On the return march conditions were harder than before. To the arrows and repeated attacks of the enemy were added dust, heat, and thirst. At one stage of the march the enemy employed a stratagem used during the battle outside Antioch on 28 June 1098 and to be repeated at Hattin in 1187: they set fire to the dry vegetation so that the Latin column was oppressed by flames and smoke.[3]

During these varied trials the Franks were careful to maintain their close formation. The bodies of the dead and wounded were brought along with the column, in order that the morale of the enemy should not be raised by the knowledge of the losses they had inflicted. Before all, the strictest measures were taken to ensure that the order of march offered no opening for the irruption of the Turks. Any man who left his place in the ranks was threatened with severe penalties.

It was, however, the disobedient but successful sortie of a single Turk which relieved the Latin column from the worst enemy pressure; and when, as the Franks approached their own territory, the Turks intensified their pressure on the rear of the column, they won no success. When the Franks dispersed to their homes, the Franks were still without Bosra, but for twelve days they had maintained themselves against the attacks of a persistent enemy.

Three years later the king was involved in a similar action. In 1150 a controversy arose in Antioch concerning the future of the places in the county of Edessa which had survived the loss

---

[1] WT, pp. 720-1.   [2] WT, *ibid.*   [3] WT, p. 723; IQ, p. 278.

of the capital four years before. The Byzantine emperor, Manuel
Comnenus, was anxious to acquire them; some Syrian Franks
were of the opinion that they themselves could no longer hold
them against the attacks of Mas'ud, Qara Arslan, and Nur al-Din;
others considered that they should remain as part of the Latin
states.[1] Baldwin III decided that they should be ceded to the
Greeks.[2] At the head of a military force he met Manuel's representatives at Tell Bashir, where the transfer of the places in question was negotiated. Those of their inhabitants, whether Frank
or Armenian, who wished to remain under Latin rule, prepared
to march with the king, accompanied by their families and household possessions. The column was therefore made up of a multi-
tude of unarmed people with their household goods, and the 500
milites under Baldwin's command.[3]

Nur al-Din mustered troops to hinder this evacuation and his
first attacks were made between Duluk and 'Aintab.[4] The Franks
prepared to meet these by drawing up their troops in battle order;
in this way they were able to reach 'Aintab. Next day the Turks
appeared on either flank of the Frankish column and were prepared to attack it from any direction. Accordingly the Frankish
leaders took measures very similar to those ordered in the French
host at the crisis of its march across Asia Minor nearly three years
before. The knights were organized so that each had his appointed place in the column. The king commanded an advance-guard;
the knights of Antioch were on either flank; and, presumably because it was known that the Turks made their greatest effort
against the rear of the column, Raymond II of Tripoli and Humphrey of Toron, 'cum majoribus et fortioribus militum copiis',
were appointed to command the rear-guard.[5] The unarmed multi-
tude and the baggage was therefore protected by its escort on all
sides; William said nothing of the role played by *pedites* in the
action.

---

[1] WT, p. 785.

[2] WT, *ibid.* Baldwin considered that the Muslims were certain to conquer
them within a short time. He preferred this to happen when Manuel, rather
than he himself, was responsible for their defence. See also Chalandon,
Jean II Comnène et Manuel I Comnène, p. 425.

[3] WT, pp. 786–7.

[4] WT, *ibid.* For the two places see Rey, *Colonies*, pp. 315, 322; Dussaud,
Topographie, pp. 472, 478; Cahen, *Syrie du Nord*, pp. 115 *et seq.*

[5] WT, p. 788.

For the whole of the day on which they left 'Aintab the Franks were assailed by Turkish troops who fought in the traditional manner of their race: repeated attacks and skirmishes; arrows in such showers that the appearance of the baggage soon resembled a porcupine; and all this endured in the heat, dust, and thirst of a Syrian August day. But the careful organization and the resolute advance gave no opportunity to the enemy to force a decisive engagement. He was himself discouraged and short of supplies, and after sunset on that day he troubled the Franks no more.

Forty years later, during the siege of Acre, the Franks undertook a march which exhibited many of the same tactical features as that made to Bosra. On 12 November 1190, urged on by lack of food and the unrest of the rank and file, the Christian army marched against Saladin's camp.[1] Saladin withdrew before them[2] and there was no action until a Latin column marched towards Haifa in an attempt to find provisions there. It camped at the head waters of the Nahr N'amein, between the spring of Ras al-'Ain and Tell Kurdaneh.[3] When their hopes of finding supplies were disappointed the Latins began the return march to their camp, following the course of the river, which appears to have given them protection on one flank.[4]

Saladin ordered his men to hem in the Franks on all sides. His horsemen kept close to the Latin column, and his mounted archers were constantly reinforced throughout the day.[5] Despite the Muslims' arrows, and the repeated short attacks at close quarters to which they were subjected,[6] the Franks, grouped around their standard, marched slowly forward in close order. The foot-soldiers protected the knights like a wall[7] and, together with the archers, especially distinguished themselves in the rear of the column. It was here that the Turks followed their normal practice and developed their heaviest attacks, and often, as at Arsuf in the following year, forced the Christian infantry to face about and to

[1] *Itin.* pp. 115–19; *Est.* 3961–4090; BD, pp. 195–201; al-Imad in AS, pp. 510–13; *RGKJ*, pp. 535–7; Grousset, III, pp. 39–40.

[2] BD, p. 196; *Itin.* p. 116; *Est.* 3992–4.

[3] BD, pp. 197–8; *Itin.* p. 117; *Est.* 4007.   [4] *Itin.* p. 118; BD, p. 199.

[5] BD. p. 199; AS, p. 512.

[6] Ibn al-Imad in AS, p. 512: 'We hoped that, carried away by blind fury, they would attack us and in this way would give us the opportunity to divide and to break their mass.'

[7] BD, p. 199.

fight while marching backwards.[1] As in 1147 they concealed their losses by carrying their wounded, and by burying their dead as they marched.[2] At certain points it was necessary for the knights themselves to take part in the fight, either because the weight of enemy attack made this necessary, or for some special purpose, like the clearing of the D'auk bridge.[3]

The foot-soldiers played an equally distinguished part in the battle of Arsuf fought on 7 September in the following year.[4] This engagement has been very fully reconstructed by modern historians, and primarily by Oman and Grousset. It is discussed here not because new material is available or a new interpretation possible, but in order to demonstrate that it was a normal type of engagement in Latin Syria, resulting from the meeting of antagonists whose military methods had remained essentially unchanged throughout the century. Because it was fully described by contemporaries, and because it was the major engagement of a campaign, it has been treated by modern historians as a set piece, affording opportunities for detailed study and fine writing. This obscures the important fact, however, that the whole operation, of which Arsuf was the climax, displayed many characteristic features of warfare in Latin Syria which have already been discussed.

After the capture of Acre the next military objective of the Franks was to establish a base from which they might attack Jerusalem. A march was therefore undertaken from Acre to Jaffa by the coast road. Throughout its course the march was harassed by Saladin's army,[5] but these Muslim attacks became

---

[1] *Itin.* p. 118: 'A tergo nihilominus nostros quidam persequentes ultra modum fatigabant, ita quod pedites nostros satellites et sagittarios qui fuerant extremi deputati, oportuit continue versa retrorsum facie progredi post tergum sine intermissione in persequentes immittentes sagittas.' See also *Est.* 4060–4.

[2] BD, p. 199; AS, p. 513.   [3] *Itin.* pp. 118–19; *Est.* 4039–42, 4070–90.

[4] *Itin.* pp. 249–75; *Est.* 5669–6658; BD, pp. 244–61; AS, v, pp. 33–40; IA, II, pp. 48–50; *RGKJ*, pp. 578–90; Grousset, III, pp. 62–71; Delpech, I, pp. 375–93; Köhler, III, pt. 3, pp. 234–48; Oman, I, pp. 305–18; Delbrück, III, p. 427; Lot, *L'Art militaire* I, p. 163.
'Epistola regis Angliae ad abbatem de Claravalle' in *Rogerus de Houeden, Chronica* (ed. W. Stubbs, Rolls Series), III, pp. 131–2.

[5] On the very first day of the march the Latin column was attacked and there was heavy fighting before the Muslims were beaten off: *Itin.* pp. 250–1; *Est.* 5759–99; BD, p. 245; IA, II, pp. 48–9.

heavier on 1 September, when the Franks left Caesarea.[1] Both Beha ed-Din and the author of the *Itinerarium* have left vivid accounts of the fighting during the two days' march between Caesarea and the Salt River. The horsemen in the Frankish army were organized in three divisions, and the main standard was in the midst of the host. The army's outer line of defence was provided by the armed men on foot; half of them marched between the knights and the Muslims, while the remainder rested from the combat by marching between the knights and the seashore. They wore efficient protective garments, and those armed with bows inflicted casualties among the Muslims. These on their part attempted by archery to provoke the Franks to a premature charge; but the Christians, although the pace of their advance was reduced by the Turkish tactics, advanced while fighting, and displayed an admirable discipline and self-control.[2] On the following day Muslim attacks were even more intense. Saladin urged his squadrons to close quarters, and a number of charges were made.[3] The Frankish knights, among them King Richard, were forced to fight back,[4] and some Frankish knights left the column to attack the Turks.[5] Yet the principal defence of the Christians was their own close order, which on that day was even more solid than usual.[6]

The battle of Arsuf was the climax of this protracted operation.[7] The general conditions were the same as they had been on 1 and 2 September; but on 7 September Saladin, who saw that the enemy were nearing Jaffa, urged his men to greater exertions,[8] while Richard, expecting an intensified Turkish attack, organized the line of march even more elaborately.[9] The method

---

[1] *Itin.* p. 256: 'Ea itaque die, solito vehementius infestabant exercitum.' BD (p. 246) recorded that Saladin had been reconnoitring ground for a pitched battle, and from BD's account on p. 251 it appears that he had chosen the country immediately south of Caesarea.

[2] All this in BD, pp. 251–2; al-Imad in AS, v, p. 34.

[3] BD, p. 253.   [4] *Itin.* p. 258.   [5] BD, p. 253.

[6] *Itin.* p. 257: 'Per turmas etiam solito densiores se cohibebat itinerans exercitus. Deducendae extremae legioni praefuerant Templarii, qui tot equos ea die, Turcis irruentibus a tergo, amiserunt quod fere desperati sunt.'

[7] *Itin.* pp. 260–75; *Est.* 6126–658; BD, pp. 258–61.   [8] BD, p. 258.

[9] *Itin.* pp. 260–1: 'Ita se agebat exercitus sensim progrediens et paulatim, ne forte disgregarentur; quia minus cohaerentes acies ordinatae, minus ad resistendum valerent.' The military ideas implicit in this sentence have been discussed above, pp. 127 *et seq.*

employed by both sides was the same as on previous days, and on former occasions in Syria during the preceding three generations. The Muslims urged on by their commander, sought to provoke and weaken the Latin formation by archery. They supplemented their efforts by a number of charges and spells of fighting at close quarters;[1] they made their principal efforts against the rear of the Latin column.[2] On their part the Franks suffered the attacks, although many individual knights, especially among the Hospitallers in the rear-guard, displayed violent impatience with orders which compelled them to endure attack without retaliation.[3] For hours they maintained their formation and continued their march. The foot-soldiers and archers fought magnificently in warding off the Muslim attacks, and especially those against the rear.[4]

The most stirring and effective action of the day, which was the irresistible charge of the Christian knights, was a natural event in the circumstances just described.[5] First, it was normal for the knights to take an active part in fighting on the march when the enemy pressed too closely on the column; second, the charge was normally delivered when the enemy was so heavily committed that he could not avoid taking its full impact; third, there was a limit to the restraint and endurance of individual knights, and this was reached on the day of Arsuf. For all these reasons it was inevitable that the foot-soldiers should be called upon to open their ranks, and to make way for the mounted onslaught which swept the Turks far from the Latin column.

[1] As usual, they slung their bows and came to close quarters: *Itin.* p. 265; *Est.* 6374.
[2] The familiar phrase 'a tergo' to indicate the direction of the Turkish attack is used throughout the account in *Itin.*; see pp. 264, 266, 267. See also 'Epistola regis ad abbatem', p. 131.
[3] *Itin.* pp. 267-8; *Est.* 6377-82.
[4] *Itin.* pp. 263-4. As usual the heaviest attacks were on the rear of the column: 'O quam necessarii fuerunt ea die validissimi balistarii, et sagittarii, satellites rigidissimi, qui concludentes extremitatem exercitus, continuis pilorum jactibus, in quantum dabatur, Turcorum retundebant pertinaciam. . . infatigabili contendebant virtute, ut versa facie in imminentes a tergo Turcos obtundendos, tanquam cedentes ambularent retrogradi in tergum, ne forte minus provide sibi praecaverent aversi. Tota quidem illa die, quia Turci imminebant a tergo, apud eos versa facie itinere praepostero potius viam carpendo quam eundo, proficiebant.'
[5] *Itin.* p. 269; BD, pp. 258-9; IA, II, p. 49; al-Imad in AS, v, p. 38.

The result was a striking and temporary tactical success, but nothing more. The charge was on a grand scale, but it achieved no more than had the knights in 1111, 1182, 1183, and 1190: it relieved pressure on the marching army. The pursuit was not pressed,[1] because they feared an ambush,[2] so that on the same day Saladin rallied his men;[3] on the next he was ready for battle;[4] and on the day after, as the Franks approached the Nahr Auja, he was once more harassing their march.[5] Arsuf was a magnified but normal episode in a normal type of military encounter. Any attempt to present it as a signal victory, or as 'a crushing blow'[6] is to misunderstand its place in the warfare of the period.

IV. PITCHED BATTLES

The subject-matter of this section is provided by the pitched battles fought by the Syrian Franks between 1097 and 1192. These engagements are considered here more briefly than in most writing on military history, because they have already attracted a disproportionate amount of attention and have been the subject of notable researches. Historians of warfare, and especially those writing under the influence of nineteenth-century ideas, have regarded events on the battlefield as that part of war most worthy of their study. They have applied to medieval accounts of battles all the technical resources of their scholarship and have analysed and collated the available sources with outstanding skill. As a result they have arrived at detailed and far-reaching conclusions on the tactical methods employed by the contesting armies. Battle, however, is only one of the available methods of waging war, and one which in twelfth-century Syria was employed by most commanders with a caution which at times approached reluctance. Furthermore the sources are of a nature which cannot yield results commensurate with the patient and expert analysis to which they have been subjected.

There are two principal reasons which explain why literary descriptions and official accounts of battles cannot be regarded as an exact record of military events. The first arises from the

---

[1] *Itin.* p. 272; , 6540.   [2] BD, p. 260; IA, II, p. 50; *Est.* 6561–2.
[3] BD, *ibid.*; *Itin.* pp. 273–4.   [4] BD, p. 261.
[5] BD, p. 262; *Itin.* p. 281; *Est.* 6918–22   [6] Oman, I, p. 263.

temptation felt by any narrator of violent action, and especially of deeds done on the fields of sport or battle, to tell a tale which will stir his audience. And for their part audiences have expected to be stirred in this way; for, until our own day, military action has been conventionally regarded as something which is necessarily vivid and exciting. Narrators have been influenced by this convention, and have achieved their effect by exaggeration and distortion.[1] And they have been exposed to a second and equally strong temptation. The events of a battle are often confused and fall into no very clear pattern. It is natural that the historian should so arrange them that they form a consecutive story. He rationalizes the irrational and in the interests of clarity deviates from the exact and too complicated truth.

The twin temptations to dramatize and to rationalize both provide elements of distortion. They are both present to some extent even in the accounts of eyewitnesses of medieval battles, which are the best sources of our present knowledge. Next best is the writer whose information was acquired direct from the eyewitness, but if he too wishes to dramatize and to rationalize then the distortion becomes more pronounced. The descriptions of the battle of Ramla fought in 1101 furnish an example of this process. One was given by Albert of Aix, who gained his knowledge of events in the Holy Land from pilgrims who had been there,

---

[1] Tolstoy makes many acute comments on military affairs which are no less applicable to modern armies than they were to those of Kutuzov and Bagration. In *War and Peace* he refers more than once to the difficulty experienced by human beings in giving an accurate account of military actions, and especially of those in which they themselves have taken part. He describes this aspect of man's nature in the episode in which Nicholas Rostov tells his friends of an action between the French and the Russians in 1805:

'He told them of the Schon Grabern affair just as those who have taken part in a battle generally do describe it, that is, as they would like it to have been, as they have heard it described by others, and as sounds well, but not at all as it really was. Rostov was a truthful young man and would on no account have told a deliberate lie. He began his story meaning to tell everything just as it happened, but imperceptibly, involuntarily, and inevitably he lapsed into falsehood. If he had told the truth to his hearers—who like himself had often heard stories of attacks, and had formed a definite idea of what an attack was and were expecting to hear just such a story—they would either not have believed him or, still worse, would have thought that Rostov was himself to blame since what generally happens to the narrators of cavalry attacks had not happened to him.' (*War and Peace*, trans. Louise and Aylmer Maude, p. 258.)

and so by normal standards may be reckoned as an authoritative source. But Fulcher, chaplain to Baldwin I, rode with the king throughout the day and was in the thick of the fight; therefore his account has to be accepted before that of Albert. Since the descriptions given by these two writers differ in nearly all respects, Albert's account has been rejected by the best modern historians,[1] although, but for the accident of Fulcher's presence at the battle, Albert's evidence would still be regarded as a trustworthy source.

The same progressive distortion may be followed in the work of Delpech. In his *Tactique au treizième siècle* he reconstructed three battles fought in the principality of Antioch in 1115 and 1119, those of Sarmin, the Ager Sanguinis, and Hab. Walter, chancellor to Roger of Antioch, was present at the second of these battles and probably at the first,[2] while he had information of the battle of Hab from men who had taken part.[3] The same events were more cursorily recorded by Fulcher, who was himself in Jerusalem when they took place. The evidence provided by these two men is therefore the best material for a subsequent study of the three battles, and it was used two generations later by William of Tyre in the composition of his own history.[4] William gave a clear description of the battles; but it is significant that, although he reproduced words and phrases of the earlier writers and intended to repeat their accounts, the picture he gave differed in many respects from that given by Walter.[5] When, seven centuries after William, Delpech reconstructed the same battles, he used as a source the work not of Walter, but William. The result is that if the work of Delpech on these three battles is compared with that of Heermann, who relied on Walter, they are hardly recognizable as the same engagements.[6]

It is likely, therefore, that a first-hand account of battle will but imperfectly represent the original events, while one composed

---

[1] Heermann, p. 58; Köhler, III, pt. 3, p. 182.
[2] Hagenmeyer in Galt. p. 6.   [3] Heermann, p. 78.
[4] Hagenmeyer in Galt. p. 48, n. 93.   [5] Heermann, p. 78.
[6] Delpech, II, pp. 182–4, 195–7; Heermann, pp. 76–95. In the same way the battle of Arsuf as described by Delpech (I, pp. 381–93) and Köhler (III, pt. 3, pp. 234–48) has little in common with that of Oman (I, pp. 305–18) or that above, pp. 162–5. Delpech and Köhler relied principally on the author of the *Gesta Ricardi* who was well informed of events in Palestine, but the author of the account in the *Itinerarium* was present at the battle. See Köhler, III, pt. 3, p. 238, n. 1; Oman, I, p. 308, n. 1; Delbrück, III, p. 427.

from second- or third-hand information will deviate even further from the truth. It is right that the resources of modern scholarship should be brought to bear on such accounts, defective as they are; but the words and phrases of highly coloured battle-pieces based on hearsay ought not to be assessed as if they were taken from a carefully drafted legal document, and so made the basis for exact and detailed conclusions on tactical methods and formations. Instances of such excesses will be demonstrated in the discussion which follows.

The Franks met the Turks in battle for the first time at Dorylaeum.[1] Modern historians have used the many available sources to reconstruct this battle in great detail, and have found evidence of a number of tactical movements and formations.[2] In fact, like

---

[1] Sources are *Anon.* pp. 44–50; Fulcher, pp. 334–6; RA, p. 240; *HEp.* p. 145 (Anselm). All were present at the battle. RC (pp. 620–9) was informed in later years by Tancred. AA (pp. 328–32) was probably informed by men present at the battle. WT, pp. 129–34; Delpech, II, pp. 150–4; Heermann, pp. 5–24; Köhler, III, pt. 3, pp. 140–9; Oman, I, pp. 273–8; Delbrück, III, p. 421; Chalandon, *Première Croisade*, pp. 169–70; Grousset, I, pp. 31–6; Runciman, I, pp. 184–6.

[2] Delpech's reconstruction of this battle furnishes an excellent study in the process of distortion. Despite the fact that no battle during the century was described by more eyewitnesses, Delpech relied on Tudebod, RC, and WT, none of whom were present. He used WT's description of Turkish methods of attack (WT, p. 131), together with two references by WT to the 'agmina Turcorum' (WT, pp. 130, 132), to present a picture of the 'successives charges en colonne' of the Turkish mounted archers. This instance is typical of Delpech's method. By assigning a precise meaning to 'agmen', a word used by medieval writers in a general sense and as a rough equivalent to 'acies', 'turma', 'caterva' (on this point see Frauenholz, *Heerwesen*, pp. 110, 113). Delpech achieved an over-formalized and therefore distorted reconstruction. See criticism by Heermann, p. 18, n. 1.

A further instructive demonstration of the methods of writing military history was given by Köhler, III, pt. 3, pp. 145–6. When he was hard pressed by the Turks, Bohemond sent for help to the leaders of the other part of the crusader army, which the Turks had not attacked. *Anon.* (p. 46) described their arrival on the battlefield in these general terms: 'Dux itaque Godefridus . . . ac Hugo Magnus simul venerunt prius . . . episcopus quoque Podiensis prosecutus est illos . . . et comes de Sancto Egidio . . . juxta illos.' By assigning an exact meaning to 'prius', 'prosecutus est', and 'juxta' and then by straining that meaning to its utmost, Köhler was able to conclude that 'die Fürsten der rechten Kolonne marschirten in voller Schlachtordnung. . . Der Bischof von Puy diente als Reserve . . . der Flankenangriff derselben ist von vornherein beabsichtigt worden' (pp. 145–6). It is suggested that the leaders carried out Bohemond's urgent instructions to come as quickly as they could (*Anon.* p. 46) and that they arrived in the best order they could. Like Delpech, Köhler appears too ready to over-formalize and to distort.

most battles of the period, it can be traced only in its main out-
lines. After they had left Nicea, the Franks had divided into two
columns, of which one was attacked by the Turks on 1 July 1097.
The Franks, under Bohemond's command, did not hesitate to
give battle, nor the Turks to accept it.[1] While the infantry pitched
camp, the Western knights attempted to attack the enemy;[2] but
the Turkish elusiveness, mobility, and archery were alike unknown to them,[3] and as a result the crusading horsemen were
forced back into the mass of armed and unarmed pilgrims.[4] For a
time the Franks were close packed and in confusion, and the more
adventurous knights who still attempted to close with the Turks
failed to do so.[5] Yet significant for future development of Frankish methods was the fact that when massed together, although
they could not organize an ordered defence and had lost all
power of striking back at the enemy, the Turks could not destroy
them.[6] The very mass of the Franks represented a formidable
defensive power. The battle remained in this suspended state for
two or three hours, until the deadlock was broken by the arrival of
the knights from the other Frankish column. These reinforcements, led by Godfrey, Raymond of Toulouse, and the bishop of
Puy completely surprised the Turks, who fled at once from the
field.[7]

It was soon clear to the leaders of the crusade that, in order to
defeat an enemy whose military methods were unknown to them,

It was right that he should have carefully examined every word of the text;
but at the same time he should have been prepared to admit that in fact the
available evidence simply does not reveal whether the relieving force came
on to the field in battle order, or whether it took the Turks in the flank.

[1] *Anon.* p. 44; Fulcher, p. 334. In future years, when they learnt more
about each other, the Franks were to use their solidity and to continue their
march in the midst of the enemy; the Turks were to weaken the Franks by
harassing and by denying them supplies before attempting the *coup de grâce.*

[2] *Anon.* p. 44.   [3] *Anon.* p. 46; Fulcher, p. 335; WT, p. 131.

[4] *Anon.* p. 46; Fulcher, p. 335; RC, pp. 621–2.   [5] RC, p. 623.

[6] The Franks were, in the words of Fulcher (p. 335), 'omnes in unum
conglobati, tanquam oves clausae ovili, trepidi et pavefacti ab hostibus
undique circumvallabamur, ut nullatenus aliquorsum procedere valeremus'.
Köhler (III, pt. 3, p. 142) distorts this confusion into a formal military
manœuvre: 'Bohemond beschloss daher, sich auf die Vertheidigung zu
beschränken und liess, wie das gebräuchlich war, von den einzelnen
Schlachthaufen die runde Ordnung einnehmen, um den Feind mit vorge-
streckten Spiessen abzuwehren.'

[7] *Anon.* pp. 48–9; Fulcher, p. 335.

it was necessary to devise tactical counter-measures.[1] The most
immediate requirements were to avoid encirclement by the
Turks, and to ensure that, when the Latin charge was delivered,
it struck the main body of the enemy. Common sense dictated
the further precaution of holding part of the force in reserve, in
order to combat any Turks who did work their way round the
flanks, and to carry help to any hard-pressed sector of the line
of battle.[2] During the months which followed Dorylaeum, the
leaders made an intelligent appreciation of the problem. Encirclement was avoided by seeking the protection of natural
obstacles for the flanks of the crusaders' line of battle. In the
three principal engagements fought in the neighbourhood of
Antioch the field commander took no part in the first assault, but
remained at the head of a tactical reserve. It is significant that on
each occasion the commander was Bohemond, and it seems clear
that, so long as he remained with the main expedition, he took
the lead in military affairs. If the evidence for this were provided
only in the account left by the anonymous knight in his following,
it would be suspect; but there is ample corroboration elsewhere,
and especially in the pages of Raymond of Agiles. Bohemond
may fairly be credited with working out means of counteracting
Turkish methods, means which were not mere exercises in
theory, but which were such as could be used in the field by a
force encumbered by unarmed pilgrims, and which had little
enough of discipline, organization, or military training. It was an
impressive performance which stamps Bohemond as one of the
foremost commanders of the age, and which tells us as much of
the qualities of medieval generalship as the victory of another
great Norman in England a generation earlier.

On 31 December 1097 a large foraging party led by Bohemond

---

[1] Fulcher in describing Dorylaeum admitted that 'nobis omnibus tale
bellum erat incognitum'. In their letter to Pope Urban II, the Latin princes
described their effort to adjust their own methods in order to counteract
those of the Turks (*HEp.* p. 163): 'Sed nobis multis bellis contra eorum
calliditates et ingenia edoctis. . . .

[2] The use of a reserve was normal in medieval armies. See the role assigned
to Louis VII in Asia Minor in 1147 (Odo, p. 72); and the description by
WT, of the marshalling of Baldwin's army at Mont Gisard in 1177 (WT,
p. 1042): 'Ordinant et ipsi nihilominus acies suas, et juxta militarem disciplinam agmina digerunt, disponentes qui primi aggrediantur et qui eis
sint subsidio.' See also Delbrück, III, p. 307.

THE LATIN FIELD ARMY IN ACTION

and Robert of Flanders met a Muslim force east of the Orontes, probably near al-Bara.[1] The best accounts of the battle show that, despite Turkish attempts to encircle them, the Franks were able to come rapidly to close quarters and to disperse the enemy by a charge led by Robert of Flanders. According to Raymond, Bohemond remained in the rear and so foiled Turkish attempts to outflank.

In a battle fought six weeks later against an army attempting to relieve Antioch, the precautions taken by the Franks against encirclement were even more elaborate; Bohemond appears both as the author of the plan, and as the leader of the squadron which was at once reserve and rear-guard.[2] As at Dorylaeum different functions were assigned to foot-soldiers and knights.[3] The former were left to guard the camp, and only the mounted men were sent against the relieving force. The Franks decided to meet the approaching enemy some miles from Antioch, at a point where the river Orontes approached to within a mile of the shores of the lake.[4] Their choice was due to their wish to prevent co-operation between the garrison of the town and the force relieving them,[5] and by means of the natural obstacles provided by river and lake to cover their flanks against any attempt by the Turks to encircle them.[6] The plan was successful and from the first they were able to engage the Turks at close quarters.[7] At first the seven hundred Franks yielded before the assault of the Turkish main body; but Bohemond sent help from the rear-guard, and a final Frankish attack carried the fight.[8]

[1] *Anon.* p. 72; RA, pp. 244-5; Chalandon, *Première Croisade*, pp. 188-9; Grousset, I, p. 77; Runciman, I, p. 221.
[2] For this battle fought near the Lake of Antioch on 9 February 1098 see *Anon.* pp. 82-6; RA, pp. 246-7; *HEp.* pp. 150, 158.
Delpech, II, pp. 161-6; Heermann, pp. 25-33; Köhler, III, pt. 3, pp. 155-9; Oman, I, pp. 279-81; Delbrück, III, pp. 421-2; Chalandon, *op. cit.* pp. 194-6; Grousset, I, pp. 85-8; Runciman, I, pp. 225-6.
[3] Above, p. 118.   [4] RA, p. 247.   [5] RA, p. 246.
[6] RA, p. 247: 'Contigit autem in eo loco bellum fieri, quo palus et fluvius quae per milliarum vicina sunt. Hoc autem hostibus evagandi licentiam vetuit, ne more suo accingere possent.'
[7] *Anon.* p. 84: 'Junctis igitur prospere nostris, unus cominus percutiebat alium.'
[8] *Anon.* pp. 84-6. Heermann's work on this battle shows how an able and accurate scholar can reduce the value of his work by attempting to read too much into the available evidence. Heermann considered that his researches

After they had taken Antioch the crusaders were themselves besieged in the city by Karbuqa's army. On 28 June 1098, unable any longer to endure the blockade, they staked everything on a sortie and battle.[1] Their plan was limited by the necessity of the whole fighting force leaving the town by a single gate; they came on to the battlefield in column with the main body of the enemy awaiting them on their right flank. During this deployment they were vulnerable to attack, but according to contemporary opinion Karbuqa was content to let the whole force leave the city that his victory might be the more complete.[2]

---

revealed two important characteristics of the Frankish *Gefechtsführung*: first, that before battle the available force was normally organized in three divisions ('drei Treffen'); second, that the various squadrons were formed up and attacked in echelon ('staffelförmig'). See Heermann, pp. 111–12, 113–14.

He considered that he had found both arrangements in the contemporary accounts of this battle. His reasoning is to be found in his *Gefechtsführung*, p. 30, n. 3. RA (p. 247) referred to the ordering of the army ('ordinatio'). Since in another passage (p. 303) he used the noun 'ordo' in the sense of division, Heermann considered that 'ordinatio' means organization into divisions. That these numbered three he deduced from the evidence of RC (p. 647) who was not present at the battle, 'praecedit Boamundus, subsequitur Godefridus, in subsidio est Stephanus'. Since it is known from the better sources that Bohemond led the reserve, Heermann has to admit that RC's account was 'ganz fehlerhaft' and 'weniger zuverlässig'; but since he wrote 'aus einer allgemeinen Gefechtskenntnis', Heermann was disposed to accept his evidence on this point. He fortified his conclusion from equally slender evidence from Tudebod, who was a less trustworthy source than RC.

From the same texts Heermann argued that the Franks were not formed in a line of battle but that the first division was nearer and the reserve further from the enemy than the middle division. They could not, however, have been formed directly behind each other because it was necessary to occupy the whole breadth of the plain between lake and river. The formation was therefore an echelon. See Heermann, p. 30, n. 3, pp. 112, 114.

Reasoning of a similar kind enabled Heermann to deduce the formation of three divisions at Dorylaeum. His fragile argument is contained in his *Gefechtsführung*, p. 13, n. 3.

Heerman's method in this research was beyond reproach, but in his conclusions he was vulnerable to arguments based on the most authoritative sources and on common sense. See Köhler, III, pt. 3, p. 159, and Delbrück, III, pp. 421–2.

[1] The sources were the same as for the battles already described. Eyewitnesses were RA, pp. 259–61; *Anon.* pp. 150–6; *HEp.* pp. 163, 167. Based on hearsay from eyewitnesses were: RC, pp. 666–8; AA, pp. 421–8. See also IA, pp. 194–6; KD, pp. 582–3; ME, pp. 42–3; Delpech, II, pp. 155–61; Heermann, pp. 35–49; Köhler, III, pt. 3, pp. 165–75; Oman, I, pp. 282–6; Delbrück, III, pp. 422–4; Grousset, I, pp. 104–7; Runciman, I, pp. 247–9.

[2] *Anon.* p. 152; RA, p. 260; Heermann, p. 46.

The Franks were marshalled in four divisions, each of two squadrons, in which were both horse- and foot-soldiers. The infantry were arrayed in front of the knights so that they stood between the knights and the enemy.[1] For the first time on a Syrian battlefield, they were posted in a battle station which was to be normal to them throughout the century.[2] Bohemond was again commander and probably planned the operation;[3] he led the fourth and last division, which was to be in reserve to the three which formed the main line of battle.[4] As soon as the first division had passed through the gate and crossed the Orontes bridge, it was to turn into line, and to march up stream with its right flank on the bank of the river. The second division marched across the rear of its predecessor, and turned to face the enemy in line when it was in a position to advance in line with and on the left of the first division. The third did likewise and came into line on the left of the second.[5] The plan ensured that each division as it left the city changed its formation from column into line at the earliest possible moment, so that it faced the enemy ready to attack, and covered the deployment of the succeeding column as it emerged from the gate.

The precautions against encirclement were repeated by Bohemond in this battle. The flanks were covered by natural obstacles, and plans were ready to oppose any Turkish detachment which might nevertheless attack the Latin rear. Some two miles ahead of the Franks as they left the city was high ground.[6] The head of the third division was ordered to reach this before it turned into line; after it had done so the left flank of the Franks was protected, just as its right was covered by the river. Bohemond himself watched the rear.[7]

The battle developed almost in accordance with Bohemond's

---

[1] RA, p. 259.   [2] Below, pp. 199–200.   [3] RA, p. 258.
[4] RA, p. 259. Heermann (p. 41) once more betrayed his anxiety to fit all battle formations into the pattern of 'eine Staffel von drei Treffen', which he considered normal. It is true that there were 'vier Treffen' but Heermann is able to reconcile this fact to his generalization because the fourth under Bohemond acted as reserve.
[5] The sources give more exact detail concerning this battle than of any other fought in Latin Syria during the twelfth century. It is also the subject of Heermann's finest piece of research, and the details given above follow his work in every particular.
[6] RA, p. 260.   [7] RA, p. 259; Heermann, p. 41

plan. The Turks resisted the attempts of the third division, led by the bishop of Puy, to reach the high ground, and were able to send a detachment across the head of the Latin column. When the Franks turned into line to face the Karbuqa's main army, the Turkish detachment was therefore in their rear. A body of crusaders was detailed to meet its attack, and in the resulting encounter the *pedites* showed that they were well able to defend themselves.[1] Their rear thus covered, the three leading divisions of crusaders were able to attack in echelon.[2] The Turks, whose morale had been sapped by the desertion of many Turkmen auxiliaries and by quarrels among the leaders,[3] fled with little resistance to the Latin charge.[4]

Immediately after they had captured Jerusalem the Franks had to face a counter-attack by the Fatimids of Egypt, and on 12 August 1099 the two armies met near Ascalon.[5] It has already been stated that the Arab and Berber horsemen of the Egyptian armies did not fight in the same way as the Turks. Superior numbers sometimes enabled them to outflank the Franks, but they were not an army of mounted archers, and their principal weapons were lance and sword. They did not use dispersal as a tactical device, and therefore offered a solid target for the Latin charge.[6] This was the deciding factor at Ascalon. The battle is not capable of detailed reconstruction. The only certain facts are: the carefully devised order of march, providing an all-round defence, which was adopted by the Franks during their approach to the enemy;[7] the posting of the foot-soldiers in front of the

[1] RA, p. 260, '. . . pedites vero illi facto gyro impetum hostium sustinuerunt viriliter. Cum vero Turci nullo modo eos propellere possent. . . .'

[2] Heermann, pp. 41–2, and sketches facing pp. 42 and 43.

[3] KD, pp. 582–3.   [4] RA, p. 261; *Anon.* p. 156.

[5] *Anon.* pp. 208–18; RA, pp. 303–5; *HEp.* pp. 171–2 (Daimbert); Fulcher, pp. 362–3; RC, p. 703; AA, pp. 490–7; WT, pp. 380–2; Heermann, pp. 49–58; Köhler, III, pt. 3, pp. 175–9; Oman, I, pp. 288–91; Delbrück, III, pp. 424–4; Grousset, I, pp. 175–6; Runciman, I, p. 296–7. AA (p. 497) included in his account a special note that he had information of the battle from men who were there. In view of the arguments advanced on pp. 166–7 above, it is interesting to recall the comment of Heermann, p. 49: 'Alberts Erzählung . . . die ausführlichste von allen, ist, wenn sie auch in einigen Einzelheiten unzweifelhaft Richtiges enthält, doch im Ganzen und Grossen so verworren, dass sie nur mit grösster Vorsicht zu benutzen ist.'

[6] Above, p. 86.

[7] RA, p. 303. In view of the contrary evidence of *Anon.* p. 212, who was the

knights;[1] the decisive charge which the squadrons of knights, after their *pedites* had engaged the enemy with their bows, launched in succession at the enemy.[2] The charge alone secured a Latin victory, and the best sources agree that the duration of the battle was brief.

Further counter-attacks, launched through Ascalon by the Fatimid army in the years which followed, resulted in more battles of a similar kind. The first of these was fought near Ramla on 7 September 1101.[3] Despite the researches of Heermann, it can still be said that nothing is known of the formation adopted by the Franks before battle.[4] Fulcher, who was present, and whose account is the only trustworthy source of information, recorded that the Latin force of 260 mounted and 900 foot-soldiers were divided into six *acies*, and, so formed, launched themselves into the midst of the enemy. The squadrons did not attack simultaneously,[5] for two of them were in the fight before the rest, and

---

best source for the battle, Köhler's statement, III, pt. 3, p. 177, that the march formation was also the battle formation is no more than an assumption.

[1] *Anon.* p. 212; Fulcher, p. 362.

[2] *Anon.* p. 214; Heermann, p. 54. Heermann's reconstruction of this battle provides another interesting demonstration of his method as a military historian. Fulcher, who at the time of the battle was in Edessa, was adopted by Heermann as his principal source; *Anon.*, who was probably present at the battle, was regarded as of lesser importance. From Fulcher's evidence Heermann (pp. 52–4) deduced that the Franks were in three divisions, arranged in echelon, with Godfrey leading the rearmost. Heermann then turned to *Anon.* to provide the evidence that Godfrey commanded on the Latin left, Raymond on the right, and that the other princes were in the centre. The argument is not convincing.

[3] Fulcher, pp. 391–5; AA, pp. 549–53; WT, pp. 424–7; Heermann, pp. 58–63; Köhler, III, pt. 3, pp. 180–2; Oman, I, pp. 292–4; Delbrück, III, p. 425; *RGKJ*, pp. 25–7; Grousset, I, pp. 225–8; Runciman, II, pp. 74–5.

[4] Heermann again argued that the Franks were drawn up in three divisions which attacked in echelon. A comparison of his argument with the two sentences from Fulcher on which he relied will show the fragility of his argument. Köhler showed five squadrons in line and one in reserve: this again was a hypothesis, and there is no means of deciding which of these entirely different reconstructions is the more accurate. See following note.

[5] Köhler (III, pt. 3, p. 180) interpreted Fulcher in the sense that five of the Latin squadrons were in line, and that led by the king in reserve. His only argument in support of this assertion was that such a formation was adopted by the Franks in order to present an extended front and so to avoid being outflanked. This is an unsupported hypothesis. Köhler's use of his own conclusions demonstrates another characteristic of military historians: the transmutation of hypothesis into accepted fact. In summarizing the results of his

when these leading units were shattered by the fiercely resisting Muslims, the king came 'a parte postrema' to restore the situation and to win the battle. A part of the Egyptian force had found its way to the rear of the Latin formation, where it had attacked and decimated the Christian foot-soldiers. Thinking that the battle had everywhere gone in their favour, these Muslims had ridden on to Jaffa; but when next day they returned expecting to rejoin their main body, in fact they met the victorious Baldwin, and were themselves scattered. Little more is known of the military methods employed in this battle, therefore, than that the Franks won the day through the efforts of their horsemen. The enemy mass absorbed the charge of the leading squadrons, but could not survive the supporting attack of the king.

Victory, however, even against the Egyptians, was not to be won by a sole charge unsupported by any intelligent plan of action. To meet the Egyptian attack in 1102, an over-confident Baldwin attacked the enemy without all his available forces, without his foot-soldiers, and without putting his small force into battle formation.[1] As a result he lost his army, and himself fled from the field almost alone.

More fortunate than his followers, the king escaped to Arsuf, and so to Jaffa. He received reinforcements from Galilee and Jerusalem, was able to leave the shelter of the town, and, by offering battle, to interrupt the preparations of the Egyptians to besiege it. The best account of the engagement which followed was given by Fulcher, but he did so in general terms which do not allow a detailed reconstruction.[2] Because of the numerical superiority of the enemy the Franks were surrounded. Heavy pressure was exerted on the Latin infantry, but many of these wore adequate protective clothing and were armed with the bow, and thus not only withstood the arrows of the Muslim archers, but

---

research, Köhler used the supposed fact that the Latin squadrons were in line at Ramla as part of his general arguments; III, pt. 3, pp. 204–5.

[1] Above, p. 125. For the two battles fought by Baldwin against the Fatimid army in 1102 see Fulcher, pp. 400–5. He was an eyewitness of neither, but was in Jerusalem at the time. See also AA, pp. 592–7; WT, pp. 429–35; Delpech, II, pp. 187–93; Heermann, pp. 65–9; Köhler, III, pt. 3, pp. 182–4; Oman, I, pp. 294–5; Delbrück, III, pp. 425–6; *RGKJ*, pp. 36–40; Grousset, I, pp. 229–36; Runciman, II, pp. 76–80.

[2] Fulcher, pp. 404–5.

effectively returned their fire.[1] By virtue of that defensive ability to be displayed throughout the century by bodies of armed, dismounted Franks in close formation, and of the relief afforded them by the attacks of the Christian knights, the foot-soldiers maintained their cohesion. When the knights succeeded in breaking through to the Egyptian camp, the enemy fled.[2]

Equally little is known in detail of the repulse of an army sent from Egypt in 1105.[3] Baldwin met the enemy in the district of Ramla, and subdivided his army in the normal way into squadrons composed both of knights and infantry. Once more the Franks were outflanked, possibly because the enemy was in greater numbers, and certainly because he was assisted by a contingent of Turks sent by Tughtagin of Damascus.[4] The Franks appear to have owed their victory to the activity of Baldwin. He vanquished the Turks when they were becoming a serious threat to his rear, and returned to the main battle to lead the decisive charge which defeated the Egyptians.[5]

Meanwhile the Franks in northern Syria had been engaged with Turkish forces. The surviving accounts of the great defeat they suffered at Harran in 1104,[6] and of Tancred's victory over

[1] Fulcher, p. 405.
[2] Fulcher, p. 405; Delpech (II, pp. 191–3) saw in this fight a turning-point in the history of medieval 'infantry'. Note his division of the century into periods of tactical development; II, pp. 185–7. He regarded the fight at Jaffa as the starting-point in the development of the tactical combination of horse and foot, and in which the knights took up a position within the circle of 'infantry', left it only in order to charge, and when the charge had been made, returned to its shelter. There is in fact no evidence that such tactics, which demanded a high standard of training and control, were ever used by the Franks during the twelfth century.
[3] Fulcher, pp. 411–14; Fulcher was in Jerusalem at the time of the battle. AA, pp. 621–3; WT, pp. 454–6; Delpech, II, pp. 193–5; Heermann, pp. 72–6 Köhler, III, pt. 3, pp. 184–6; Delbrück, III, p. 426; *RGKJ*, pp. 56–8; Grousset, I, pp. 242–5; Runciman, II, pp. 89–90.
[4] Fulcher, p. 413; IQ, p. 71.
[5] Fulcher, p. 414. Heermann again was able to find that the Latins formed up for the battle in three divisions arranged in echelon. His reasoning is open to the same general objections as before. It was technically skilful, but failed to pass the test of common sense, as any reader of Heermann will see for himself. Heermann agreed that his proof was not conclusive, yet on p. 114 he adds the evidence of this battle to the impressive list of examples quoted in support of his thesis. Köhler (III, pt. 3, p. 186) concluded, without a shadow of evidence, that the Latin horsemen protected their formation by surrounding it with the *pedites*.
[6] Almost nothing is known of the course of this important battle, which at

Rudwan of Aleppo at Artah in 1105,[1] give little information on
the tactical methods employed during the period. But when, in
1115, Bursuq b. Bursuq and, in 1119, Il Ghazi b. Ortuq invaded
the territories of Antioch, the chancellor of Prince Roger was
available to report three battles, of two of which he was an eyewitness.

The circumstances have already been described in which Roger
of Antioch, aided by Baldwin of Edessa, defeated the army of
Bursuq near Sarmin.[2] Roger completely surprised his adversary
and this was the reason for his easy victory. From Walter's account, Heermann skilfully reconstructed the formation in which
the Franks entered the battle. Their force was divided into left
and right wings and centre, which was commanded by Prince
Roger himself. The count of Edessa was given the honour of
opening the attack by leading the left wing into action. This
division therefore went in advance of the centre, but the right
wing lay still further back; for when it was attacked by a band of
300 Turks, we are told that these passed 'post aciem principis'.
The three divisions of the Christian army therefore approached
the enemy in echelon with the left wing thrown forward and the
right drawn back.[3] Once the fighting began, the issue was not
long in doubt. On the left the Franks soon broke the main
strength of the Turks, who had withdrawn to a hillside behind
their camp, while Roger occupied the camp itself. Only on the

---

a stroke undid the work of conquest achieved by Bohemond and Tancred
during the five preceding years, and ended for ever Frankish expansion to the
Euphrates. See RC, pp. 710–11; Fulcher, pp. 408–9; AA, pp. 614–16;
WT, pp. 443–7; ME, pp. 71–2; IA, pp. 220–2; IQ, pp. 60–1; Heermann,
pp. 69–72; Oman, I, pp. 320–4; *RGKJ*, pp. 49–50; Grousset, I, pp. 405–6;
Cahen, *Syrie du Nord*, pp. 237–8; Runciman, II, pp. 41–4. In the words of
Cahen, p. 237: 'les divers compte-rendus [de la bataille] sont inconciliables'.
The same conclusion also in Heermann, pp. 69–72. Oman produced a good
story of the battle, but without references to the sources, and he ignored the
difficulties which they present.

[1] RC, pp. 714–15; Fulcher, p. 411; AA, pp. 620–1; WT, p. 453; IQ,
pp. 69–70; IA, pp. 227–8; KD, p. 593; *RGKJ*, p. 56; Grousset, I, pp. 420–1;
Cahen, *Syrie du Nord*, p. 242; Runciman, II, p. 52. RC gave the detail that
Tancred gained his victory by the skilful use of ground.

[2] Above, p. 147; Galt. pp. 72–6; Fulcher, p. 430; AA, p. 702; ME, pp.
115–16; WT, pp. 497–8; KD, p. 609; IA, pp. 297–8; Heermann, pp. 78–83;
Köhler, III, pt. 3, pp. 187–90; *RGKJ*, pp. 110–12; Grousset, I, pp. 506–9;
Cahen, *Syrie du Nord*, p. 274; Runciman, II, pp. 132–3.

[3] Heermann, pp. 80–1, using Galt. pp. 74–5.

right were the Franks ever in difficulty. There the Turcopoles, who were used by the Franks as archers and who may also have been mounted, yielded before the first enemy counter-attack and were driven in on the knights who followed. For a time there was confusion in these Christian ranks, but by hard fighting they were able to recover, and their sweeping success in the centre and on the left gained for them a decisive victory.

Four years later, on 28 June 1119, Roger lost his army and his life at a battle so disastrous that Latin writers called its site Ager Sanguinis.[1] He was not only the victim of surprise, but he allowed himself to be trapped in a valley with steep, wooded sides.[2] Il Ghazi and his Turkmens, approaching rapidly by little-used paths, appeared on all sides of the valley, leaving Roger with barely sufficient time in which to marshal his troops. He had with him 700 knights and some 3000 foot. He sent a strong detach-ment under Renaud Mansoer to oppose an enemy force moving against his rear, and drew up the rest of his men in five squadrons. Horse- and foot-soldiers were associated for mutual protection. The foot were posted nearer the enemy, for it was they who opened the battle, 'ut mos bellantium exigit', with an archery duel against the Turkish bowmen.[3]

The battle formation of this main Frankish force, as described by Walter, appears to have been in the shape of the letter **V**, with its point furthest from the enemy. The squadrons on the extreme right—the 'acies beati Petri'—and that on the extreme left, com-manded by Robert de St Lo, were first in action. They were respectively supported by the divisions of Geoffrey the Monk and of Prince Roger. These second line contingents were not drawn up immediately behind the first, but rather to a flank, for Geoffrey led his men to the assault not only after the 'acies beati Petri' had gone into action, but against a different part of the enemy force; and when on the left Robert de St Lo's Turcopoles, like their predecessors at Sarmin four years earlier, were driven back, they carried with them into confusion a part of Robert's

---

[1] Above, p. 29; Galt. pp. 86–91; Fulcher, p. 442; WT, pp. 523–6; ME, pp. 122–3; IQ, p. 160; IA, p. 324; KD, pp. 617–18; Delpech, II, pp. 182–4; Heermann, pp. 83–9; Köhler, III, pt. 3, pp. 190–4; Delbrück, III, p. 426; *RGKJ*, pp. 132–5; Grousset, I, pp. 552–8; Cahen, *Syrie du Nord*, pp. 285–6; Runciman, II, pp. 148–51.
[2] IA and KD both emphasize the elements of surprise.   [3] Galt. p. 87.

squadron. Meanwhile the fifth and last squadron, that of Guy de
Frenelle, had attacked after that of Geoffrey and had struck yet
another section of the enemy. This threefold attack on the right
met with considerable success. The 'acies beati Petri' and
Geoffrey's squadron both vanquished their immediate opponents. Guy, however, encountered greater difficulties, and before
these could be resolved, the fate of the whole battle was decided
on the left. The defeated Turcopoles of Robert de St Lo so disorganized Prince Roger's squadron that the Franks were unable
to recover. They were the worse confounded by a wind from the
north which drove a column of dust into their faces. The Turks
were always quick to exploit any loss of order or morale on the
part of their opponents, and this occasion provided no exception.
They extended their attack to the flanks and rear of Roger's
force. The Christians' camp was occupied and, since avenues of
escape were few, the bulk of their army was either killed or taken.
Roger himself was among the dead. The heavy defeat was due
first, to his disregard of the cautious methods normally adopted
by the Latin princes in the face of invasion; second, to the tactical surprise achieved by Il Ghazi on the morning of the battle.

The arrival in the principality during the following month of
King Baldwin and Pons of Tripoli checked Il Ghazi's victorious
progress. They marched from Antioch in an attempt to raise the
siege of Zerdana. When, encamped on Tell Danith, they heard
that the place had fallen to Il Ghazi, the king decided to retire to
Hab. He expected opposition from Il Ghazi and, as the march began at dawn on 14 August 1119, the first Turkish attacks were
made.[1] Walter the Chancellor described, in greater detail than
was usual in the writing of his contemporaries, the order in which
the Latin squadrons were arrayed.[2] In his account of the ensuing

---

[1] Galt. pp. 102–5; Fulcher, p. 443; WT, pp. 529–30; ME, p. 124; KD,
pp. 620–1; Delpech, II, pp. 195–7; Heermann, pp. 89–95; Köhler, III, pt. 3,
pp. 196–203; Oman, I, pp. 297–301; Delbrück, III, p. 426; *RGKJ*, pp. 139–40;
Grousset, I, pp. 567–70; Cahen, *Syrie du Nord*, p. 289; Runciman, II, pp.
153–4.
[2] Galt. p. 103, and see my next paragraph. This passage from Galt. is
perhaps the clearest description of an order of battle given by a twelfth-
century Latin writer in Syria. Modern military historians treat such texts
as exact statements of fact, and it is significant that each of those who have
used Galt.'s account of the battle of Hab has produced a different picture
of the Latin formation. Cf. Heermann's plan (p. 91) with that of Oman

fight the normal tactical characteristics of the Turks are apparent: the attack from all sides; the use of archery and missiles when battle was first joined; the subsequent attack at close quarters in an effort to force a decision.[1]

The Franks had three squadrons of knights in advance, and behind them the whole mass of the foot-soldiers. Pons of Tripoli with his contingent was posted on the right flank, Robert Fulcoy with a body of Antiochene knights on the left, while other squadrons provided by Antioch brought up the rear. The king with his following was so posted that he could carry help to any part of the field. His ability to do this was in fact to save the day for the Franks. The Turks launched their first attack at the Latin foot, who for a time showed their usual collective power of resistance. Soon, however, the three advanced squadrons of knights, who covered and were covered by the foot-soldiers behind them, were scattered by the enemy. Deprived of their support, the infantry suffered heavy casualties. The flank-guards had likewise disappeared. The contingent under Pons had been destroyed as a fighting force. Many of his knights were soon fugitives who spread news of Latin defeat in Hab, Antioch, and even in Tripoli. Others were driven in on the squadron commanded by the king, where Pons with a few followers continued the fight. On the right Robert Fulcoy had defeated the troops immediately opposed to him. After the pursuit he did not return to the battle, but rode to his castle at Zerdana, only recently lost to the Turkmens.[2] The fortunes of the Christians were maintained by the skill and energy of King Baldwin, who led reinforcement where it was most needed. He met attacks both in the van and rear of the Latin array, and it was due to his efforts that the enemy left him at length in possession of the battlefield.

(1, facing p. 290). Köhler (III, pt. 3, pp. 197–8, 201), considered, without convincing reasons, that the three forward squadrons of Frankish knights were an advance-guard and were withdrawn to the rear at an early stage in the battle. Delbrück (III, p. 426) agreed generally with Heermann, but argued that the squadrons marched not in line but in column. There is no means of deciding between these various interpretations. Since the Franks were on the march to Hab, the writer, after walking over the ground, is more impressed by the argument of Heermann than by that of Oman.

[1] Galt. p. 103.

[2] This paragraph is based on Galt. pp. 103–4; the incident of Robert Fulcoy is recorded by KD, p. 621.

Far less is known of the only other two battles in which Baldwin was engaged, at 'Azaz on 13 June 1125[1] and at Marj es-Suffar on 25 January 1126.[2] From the meagre information provided by Fulcher it is known that in both engagements the Latin army was organized in squadrons of horse- and of foot-soldiers, but the order of battle cannot now be determined.[3] At 'Azaz the Turks offered or were compelled to accept close combat in an early stage of the battle and as a result were defeated.[4] At Marj es-Suffar the Franks suffered heavily from enemy archery, but a strong attack made late in the day gave them a hard-won victory. Their tactical success left them unable to achieve their object in undertaking the campaign, which was the conquest of Damascus.

The battles fought in the middle years of the century were less frequent and less fully described than those of the first generation of the Latin occupation.[5] In 1149, for example, Raymond of Antioch was defeated in circumstances which recalled those of the Ager Sanguinis thirty years earlier.[6] Like Roger, Raymond was

---

[1] Fulcher, pp. 471–2; WT, pp. 579–80; Delpech, II, p. 199; Heermann, pp. 95–8; Köhler, III, pt. 3, p. 206; Oman, I, pp. 301–2; Delbrück, III, p. 426; *RGKJ*, p. 176; Grousset, I, p. 634; Cahen, *Syrie du Nord*, p. 302; Runciman, II, p. 173.

[2] Fulcher, pp. 477–8; WT, pp. 582–5; IQ, pp. 174–7; IA, pp. 372–3; Delpech, III, pp. 200–1; Heermann, pp. 98–100; Köhler, III, pt. 3, p. 206; Oman, I, pp. 302–4; Delbrück, III, p. 427; *RGKJ*, pp. 178–9; Grousset, I, pp. 639–40; Runciman, II, p. 174.

[3] In his plan, p. 97, Heermann showed the knights formed in front of the foot-soldiers. There appears to be no good reason for his reversal of the normal order, especially as it contradicts his written statement on the matter. See Delbrück, III, p. 426.

[4] According to Cahen, *Syrie du Nord*, p. 302, 'l'armée de métier de Boursouqî pratiquait non la tactique de l'attaque dispersée avec pluie de flèches, mais le corps à corps à cheval à la lance ou à pied à l'épée'. The source of this surprising statement is not given. The writer can only surmise that it is based on Fulcher, p. 472: 'Jamjamque arcus tentos in brachia de manibus deponebant, et cominus ensibus extractis nudatisque dimicabant.' The interpretation given above is rather more in keeping with the warfare of the period.

[5] For example, the repulse of the Franks before Damascus in 1129 and the defeat by Zanki of the army taken by King Fulk to the relief of Ba'rin in 1137, are known chiefly from the description of WT, pp. 595–8 and 643–5. He gave no tactical information, and neither did the Arab historians. For 1129 see IQ, pp. 195–9; IA, pp. 385–6; *RGKJ*, pp. 186–7; Grousset, I, pp. 662–5. For 1137 see IQ, pp. 242–3; IA, p. 421; KD, p. 673; *RGKJ*, p. 205; Grousset, II, pp. 72–3.

[6] The battle of Fons Muratus was fought on 29 June 1149; WT, pp. 771–3; IQ, pp. 291–2; *RGKJ*, p. 260; Grousset, II, pp. 275–8; Cahen, *Syrie du Nord*, p. 383; Runciman, II, p. 326.

killed, and the consequences to his principality were even more severe, since Baldwin III was unable to repeat the work of his grandfather and to make good the consequences of defeat. The errors made by Raymond on this occasion have already been discussed.[1] When he had forced Nur al-Din to raise the siege of Inib, he remained encamped with his force in open country. Nur al-Din was from a distance watching the movements of the Franks. When he saw that they had received no reinforcement, he surrounded their camp by night, and next day annihilated their army.[2]

This defeat sensibly weakened the ability of the principality of Antioch to resist Muslim attack, and after the even greater disaster before Harim in 1164, she ceased to exist as a military power.[3] It is known that the Christian coalition which opposed Nur al-Din on that occasion were not content with forcing him to abandon the siege of Harim, but they followed his army as it withdrew.[4] During this phase of the campaign the Franks were attacked by the enemy and were decisively defeated. The reason lay in their loss of formation, and in their surprise by the enemy in difficult country;[5] but whether this was due to their own carelessness in pursuit, or to the military art of Nur al-Din, must remain uncertain.[6]

In 1167 King Amalric attempted to destroy the army, organized by Nur al-Din and led by Shirkuh, which was disputing with him the possession of Egypt. After a long pursuit up the Nile valley, in which the king took with him only his mounted forces, he found that the Muslims had turned to face him on skilfully chosen ground where cultivation ended and the desert began.[7]

---

[1] Above, pp. 33, 126.   [2] WT, p. 773.

[3] Cf. Cahen, *Syrie du Nord*, p. 409.

[4] Above, pp. 134-5. For the battle of Harim (11 August 1164), see WT, pp. 895-7; letter of Amalric to Louis VII of France in Bouquet, *Recueil des Historiens des Gaules*, p. 79, no. 243; IA, pp. 538-40; *AM*, pp. 219-23; Delpech, II, pp. 207-8; Köhler, III, pt. 3, pp. 211-13; *RGKJ*, pp. 317-18; Grousset, II, pp. 460-4; Cahen, *Syrie du Nord*, pp. 408-9; Runciman, II, p. 369.

[5] WT, p. 896; letter of Amalric to Louis VII in Bouquet *op. cit.*

[6] The evidence of IA (pp. 539-40) is not decisive. He was writing long after the battle, and was exposed to the double temptation of reducing events to a pattern and of exalting the military skill of Nur al-Din.

[7] On the battle of al-Balbein (18 or 19 March 1167), see WT, pp. 925-7; IA, pp. 547-9; AS, pp. 131-2; Delpech, II, pp. 209-13; *RGKJ*, pp. 326-7;

The steep slopes and soft sand were calculated to reduce the force
of the Latin charge.[1] Amalric, whose army had been weakened by
detachments,[2] commanded 374 armed Frankish horsemen of all
kinds, together with Turcopoles and Egyptians, who were many
in number and slight in military value.[3] Shirkuh's plan for the
battle was so to deceive the Franks that they would think him to
be posted with his best troops in the centre of his line. In fact
Saladin was placed there with a small following, and with orders
to retreat before the Franks who attacked him, and to draw them
away from the battlefield.[4]

Shirkuh's plan was a variant of the usual Turkish efforts to
ensure that the Latin charge found no worthy target, and it was
almost completely successful. Amalric decided that the main
strength of the enemy lay in the centre and that Shirkuh commanded there.[5] Thither he directed his main attack and, since
Saladin executed his orders efficiently, was duly drawn away from
the rest of his force. These were routed by Shirkuh, who also captured the Franks' baggage.[6] On the broken ground the battle resolved itself into a number of small fights, in some of which the
Franks, in others the Turks, were successful. William of Tyre has
left a fine picture of this soldiers' battle amid the sand dunes, in
which no man could tell how the day had gone.[7] When Amalric
returned from pursuit he displayed his standard and rallied as
many as possible of his men. He formed a column which, with the
familiar slow pace and compact formation, marched through the
Turks and off the battlefield.[8] Neither side had won a complete

---

Grousset, II, pp. 489–93; Schlumberger, *Campagnes du roi Amaury*, pp.
136–46; Runciman, II, p. 374.

[1] WT, p. 926.

[2] Not only of the *pedites*, but of a contingent on the far bank of the Nile;
WT, pp. 927–8.

[3] WT, p. 925.   [4] IA, pp. 548–9.

[5] When he wrote William still thought that Shirkuh had been in the
centre; WT, p. 926.

[6] WT, p. 926.   [7] WT, pp. 926–7.

[8] WT, p. 927: 'Habentes ergo redeundi propositum, in aciem ordinati per
hostes medios, quos a dextra laevaque contuebantur, iter agunt, gradu lento.
Contra quos cum tanta constantia proficiscentes, nil ausi sunt adversitatis
hostes moliri; sed juncto agmine, viris fortioribus et armatis optime per
gyrum locatis, ad quandam fluminis portionem pervenerunt. . . .'

It is yet another description of the Frankish tactics employed on an
opposed march and described in the preceding section.

victory; but the Franks had lost one hundred knights and, by failing to destroy Shirkuh's army, had lost an opportunity to become undisputed masters of Egypt.

In 1177 Saladin suffered the heaviest defeat of his career at Mont Gisard.[1] Once again the medieval records give no tactical information, but only how the battle came to be fought, and why Baldwin IV was the victor.

Saladin entered Palestine from Egypt by way of the coastal route. Baldwin had sent a contingent of his knights to Antioch with Philip of Flanders, but, despite his reduced resources, he immediately challenged the invader.[2] Impressed by the numerical superiority of Saladin's forces, he decided against battle, and took shelter with his forces in Ascalon. Saladin then decided to ignore the Franks. He marched north to lay waste the countryside and to cut communication between Jerusalem and the coast.[3] Baldwin's subsequent action revealed his own conception of his military duty. He had shown at Ascalon that he was not prepared to undertake battle against heavy odds: now he showed that he would rather fight than tolerate the unchecked devastation of his subjects' property.[4] Therefore he hastened after Saladin, and attempted to surprise him[5] while his men were scattered in their search for plunder.[6] He was not completely successful; but when the battle, of which there exists no detailed account, was fought, Saladin had not been able to recall all his detachments. Baldwin achieved partial surprise, and drove the shattered Muslim army back into Egypt.[7]

---

[1] On 25 November 1177. See WT, pp. 1041–5; *Ernoul*, pp. 41–5; letter of Roger des Moulins, master of the Hospital, in Röhricht, *Beiträge zur Geschichte der Kreuzzüge*, II, pp. 127–8; BD, pp. 63–4; AS, pp. 184–9; IA, p. 628; Delpech, II, pp. 214–15; *RGKJ*, pp. 376–80; Grousset, II, pp. 650–62; Runciman, II, pp. 416–17.

[2] WT, p. 1038.   [3] WT, p. 1039.

[4] WT, p. 1041: '. . . rex . . . ex Ascalona cum suis egreditur; hostibus ire obviam parat, satius ducens cum hostibus etiam dubio eventu praeliandi fortunam tentare, quam praedam, incendia, suorum stragem sustinere.' The idea is clearly expressed here that in certan circumstances the undoubted risks of battle ought not to be avoided. Unchecked devastation by the enemy provided such an occasion. It was probably against such standards that William measured and condemned the otherwise sound military plan of Guy de Lusignan in 1183. See above, pp. 155–6.

[5] WT, p. 1041: 'ut subito et occultus posset inimicis occurrere. . . .'

[6] This was stressed by WT, pp. 1039–42; IA, p. 628; AS, p. 184.

[7] That a degree of surprise was achieved is clear from all accounts of the battle.

At that stage in the history of Latin Syria victory in the field ended the campaign but little more. In 1179 Saladin was again at the head of an army. He based his main force on Banyas and sent detachments to raid towards Sidon and the coastal plains.[1] True to the military ideas of the Latin kings, Baldwin took a force to the threatened areas. From Tiberias he marched by way of Safad and Toron to a point on the eastern edge of the coastal range from which he could overlook the Marj 'Ayyun, and could see in the distance the tents of Saladin's main army.[2] The Franks decided to descend to the plain without delay, and in the hurried march down the steep slope, only the most active of the foot-soldiers could keep pace with the mounted men. The remainder, already tired by the long march, followed as well as they could, and were for a time separated from the knights.[3]

When the mounted men and their companions reached the plain, there was a delay of some hours.[4] When fighting began it was against Muslim detachments returning from the raids they had made further to the west, and since these were neither prepared nor formed for battle, they were easily defeated. After this episode the Franks behaved as if the battle were over and won. Some pursued the Muslims towards their camp; Raymond of Tripoli and the master of the Temple led their men on to the high ground between the Marj 'Ayyun and the Litani gorge; the infantry collected spoil and rested. When therefore Saladin came to the attack with the bulk of his forces the Latins were defeated, not because some hours before their horse and foot had been separated, but because they were entirely unprepared for battle.[5]

---

[1] For the fighting on Marj 'Ayyun on 10 June 1179 see WT, pp. 1054–7; IA, pp. 636–7; AS, pp. 197–203; Delpech, II, pp. 216–17; *RGKJ*, pp. 384–6; Grousset, II, pp. 672–7; Runciman, II, pp. 419–20.

[2] WT, p. 1055.   [3] *Ibid.*

[4] WT, p. 1055: 'Per aliquot ergo horas, ut plenius deliberaretur quid facto opus esset, ibi substiterunt.' A point clearly overlooked by Delpech, II, pp. 216–17, who ascribed the Latin defeat solely to the separation of knights and *pedites* during the rapid descent of the hillside, and by La Monte, *Feudal Monarchy*, p. 219, who described the charge of the master of the Temple 'that by its sheer force so divided the Christian ranks that the battle was lost'. The source of this statement is not clear, unless he too had in mind the descent, which in fact preceded the fighting by some hours.

[5] WT, p. 1056: 'At vero pedites nostri de spoliis eorum qui interfecti fuerant ditati, putantes nihil superesse ad consummatam victoriam, secus ripam fluminis castrametati, quieti consederant: equites vero hostes super

The fight at Cresson on 1 May 1187, and the great battle at Hattin which followed two months later will be discussed in the final section of this chapter; thereafter the next major conflict was incidental to the siege of Acre. In the second month after they had formed the siege in 1189, the Franks attempted to rid themselves of the attentions of Saladin's field army. The battle fought on 4 October was described by more than one eyewitness, and the details they gave have enabled historians to reconstruct the engagement at length.[1] It provides a good story, but little more information on the military ideas and methods of the age than was given in the single sentence devoted to the battle by Delbrück.

The Latin army was formed in four divisions, in each of which the foot-soldiers, many of whom were armed with bow or crossbow, marched in their usual station before the knights.[2] All accounts agree that two battles developed: in the one the Templars on the left wing engaged Taki ed-Din's command on the Muslim right; in the other the centre of each army was engaged. This division of effort arose through the early success of the Templars, who either by the weight of their charge,[3] or because Taki ed-Din retreated by design to draw them from the battlefield,[4] pursued their immediate opponents for a distance which observers thought too great. In the centre the Franks had advanced until, at a suitable distance from Saladin's line, they delivered their charge. Saladin had already sent troops from the centre to assist his retreating left wing,[5] and thus weakened, his line broke before the Latin onset. The Christians, both knights and foot, penetrated to his camp on Tell Ayadiya.[6]

---

se, quos devictos putabant, reparatis viribus videntes irruere, non habentes ferias vel otium, ut, juxta militarem disciplinam, acies instruerentur, ordinarentur agmina, ordine confuso decertantes, resistunt ad tempus, et hostium perseveranter sustinent impetus. Tandem viribus impares, nec se cum dispersi essent inordinatius, mutuo juvantes, in fugam versi succumbunt turpiter.'

[1] 'Epistola Theobaldi praefecti et Petri Leonis Domino Papae' in Radulfus de Diceto, *Ymagines Historiarum* (ed. W. Stubbs), II, pp. 70–1 (Rolls Series); *Itin.* pp. 68–72; *Est.* 2957–3054; *Eracles*, pp. 129–30; BD, pp. 140–6; AS, pp. 415–21, 424–5; IA, II, pp. 9–13; Köhler, III, pt. 3, pp. 228–34; Oman, I, pp. 334–40; Delbrück, III, p. 427; *RGKJ*, pp. 507–10; Grousset, III, pp. 24–6.
[2] *Itin.* p. 69; BD, p. 142.   [3] *Itin.* p. 70.   [4] BD, p. 141.
[5] BD, p. 142; IA, II, pp. 10–11.   [6] BD, p. 142; *Itin.* p. 69.

At this stage the fortunes of the battle changed. Contemporaries differed in assigning a reason for the final defeat of the Franks. The author of the *Itinerarium* recorded that after their successful charge the Franks in the centre looked for spoils and lost interest in continuing the battle.[1] With Ambroise and the author of the *Eracles*, he emphasized the cumulative effect of the panic among the Christians caused by a runaway horse;[2] with Theobald and Leo, he assigned prime importance to the successful sortie made by the garrison of Acre.[3] From all available accounts, both Christian and Muslim, it is clear that the Franks, while held on each wing of the battle,[4] won a decisive success in the centre, but that their lack of concentration and discipline enabled Saladin to organize a counter-attack which drove them back into their camp.

The last fight before the Third Crusade ended and King Richard departed from Syria was that in which he was involved outside Jaffa on 5 August 1192.[5] He was then encamped with a small force outside the walls of the town. Not more than ten of his knights had horses, but of the 2000 men who fought on foot a proportion, perhaps one-fifth, were armed with the crossbow.[6] The Muslims attempted a surprise attack at dawn, but by good fortune the alarm was given just in time for Richard to organize resistance.[7] He posted his men in a solid, static, defensive formation. The front rank was of men who knelt side by side, each protected by his shield, the butt of his lance based firmly on the ground, with the shaft inclined upwards and the point towards

[1] *Itin.* p. 69.   [2] *Itin.* p. 70; *Est.* 2997–3004; *Eracles*, p. 129.

[3] *Itin.* p. 69; Epistola Theobaldi, Diceto, *op. cit.* p. 71.

[4] BD, pp. 142–3; AS, pp. 424–5.

[5] *Itin.* pp. 413–24; *Est.* 11345–652; Radulphus de Coggeshall, *Chronicon anglicanum*, pp. 41–51; BD, pp. 337–8; IA, II, pp. 64–5; Delpech, I, pp. 284–90; Köhler, III, pt. 2, pp. 266–7; Oman, I, pp. 318–19; Delbrück, III, pp. 427–8; *RGKJ*, pp. 641–3; Grousset, III, pp. 114–16.

[6] *Itin.* (p. 413) gives the numbers as about fifty-five knights and up to 2000 *pedites*, who included 'crossbowmen and men-at-arms, Genoese, Pisans and others'. Rad. de Coggeshall (pp. 44, 50) gives the total number of knights as eighty, and the number of crossbowmen (p. 44) as 400. *Itin.* (p. 413) states that the army had at first fifteen horses, but that on the morning of the battle only ten of the king's companions were mounted, some of them indifferently (pp. 415–16; *Est.* 11413). Coggeshall (p. 46) says that on the day of the battle the king disposed of only six horses and a mule.

[7] *Itin.* pp. 415–16; *Est.* 11351–408.

the enemy. Each of these men was close to his neighbours on either side; the king himself stressed the necessity of a close order which should offer no gap for enemy penetration. In the second rank, with a man covering each space between the heads of the kneeling spearmen, Richard placed his archers. They worked in pairs; while the foremost discharged a bolt from one crossbow, his mate wound the other; they then exchanged weapons and so continued, the one as marksman and the other as loader, throughout the action.[1] The ten mounted men were posted behind this formation, which may have been further protected by a rough barricade of wood collected from the bivouacs.[2]

The Muslims never closed with this formidable array.[3] They may have been intimidated by the line of spearheads and by the sustained archery, but it is probable that their morale had been even more adversely affected by their grievances against Saladin.[3] Certainly, they never attempted to ride down the Christian force,[4] and finally it was Richard himself who passed to the attack.[5] His personal prowess on that day helped to win him immortality.

V. HATTIN

The previous section includes no detailed account of the battle of Hattin. That work has been achieved with admirable care and skill by Professor Baldwin who, as he justly claims, is the first historian who 'treats the subject in all possible detail, or uses to the fullest extent all possible sources'.[6] But if, as he implies, he sees himself as the first to 'realize the full political, military and tactical significance of the battle',[7] his claims are not so firmly based. His knowledge of medieval warfare appears to be drawn

[1] *Itin.* pp. 415–16; *Est.* 11455–63; Rad. Coggeshall, pp. 46–7.

[2] So Rad. Coggeshall, p. 45, but *Itin.* p. 408 and *Est.* 11154–8 associate this improvised *antemurale* with the king's landing at Jaffa four days earlier. Rad. Coggeshall owed his information to Hugh de Nevill, who was one of the king's ten mounted followers on 5 August, *op. cit.* p. 45.

[3] BD, p. 337; IA, II, p. 64.

[4] *Itin.* pp. 417–18; *Est.* 11499–502; Rad. Coggeshall, p. 47.

[5] *Itin.* (p. 418) states that it was 'rex cum iis qui equos habebant' who carried out the attack. According to Rad. Coggeshall (p. 48) it was the whole force which advanced, with the crossbowmen still in the van.

[6] Baldwin, *Raymond III of Tripoli and the Fall of Jerusalem (1140–1187)*, p. 151.

[7] *Op. cit.* p. 152.

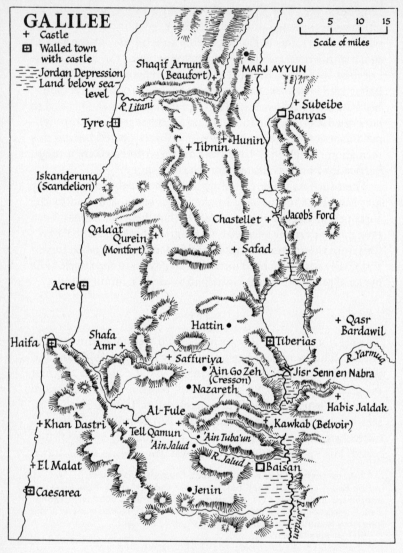

GALILEE

+ Castle
⊞ Walled town
 with castle
≈≈≈ Jordan Depression
≈≈≈ Land below sea-
 level

0   5   10   15
Scale of miles

Shaqif Arnun
(Beaufort) +
MARJ AYYUN •

R. Litani

+ Subeibe
⊞ Banyas

Tyre ⊞

+ Tibnin   + + Hunin

Iskanderuna
(Scandelion) +

Chastellet +   ⌐ Jacob's Ford

Qala'at
Qurein
(Montfort) +
                + Safad

Acre ⊞

                + Qasr
                  Bardawil

Haifa ⊞   Shafa
           Amr +
Hattin •   ⊞ Tiberias

           R. Yarmuq

+ Saffuriya
• 'Ain Go Zeh
  (Cresson)   ⌐ Jisr Senn en Nabra
• Nazareth
                Habis Jaldak

Al-Fule
+ Khan Dastri   +   +   + Kawkab (Belvoir)
    + Tell Qamun 'Ain Tuba'un
    'Ain Jalud
+ El Malat   R. Jalud   ☐ Baisan
⊞ Caesarea   • Jenin

R. Jordan

MAP II

exclusively from the pages of Delpech, which deal only with tactics and are thickly sown with error. It is agreed that the significance of the battle can be understood only against a background of the military history of Latin Syria, and an attempt has been made to provide such a background in the foregoing pages. Hattin has therefore been made the subject of this final section both for this reason, and also because it illustrates the conditions and methods of warfare in the Latin states more fully than any other military event. Its significant episodes were first, the Christian decision to relieve Tiberias; second, the Muslims' success in compelling the Franks to halt and bivouac in waterless country between Saffuriya and Tiberias; third, the collapse and destruction of the Christian army on the following morning. Each will be considered in turn, and each placed in its historical setting.

On 2 July 1187, King Guy in his camp at Saffuriya knew that Saladin had attacked Tiberias, and that Count Raymond's wife, Eschive, who was without knights to assist her and the citizens in defence of the place, had withdrawn to the citadel.[1] From that last place of refuge the lady had called on Guy for help. That same night the king turned to his magnates for counsel, and he called first on Raymond of Tripoli, who was his greatest vassal and lord of Tiberias. It is certain that Raymond gave strong reasons against relieving the town, but the arguments he used cannot now exactly be determined. In the first place, contemporary versions of them were written down after the subsequent catastrophe, and it is probable that some of the chroniclers concerned succumbed to the temptation of presenting Raymond as a prophet; in the second, those versions vary in important details, and historians have not yet been able to decide which account constitutes the

---

[1] For the battle of Hattin see *Libellus*, pp. 218–26; *Eracles*, pp. 48–64; *Ernoul*, pp. 157–70. Four important letters are 'Consules Januenses Urbano III', ed. K. Hampe in *Neues Archiv der Gesellschaft für ältere deutsche Geschichtskunde*, XXII (1896), pp. 278–80. *Reg.* no. 664a; Fratres Hospitalis ultramarini Archumbaldo, in *HEF*, pp. 2–4; *Reg.* no. 661; 'Principes transmarinae ecclesiae Frederico I', in *Mon. Germ. Hist. SS.* XXI, p. 475; *Reg.* no. 658; 'Terricus, magnus praeceptor Templi Urbano III papae', in *Mon. Germ. Hist. SS.* XVII, p. 793; *Reg.* no. 660; BD, pp. 92–6; IA, pp. 681–6; AS, 263–88; Delpech, I, pp. 369–75; Köhler, III, pt. 3, pp. 216–24; Oman, I, pp. 324–33; Delbrück, III, p. 427; *RGKJ*, pp. 430–9; Lane-Poole, *Saladin*, pp. 204–14; Stevenson, *Crusaders in the East*, pp. 240–8; Groh, *Der Zusammenbruch des Reiches Jerusalem*, pp. 16–22; Grousset, II, pp. 788–99; Baldwin, *op. cit.* pp. 96–135, 151–5; Runciman, II, pp. 455–60, 486–91.

best authority.[1] All the various arguments ascribed to the count, which almost certainly include those he in fact urged, will be considered here. All can be related to the known conditions of contemporary warfare, and therefore none are inherently im-probable.[2]

Raymond based his advice on the forecast that if an attempt were made to relieve Tiberias, the whole kingdom might be lost. The march from Saffuriya to that town could only be accomplished if Muslim resistance were overcome. Defeat in the ensuing battle could entail the loss of the army, and therefore of the kingdom.[3] All accounts agree on this point;[4] they differ in recording his prophecy of Saladin's actions after the town had fallen. According to the *Ernoul* group, Raymond considered that

---

[1] The versions of the Hattin campaign given by the continuators of William of Tyre are all closely related to a history of Saladin's conquest of the Latin kingdom written by Ernoul, a squire of Balian of Ibelin. Whether any of the continuations contain his original work has not yet been determined, for even those MSS. which mentioned his name may in their existing form be adaptations or abridgements of the history which Ernoul wrote down.

The versions of events which include the Hattin campaign fall into two main groups. The first includes the MSS. collated by Mas Latrie in his *Chronique d'Ernoul et de Bernard le Trésorier*, and those called *C* and *G* by the editors of *RHC, Hist. occ.* II; the other includes the so-called Colbert and Fontainebleau MSS., that is, the *A* and *B* of *RHC, Hist. occ.* II. Both groups are related, but the second is more detailed and more fully developed than the first. Mas Latrie, in his 'Essai de Classification' in *Ernoul*, pp. 499–501, inclines to the view that *AB* includes Ernoul's original work, of which his *Chronique d'Ernoul* and the *CG* versions are abridgements. There are also grounds, however, for regarding *AB* as an elaboration of the original history contained in the other group.

On the whole subject see Beugnot's Introduction to *RHC, Hist. occ.* II; M. L. de Mas Latrie in *Chronique d'Ernoul et de Bernard le Trésorier*, pp. 473–565; C. Cahen, *Syrie du Nord*, pp. 20–5.

[2] According to *Eracles*, pp. 48–9, Guy held two councils at which the military situation was discussed, one at Acre, and the other at Saffuriya. Raymond spoke on both occasions. Runciman accepts this account; II, p. 486.

[3] *Ernoul*, p. 160; *Eracles, C, G*, p. 50.

[4] That is, all the principal accounts. It is interesting to note, however, that according to one Latin and one Arabic source Raymond requested the king to relieve Tiberias; 'Consules Januenses Urbano' in *Neues Archiv der Gesellschaft für ältere deutsche Geschichtskunde*, XXII (1896), p. 278; AS, p. 265. It is possible that the resolution of this apparent contradiction is to be found in the most fully developed of the *Eracles* versions. *Eracles, A, B*, pp. 49, 50, record that, after Raymond had advised against the relief of Tiberias, and had been taunted with treachery by Gerard and Renaud, he called on the king to relieve Tiberias.

Saladin would not subsequently challenge the Christian army encamped at Saffuriya. The Muslims, he said, could not hold Tiberias, but would retire to their own territory. Saladin might destroy the walls of the town but these could be rebuilt; he might take captive Raymond's wife and men, but these could be recovered. The usual course of marching to the immediate neighbourhood of the enemy was on this occasion to be avoided. It entailed crossing the waterless country between Saffuriya and Tiberias where the army, its fighting efficiency reduced by heat and thirst, might not survive the inevitable enemy attacks. 'Therefore', Raymond is said to have advised, 'do not endanger the kingdom by endangering the field army; let Tiberias go; remain here at Saffuriya.'[1]

Whether or not Raymond in fact expressed such views, they were justified by many precedents. Throughout the century Frankish leaders had exploited the probability that any large Muslim force, especially when denied the profits of military success, would disperse of its own accord at the end of the campaigning season. The task of the Franks was to deny them that success, and the possibility of achieving permanent conquest, by keeping intact their own field army. Therefore it became the normal practice never to expose that army to enemy attack in conditions which might result in its destruction. The arguments here ascribed to Raymond were founded not only on the lack of water between Saffuriya and Tiberias: they were the fruit of Latin experience of conditions which had recurred throughout the century.

The same may be said of the versions given in the *Libellus* and in the Colbert-Fontainebleau group of the *Eracles* manuscripts. These credit Raymond with the prophecy that Saladin in his pride would come from newly captured Tiberias to attack the Christian army. If he did so, the argument ran, the Muslims would carry the burdens of heat and thirst, while the Franks and

---

[1] *Ernoul*, pp. 159–60; *Eracles*, C, G, pp. 50–1. It is instructive that Ibn al-Athir, who came to Palestine during this period, and was probably well informed on events in the Christian camp, credits Raymond with emphasizing that Saladin might take Tiberias, but he could not hold it. He would require his whole army to do so, and he could not maintain it in the field indefinitely, because of the natural desire of the men to return to their families and homes. IA, p. 682.

their horses would go into battle well supplied and refreshed. In
such conditions they had every chance of success, and the defeated Muslims would be caught, as Saladin had been after Mont
Gisard ten years earlier, with neither base nor refuge. If, which
heaven forbid, the Christians were defeated, then their own fortified places were near to serve, as they had so often served before
in the hour of defeat, as a shelter and rallying point.[1] Raymond is
said to have urged the exploitation of these advantages by offering
battle, according to the *Libellus*, near Saffuriya, and according to
the *Eracles*, in the plain of Acre itself.[2] Whatever his reasons, it is
certain that Raymond advised against the relief of Tiberias and
that, with the exception of the master of the Temple and possibly
Renaud de Châtillon, he was supported by the rest of the assem-
bly. Guy therefore accepted his counsel; but during the same
night he was over-persuaded by the master of the Temple, and
the bewildered knights were ordered to arm themselves for the
march to Tiberias.[3]

Historians, wise after subsequent events, have severely condemned Guy's action, and none more so than Grousset.[4] Certainly there is much to criticize in Guy's vacillation, but it is only
just to recognize the grave dilemma in which he found himself,
and which is revealed by a study of previous military events. In
1182, for example, Raymond had given similar advice to King
Baldwin IV, and that successful and energetic military leader had
rejected it.[5] In the following year Guy himself had, while com-
manding the army of Jerusalem, watched that of Saladin in the
neighbourhood of Ain Tubaniya, and had not attempted to attack
it. For this decision he was not only severely criticized, but had
soon afterwards lost his position as regent.[6] His enemies on that
occasion had said that his inaction was the more to be blamed because he was at the head of the largest Christian army ever gathered in the kingdom; in 1187 men were saying the same of the
force then gathered at Saffuriya.[7] The fact of the Lady Eschive's
appeal only added to Guy's difficulties. The oldest surviving
version of the Laws of Jerusalem states in strong terms the lord's

---

[1] Above, p. 126, n. 5.   [2] *Libellus*, pp. 221–2; *Eracles, A, B,* p. 50.
[3] *Ernoul*, p. 162; *Eracles*, all versions, pp. 52, 53.
[4] II, p. 792. He heads the relevant section of his work, 'Quos vult perdere'.
[5] Above, p. 148.   [6] Baldwin, pp. 52–4.   [7] *Eracles, C, G,* p. 52.

overriding obligation to aid a vassal attacked by the Muslims; rulers with stronger character and authority than Guy had been obliged to answer such appeals.[1]

Facts such as these must have influenced Guy as he listened to the arguments of Gerard de Ridefort. The master can have had little difficulty in persuading the king that Raymond was seeking to disgrace him. Before their reconciliation a few weeks before Raymond had been Guy's enemy and rival; he had been one of the two magnates who in 1186 had refused homage at Guy's coronation; he had lately been in close diplomatic relations with Saladin; he was urging a military plan of the kind which had discredited Guy four years before; what was more natural than to see, in the advice he offered at Saffuriya, an attempt to disgrace the king anew. This was Guy's first major campaign as king; was he, at the head of so large an army, to watch the loss of Galilee's capital but five leagues away, when the lady of the town had sent an urgent call for help? If the king persisted in such a course, he could no longer count on the support of the all-powerful Templars.[2] The true weight of such arguments becomes apparent if they are considered, as Guy considered them, in relation to past events.

As a result of these deliberations the Christian army left its camp on the morning of 3 July. Although the leaders knew that the chosen course of action must involve them in heavy fighting, their primary object was not to give battle, but to relieve the citadel of Tiberias. Their failure to do so, and the destruction of the army on the following day, were the consequences of an event which was the second turning-point in the campaign: they were forced to halt before they reached Tiberias, and to postpone continuing their march until the following day. During the remainder of 3 July and the night which followed they lay encamped without water for man or horse, their wounds and their weariness unrelieved, exposed to heat, dust, and thirst, and in the presence of an exulting enemy. All these powerful forces destroyed their morale and ensured their defeat as certainly as the arrows and onsets of the Muslims.[3]

[1] Above, p. 149, n. 1.   [2] *Ernoul*, pp. 161–2; *Eracles, C, G*, pp. 52–3.
[3] On the ordeal of that night see *Libellus*, pp. 223–4; *Ernoul*, p. 168; *Eracles, C, G*, p. 61; *A, B*, pp. 63–4; IA, p. 683.

This halting of the Christian army was a success won by the unchanging military methods of the Muslim forces. From their first moment of contact with the enemy on the morning of 3 July, the Franks were involved in a battle fought on the march. It has been seen that such engagements were not then uncommon in Latin Syria. On such occasions the Muslims exploited their normal tactical methods to halt or to break up the Latin column; the Franks attempted to preserve a solid formation, and to beat off attacks without checking their own progress towards their destination. Study of similar fighting has shown that the Muslims used their mounted archers to harass the enemy, and exerted their maximum efforts against the rear of his column. The familiar pattern was repeated on 3 July. Soon after their march began, the Franks were subjected to harassing attacks which continued throughout the day; the mounted archers of the enemy directed a heavy attack against the Latin column;[1] the Templars and Balian of Ibelin in the rear-guard were especially hard pressed. It was they who sent the message that they could no longer sustain Muslim pressure, and which finally decided Guy to halt in the neighbourhood of Lubya.[2] Heavy attacks on the rear-guard had always embarrassed Latin commanders; on this occasion they virtually decided the battle.

On 4 July the Latin army was annihilated as a fighting force. Baldwin has emphasized the importance, as an explanation of this defeat, of the separation of the infantry from the knights early in the fighting on that day. It is natural that he should do so, for the factor was stressed by Delpech, his principal secondary authority on twelfth-century military history, and by the author of the *Libellus*, his primary source; but he has rightly concluded that 'the separation of the two arms . . . was the result not of better planned or more aggressive fighting once the battle was joined, but of the sheer physical exhaustion of the Latin infantry caused by Saladin's manœuvring of the day before'.[3]

The point has been argued in a previous chapter,[4] and it was illustrated in the fight at Cresson on 1 May 1187, as well as on the

---

[1] *Libellus*, p. 223; *Ernoul*, p. 167; *Eracles C, G*, p. 54; *A, B*, p. 62.

[2] *Libellus*, p. 223. *Ernoul*, p. 163 provides evidence that Balian was in the rear-guard, and that he lost many of his knights there.

[3] Baldwin, *op. cit.* p. 131.   [4] Above, pp. 131–2.

final day at Hattin. On the first of these occasions[1] Gerard de Ridefort determined to attack a Muslim force perhaps 7000 strong, although at his disposal he had only a small hastily gathered band of 140 knights and some dismounted men. Either tempted by the planned retreat of the Muslims, or driven by the offensive ardour of the master, the Christian knights committed themselves to an outright charge; the enemy withstood the shock and thereafter annihilated both knights and foot-soldiers.[2] Certainly defeat was incurred when mounted and dismounted men were separated; but so would victory have been achieved had the charge been successful. Separation is not a sufficient explanation for the disaster; it was the result of a rash decision to undertake an ill-timed charge in unfavourable circumstances.

To say with Baldwin that, at Hattin, 'the separation of the two arms [was] . . . the really decisive factor in this battle'[3] is to overstate its importance. On the morning of 4 July the will to fight of important elements in the army had evaporated before the battle was resumed. The night-long ordeal, the prospect of renewed combat in the summer heat, and the additional burden of the heath fire, all combined to produce a spirit of defeat of which the mutiny of the *pedites*, the treason of the six knights, and the flight of Count Raymond were all symptoms. Those who with magnificent courage sustained the battle until late afternoon were too few to withstand an enemy superior in numbers and morale.

So ended a battle which could have been fittingly included in any of the three preceding sections of this chapter. Had the advice of Count Raymond been accepted, the campaign of 1187 might have been completed without battle, like those described in the second section of this chapter. Once the attempt to relieve Tiberias had begun, the Franks were involved first in an engagement fought on the march, and, finally, in a desperate battle which they waged and lost grouped round their tents and the True Cross on the Horns of Hattin.

---

[1] *Libellus*, pp. 211–16; *Ernoul*, pp. 145–7.
[2] *Libellus*, pp. 213–14.   [3] Baldwin, *op. cit.* p. 131

VI. CONCLUSIONS

Now that some significant episodes in their warfare have been studied, it is possible to comment on the methods used by the Franks to solve the military problems outlined at the beginning of this chapter.

Clearly they were well aware that it was often in their interest to avoid battle. They repelled more than one major invasion without exposing themselves to the risks of combat and to the grave consequences of defeat. As a result such campaigns have not been studied by military historians. Yet on these occasions there was intense military activity. The problems raised by the invasion were considered and a plan of operations decided upon. Measures were taken to secure early information of enemy movements. Troops were summoned to a base which was carefully chosen for its supplies and water, and for its proximity to areas into which the enemy might direct his attack. When his intentions were no longer in doubt, help might be requested from those Latin states not immediately threatened and, despite intense enemy provocation, the commander prohibited the launching of attacks before all available strength was gathered. Such decisions were unpopular, and their enforcement required inflexible resolution. There was no battle, but neither was there inaction. Important military objectives were achieved by the consistent application, in face of every difficulty, of a well-conceived plan of campaign.

The mobility of the Turks enabled them to harass a marching column. On such occasions the Franks were compelled to take measures by which they could meet attacks from any quarter, and especially from flank and rear. They had also to ensure that they would not be separated from each other, and so leave in their ranks gaps of which, as they knew, the Turks would be quick to take advantage. Therefore all fighting men were given a place on the line of march which they were forbidden to leave and they sought, by the solidity of their formation, to discourage and repel any Turkish attempt to come to close quarters. In this way they could continue their march even 'inter acies Turcorum'.

Historians have not yet remarked on the possible connexion between these measures and Byzantine military practice. In his last campaign against the Turks Alexius Comnenus adopted a formation which, his daughter assures us, he himself evolved for the express purpose of resisting their attacks. Her description of Turkish tactics tallies with that given by Frankish writers:

> ...the Turks' right and left wing and centre were quite disconnected and the phalanxes stood as if severed from each other. Consequently if you attacked the right or left wing, the centre would swoop down upon you and all the rest of the army posted behind it.... They surround the enemy completely and shoot at him with arrows, and they make this defence from a distance.[1]

In reply to these methods the emperor, who was a student of military science and an inventor of new orders of battle, adopted a formation which was 'solid and not easily broken'.[2] Captive women and children were placed in the centre and, 'had you seen it, you would have said a living walled city was walking, when the army was marching in the new formation we have described'.[3] It is not surprising to learn that the Turks, although they attacked the Roman army throughout the day, 'were unable to break it up entirely or even partially'.[4] It is probable that Turkish tactics did more to compel the Franks to adopt a close marching formation than did the advice of Alexius; but it is possible that he and other Byzantines transmitted something of Greek military experience to the crusaders.

The pitched battles of the period were not characterized by complex tactical plans and formations and, as previous students of the subject have found, comparatively few generalizations are possible. Once the all-important decision had been taken to offer battle, the arrangements were fairly simple. For victory the Franks relied on an attack by the mounted troops; but until this could be delivered, the horsemen were covered by a screen of foot-soldiers. Throughout the century these groups of archers and spearmen possessed a stubborn defensive strength which they revealed, despite themselves at Dorylaeum, by intent at Antioch and Ramla, and which they still displayed ninety years later at Arsuf and Jaffa. They were always a normal part of the Latin armies who, during the opening stages of a battle, were usually

---

[1] Anna, pp. 397–8.　　[2] *Ibid.* p. 398.　　[3] *Ibid.* p. 401.
[4] *Ibid.* p. 402; Buckler, *Anna Comnena*, pp. 393–6.

posted in front of the mounted troops with the task of holding the enemy in check until these could deliver the decisive assault.

The horsemen did not attack in a single body, but were divided into a number of squadrons. Heermann has shown that these squadrons were not uncommonly five or six in number, and that their average strength on more than one occasion was between 100 and 150. From the accounts of the chroniclers it appears that the squadrons were then nearly always brigaded into a threefold order of centre with left and right wings; but it is extremely difficult to establish whether these writers were describing tactical realities or whether they were observing a literary convention perhaps based on classical models.

Many military historians have been deeply interested in the formation in which these mounted squadrons were marshalled before battle and in the order in which they went into the attack. They have sought to draw contrasts between 'tiefe und flache Ordnung', 'ordre parallèle', and 'ordre perpendiculaire' while Heermann has sought to establish that the attack in echelon was the normal tactical procedure. In fact it appears that the consistent adoption of particular formations cannot be proved. Much of the available evidence is too vague to permit elucidation in detail, while the rest points to a variety of formations. The Franks sometimes fought in column; when attacked on the march, they were forced to do so. For the pitched battle, it appears to have been usual for the squadrons to be drawn up abreast or in echelon. On certain occasions it is beyond doubt that such a formation was adopted; on 9 February 1098 for example, and again on 28 June, they made it their object to cover as broad a front as possible so as to take advantage of natural protection on the army's flanks. Both engagements took place at a time when extreme privation had reduced to a few hundreds the number of horses sufficiently fit to take knights into battle; the necessity of occupying a broad front must have compelled the horsemen of each squadron to attack in line. And it is likely that an attack in line was often made, for such a formation allowed full use to be made of each armoured rider, on whom so much depended and who were always too few in number.

The whole mounted strength of the Franks did not go into action simultaneously. Heermann clearly shows and rightly emphasizes that on many occasions the divisions of the army charged in succession. They did not advance on the same axis, for it can be shown that they struck different parts of the enemy's line. This attack in echelon was undoubtedly a common practice, but whether the Franks formed up and approached the enemy in that formation is not so certain. Heermann brilliantly proved that an advance in this formation was adopted at Antioch and at Sarmin; but his arguments in respect of other battles are too fragile to command general acceptance.

The battles of the period clearly demonstrate the importance to the Franks of the field commander and of the tactical reserve. Of these the first might seem scarcely worthy of special remark, if it were not for the fact that the Franks have been regarded as lacking in effective leadership. It is true that there were important periods and occasions when military command was divided or non-existent. When three kings were present in the army, as they were during the Second and Third Crusades, there could be no unity of direction; and when political difficulties agitated a kingdom nearly to the point of civil war, as they did in Jerusalem in the years immediately before Hattin, faction divided the high command. Taking the twelfth century as a whole, however, it was more general for the Franks, when on campaign, to submit to the will of a single leader. In three battles fought outside Antioch in 1097 and 1098, Bohemond was in full and undisputed command; and in each of them Bohemond personally retained under his own control a tactical reserve which intervened decisively in the action. In the same way the kings of Jerusalem, before 1183, usually exercised a fully effective authority over their army, and often posted themselves on the battlefield so that they could lead the reserve division held under their immediate command to any part of the Christian lines where help was needed.

In all these matters the Franks showed a certain continuity of practice on the field of battle, but there were changes as well. From the time of their first meeting with the Turks, the Franks recognized that they were faced by new tactical problems, and that adjustments to their normal military methods were necessary. They saw that they must stand firm in the face of archery and encirclement, ignore the temptation offered by the Turks' simulated flight, preserve their solidity and cohesion until they

could choose the moment at which to deliver their charge with
the certainty of striking into the main body of the enemy. The
records of the First Crusade reveal them learning this lesson. In
September 1098 the Latin princes sent a letter to Pope Urban II
in which they described certain actions which they had fought
against the Turks. In their account of the battle of 28 June 1098,
they told how the Turks began to disperse and to encircle them,
and continued 'sed nobis multis bellis contra eorum calliditates
et ingenia edoctis, ita gratia Dei et misericordia subvenit, ut qui
paucissimi ad eorum comparationem eramus, omnes illos in
unum coegimus et coactos, dextera Dei nobiscum dimicante'.[1]
They well understood that they must manœuvre the Turks into
a mass before they themselves struck home. Two decades later
Walter the Chancellor told how attacks were made on bodies of
Turks when they were riding 'gregatim'.[2] Here again it is possible that they were aided by the advice of Alexius Comnenus and
perhaps of other Byzantine soldiers. There is some similarity between the tactics which the Emperor Leo the Wise prescribed for
use against the Turks and those which were employed by Bohemond. The emperor recommended that a general when directing
operations against the Turk should be careful to cover his flanks
and rear by natural obstacles, to avoid pursuit, to make use of
steady infantry, and to carry the fight to close quarters without
delay.[3] It has been seen that Bohemond's victories at Antioch in
1097 and 1098 were achieved by securing natural protection for
the flanks of the battle line, by the posting of a reserve, and by
a charge delivered at the earliest practicable opportunity. In his
greatest victory, too, the dismounted men were already associated
with the knights in battle and preceded them into battle. It seems
certain that he was making use of Byzantine experience. We
know that he received advice; we know from Byzantine military
writings that kind of advice which he must have received, and his
actions were in accordance with its precepts. Yet his innate military genius also made its contribution. He alone of the leaders of
the First Crusade emerges as a skilful general. For putting theory
into practice he had not the well-drilled regiments of the old East

[1] *HEp.* p. 163, 'Epistula Boemundi et aliorum principum ad Urbanum
papam'.
[2] Galt. p. 82.   [3] Oman, I, pp. 206-7.

Roman army, but a motley host of pilgrims which included many non-combatants. Among the knights were adventurers and individualists, unused to military discipline and not inclined to accept it. The development in Frankish tactics during the First Crusade owed something to Byzantine experience; but it also owed much to Bohemond's remarkable ability to adapt the defective means at his disposal to the needs of a plan for battle—an ability equalled during the century only by that of Richard Plantagenet—and something to the natural reaction of the crusaders in the face of Turkish methods.

After Bohemond had ceased to dominate the military scene, the importance of the reserve and the timing of the charge were understood throughout the twelfth century; but less was heard of the flanks protected by nature, although flank-guards were often posted. Ultimately the most fundamental tactical measure was the result of this natural reaction to which reference has just been made. It has been seen above that the Turks sought to weaken enemy morale and to loosen their formation before they themselves delivered their final assault. The Franks naturally made the attainment of these aims as difficult as possible with the means at their disposal. Therefore they adopted a close formation, making use of the defensive qualities of their foot-soldiers, and of the mutual aid which these and the knights afforded each other, until the horsemen could administer the *coup de grâce*. The plan was simple, but it taxed their leadership and discipline. If either failed, defeat was the likely result.

CHAPTER VII

THE CRUSADERS' CASTLES

A<small>LL</small> governments are to some extent based on force, and it was perhaps the principal foundation of Frankish dominion in Syria. Not only was the threat of invasion almost continuous, but many of the subject peoples never fully consented to Latin rule, and on important occasions were to show themselves either doubtfully loyal or actively hostile. That force was embodied in the twin instruments of the field army and the walled places, and of these the second is the subject of this chapter. In the first section their military functions will be discussed; in the second, their form.

I. THEIR MILITARY FUNCTIONS

The castles of Latin Syria had no more important military function than that which has just been stated, and which was discussed in an earlier chapter.[1] Historians have nevertheless preferred to consider them mainly as means of defending a frontier, and they have done so in metaphorical phrases of no very precise meaning: they have said, for example, that a castle 'guarded the frontier' or 'commanded the valley' or 'closed the route'. Since there have been epochs in which fortresses have, in time of war, literally discharged such functions, it must at once be emphasized that the medieval castle did so in only a limited sense. In the eighteenth century, for example, the life of an army in the field often depended on its communications with its magazines, and if enemy artillery, mounted on a fort, could engage traffic on the important road, then that route was literally 'commanded' by the garrison.[2] Conditions in Latin Syria were entirely different. The small field armies lived partly on the country. They were not dependent upon supplies brought up by wheeled vehicles from a base, and so were not limited to the use of certain roads. Nor

[1] Above, pp. 60–2.
[2] Spenser Wilkinson, *The Defence of Piedmont*, pp. 69–72.

could their movement be hindered by the primitive artillery of the age. Routes and areas were held or commanded by medieval garrisons only in the sense that those garrisons dominated them in time of peace and could repress civil disturbance or minor enemy raids. But when warfare was fought on a scale likely to endanger the Latin occupation, no fortress or group of fortresses could restrain the passage of an invading force.[1] It has nevertheless become customary to associate fortification in Latin Syria with the defence of a frontier, and historians have regarded certain groups of castles as constituting a system of defence. Such a view was stated in its most extreme form by Prutz. From the evidence afforded by a map of the fortified places in Latin Syria, he argued that the Franks established an outer ring of defences on the frontiers, and supported this by two inner lines of greater works. Similar ideas have found a place in the writings of Rey and Deschamps.[2]

It is true that a map of the kind on which these writers have relied, when it is the result of scholarship critically applied to the evidence provided by existing monuments and the literary sources, is historical material on which the historian may base generalizations. Yet it must be used with caution, and the views of Prutz, inasmuch as they imply a system of defence consciously planned only with reference to the frontier, are certainly inadmissible. Furthermore the map of fortification in Latin Syria is a palimpsest which records the military requirements not only of the crusaders, but of their predecessors also. The Franks occupied fortresses which had marked the north-west frontier of Islam as it had existed from the seventh until the tenth century,[3] and others which stood at the southern limits of the Byzantine duchy of Antioch established by Zimiskes and Nicephorus Phocas.[4]

It might be argued that, among the strong places they found

---

[1] Above, pp. 19–21.

[2] Prutz, *Kulturgeschichte der Kreuzzüge*, pp. 195–6; Rey, *Étude sur les monuments de l'architecture militaire des croisés en Syrie et dans l'Île de Chypre*, p. 4; Deschamps, *Le Crac des Chevaliers*, pp. 16–42.

[3] Le Strange, *Palestine under the Moslems*, p. 26.

[4] E.g. Sahyun, Bourzey, Safitha, Bikisra'il and perhaps Ollaiqa. See Dussaud, *Topographie*, pp. 119, 151–2; Cahen, *Syrie du Nord*, pp. 172–3; van Berchem, *Voyage en Syrie*, pt. 1, p. 269.

in existence, the Franks occupied only those likely to be of use against an invader. It must be repeated, however, that a medieval castle was more than a fortress in a modern military sense; it enabled its tenant to serve both the public and his own private needs. On the one hand he could maintain in it the force necessary to dominate, police, and protect the surrounding district; on the other, he used that same force to profit from that area and to exploit its population. The process of Latin settlement at the time of the First Crusade was not the result of a conquest ordered and organized by a single authority, but it was often extended by the boldness and greed of individuals.[1] In such circumstances a fortified place was occupied not by a public authority adding units to a planned system of defence, but by individuals acquiring property. The economic aspect of the castle was of more immediate importance than the purely military.

These objections to the ideas of Prutz do not apply with the same force to those of Deschamps. The French scholar points out that the Latin states were protected by the mountain and hill ranges which lay between the Syrian coastal plain and the rift valley. This barrier is, however, broken by passes and wide corridors of country offering easy communication to an enemy attacking from east to west. The protection of the coastal plain demanded that the deficiencies of nature should be made good by the works of man, and the most important fortifications constructed by the Franks were a response to that need. The evidence of the map lends support to Deschamps's views, but shows also that he overemphasized the motive of frontier defence which, like Prutz and Rey, he ascribes to the Franks. Certainly in some areas of special military importance, like that in the neighbourhood of Jisr esh Shoghr,[2] and in the wide gap north of Lebanon which gives communication between Hims and Tripoli, fortified places were unusually numerous;[3] and where the main Lebanon range afforded maximum natural protection, they were, on the frontier, few. On the other hand the map shows that there were many castles far from the frontier. They were especially

---

[1] RA, p. 275: 'Etenim mos erat in exercitu ut, si signum alicujus Franci in civitate aut castello reperiretur, a nullo postea expugnabatur.' Beyer, 'Die Kreuzfahrergebiete Sudwestpalästinas', in *Beiträge zur biblischen Landesund Altertumskunde*, 1950, p. 150.

[2] Dussaud, *Topographie*, p. 170.   [3] Deschamps, *Le Crac*, pp. 30–1.

dense, for example, on the coastal plain between Haifa and Jaffa, in the heart of the Latin kingdom, while there were important avenues of access into the kingdom which were poorly provided with fortified posts.

Throughout the period Damascus was a more important seat of Muslim political power than the towns of the middle Orontes; the defence of the easy routes from that city into the Latin kingdom was therefore a more urgent and important problem than that of the Hims-Tripoli corridor. A Muslim force marching from Damascus to Banyas was on the main road to Tyre and Sidon, while it could also thrust across upper Jordan to the plain of Acre. If Deschamps is correct in his view that the Franks built castles principally with reference to their frontiers, it is to be expected that this sector of the eastern frontier would be strongly fortified, since, by its lack of natural obstacles, it gave easy access to the principal seaports of the Latin Kingdom. The map shows that it was not; and any evidence to the contrary becomes even less impressive when it is remembered that Banyas was in Christian hands only from 1129 to 1132 and from 1140 to 1164, and that the Chastellet at Jacob's Ford was founded in 1178 and destroyed for ever in 1180. The entry into the kingdom by way of the Jordan crossing immediately south of Lake Tiberias at al-Sannabra, used during the major invasions of Mawdud and Tughtagin in 1113, and of Saladin in 1182, 1183, and 1187, was virtually undefended. There appears to have been no fort near the bridge of al-Sannabra; and if the invader, like Saladin, continued his march by way of the valley of Jezreel, he encountered no major fortified place. His route was overlooked by the Hospitaller castle of Belvoir (Kawkab al-Hawa), but on the road itself stood only the weak citadel at Baisan, and, at the head of the valley of Jezreel, the little castle of al-Fule.[1] In considering these facts it is to be emphasized that, except for the years between 1140 and 1154, the ruler of Damascus was throughout the century a potential invader of the Latin states, and a greater danger to them than any ruler or governor of Hims. The roads from Damascus into northern Palestine were more often used by invaders than that from Hims to Tripoli. Yet the frontier which they crossed was not as well provided with fortified works. Late in the twelfth

[1] George Adam Smith, *Historical Geography of the Holy Land*, p. 357.

century, as Muslim pressure from Damascus increased, the
Franks seem to have shown themselves more aware of this danger
by building new castles at Hunin and Jacob's Ford, and possibly
by strengthening the Hospitaller castle at Belvoir.[1]

Every castle dominated its neighbourhood and, whatever its
location, was essential to the maintenance of Latin overlordship.
It is therefore misleading to think of these buildings only as a
means of frontier defence; but that is not to deny a special importance to the border castles. That importance was on occasions
fully recognized by the rulers of the Latin states themselves. After
the earthquake of 1114 Roger of Antioch, in making good the
damage done to his castles, gave priority to those 'quae defensioni
suae terrae utiliora et hostibus propinquiora novit'[2] and after
Saladin acquired Aleppo in 1183, the Franks took special care of
the defences of their towns which stood 'in confinibus hostium'.[3]
The late construction of castles in Galilee, mentioned in the
preceding paragraph, also shows that they could be sensitive to
dangers on the frontiers. Border districts were exposed to sudden
and frequent attacks and the strong places which controlled them
were correspondingly more important in preventing any permanent reduction in the area under Frankish rule than those situated
at a greater distance from the enemy.

When Latin Syria was invaded the border castles enabled the
Franks to meet the enemy before he had penetrated too deeply
into Christian territory. The field army was normally mustered
at a point behind the frontier,[4] where it was joined by contingents
from the strong places, including those on the border. There
were occasions on which border garrisons rode away from the
enemy in order to join the main Latin army concentrated at some
distance from the frontier.[5] Once they knew his direction of attack, the Frankish commanders attempted to make contact with

[1] Deschamps, *Défense*, p. 14.
[2] Galt. p. 65.   [3] WT, p. 1114.
[4] For example, the use made of Rugia by Tancred in 1111 (above, p. 141)
and Roger in 1115 (above, p. 147) and of Saffuriya by the army of Jerusalem
after 1170 (above, p. 151).
[5] Galt. (p. 99) records that in 1119 Il Ghazi decided to besiege Atarib
because Alan, its lord, had gone with his knights to Antioch, where the king
was gathering all available military forces. BD (p. 74) records the destruction
of the Transjordan contingent while marching to join the general muster at
Saffuriya in 1183.

THE CRUSADERS' CASTLES 209

the invader without delay, and on such occasions a border stronghold could be of the first importance. It afforded shelter, water,
and, because it normally stood in a cultivated area, supplies. If
the enemy were too strong to be challenged in the open field, the
Latin force could take refuge within its walls, as could its survivors if it were defeated.[1] For such reasons contemporary opinion accounted it wise to face the enemy in the neighbourhood of
friendly fortresses.[2]

The strong place on the borders might, therefore, have a special
importance in military affairs, but in general the medieval castle,
unlike the modern fort, fulfilled in addition a number of functions to the variety of which some reference has already been
made.[3] The sources record occasions, however, on which the
Franks established a castle for reasons which at the time of its
foundation were purely military. Some account will be given of
these in the remainder of this section, and it will be seen that
so far as the available evidence goes, many crusader castles were
founded not for defence, but for determined and sustained
attack.

In medieval siege warfare the use of the *Gegenburg* was not uncommon. A besieged garrison did not always conduct its defence
from behind stone walls, but by sorties carried the attack into the
enemy camp. In such circumstances the besiegers themselves
might require a firm base for their operations, and therefore constructed a temporary fortification within their own lines. Such
buildings could also be used to watch the gates through which the
sorties were made, and it was for such a purpose that the Latins
built their first castles in Syria.[4] The siege of Antioch began in
October 1097, and it was probably in the following month that a
council of the leaders decided to establish a castle outside Saint
Paul's gate. 'Malregard' was the result, and its garrison were soon
able to challenge Turkish sorties.[5] The device appears to have
been successful, for in the following March it was decided to place
a similar building on a mound which stood at the western end of
the main Orontes bridge, and from which a garrison could com-

---

[1] As did Baldwin IV in Ascalon in 1177; above, p. 126, n. 5.
[2] Above, p. 126.   [3] Above, pp. 60–2.
[4] Jähns, *Handbuch*, p. 682; Prutz, *Kulturgeschichte*, p. 194.
[5] *Anon.* p. 70; RA, p. 247; *HEp.* p. 157.

mand egress from the bridge gate.[1] A third and final strong point
was established outside Saint George's gate on the southern peri-
meter of Antioch. The necessary buildings already existed in the
form of a fort and a monastery, and Tancred manned the new
castle with a force of his own followers.[2]

The Frankish settlement was developed by a series of siege
operations, some of which extended over a period of years.
Bohemond began that series of thrusts against Aleppo which was
not to fail finally for another quarter of a century, and to support
his attack he was by 1100 intending to fortify existing buildings in
the immediate neighbourhood of Aleppo, in order so to maintain
a permanent blockade.[3] Ten years later his nephew Tancred began the construction of a stronghold on Tell ibn Ma'shar as a
base for attacks on Shaizar.[4] In 1103 Raymond of St Gilles began
his siege of Tripoli. He had but few followers, while the defences
of the town were strong and its population numerous; he might
also expect attacks from the rulers of still unconquered Muslim
territories. Therefore he selected a defensible site within sight of
the walls of Tripoli and from the castle he built there disputed
control of the surrounding country-side with the city's rulers
until, cut off from their sources of supply, they surrendered six
years later.[5]

Tyre was a seaport of even greater artificial and natural
strength. It could count on assistance both from the Fatimids of
Egypt and from the rulers of Damascus, and early attempts
against it showed that it would not fall easily into Latin hands.
According to William of Tyre, Hugh of St Omer, the second
prince of Galilee, organized many attacks against Tyre, but the
distance between the city and his base at Tiberias was so great
that whenever his men were beaten in an encounter near Tyre
they had no refuge against their pursuers. Therefore, some time
before his death in 1107, he established a castle, known to the
Franks as Toron, on the hill of Tibnin some thirteen miles east of

[1] *Anon.* p. 96; RA, p. 248; *HEp.* pp. 158, 166.
[2] *Anon.* p. 98; RA, p. 250.   [3] KD, p. 589; Grousset, I, p. 377.
[4] Derenbourg, *Vie d'Ousâma*, p. 91; IQ, p. 114.
[5] Raymond's castle became the nucleus of the modern town of Tripoli.
There is still more than a mile of gardens between Tripoli and its seaport,
which was the twelfth-century town besieged by Raymond. WT, p. 441;
Cafarus, *Liberatio Orientis* (ed. Belgrano), p. 119.

Tyre.[1] In 1117 Baldwin I ordered the construction of a castle at Iskandaruna on the coast road, nine miles south of Tyre, 'ad coercendum praedictam urbem'.[2] Thus although it is true that ultimately these two Latin foundations were to 'defend his [Baldwin's] conquests',[3] they originally owed their existence to the Latin offensive against Tyre.

Tyre fell to the Franks in 1124, but Ascalon remained in Muslim hands until 1153. The Egyptian government was careful to preserve its last possession in Syria, and reinforced its garrisons and supplies at regular intervals.[4] After 1123 the Fatimids never again used it as a base for a major attack on Latin Palestine, but the garrison constantly raided towards Jerusalem and Jaffa, and so brought insecurity into the life of the inhabitants of the fertile coastal plain and of the pilgrims on the road to the Holy Places. In order to curb this activity the Franks decided to establish fortified posts in the neighbourhood of Ascalon, and between 1136 and 1149 castles were built in turn at Bait Gibrin (Gibelin), Yibneh (Ibelin), Tell es-Safi (Blanche Garde), and Gaza.[5]

Historians have related the function of these places to the need for defining and defending the southern boundary of the Latin kingdom,[6] but William of Tyre has given a more precise statement of the reasons for their foundation. First among them was the need for restraining the raids by the garrison of Ascalon. This was to be achieved not by the mere existence of the new forts, with their garrisons within them ready to meet attack; those garrisons were themselves to take the field, and to attack the men of Ascalon whenever they left the shelter of their city. It can easily be understood how this aggressive defence could become an attack on the surroundings of Ascalon, which was the first step in the process of reducing the city itself.[7] Thus, according to

---

[1] WT, p. 459.   [2] Fulcher, p. 435.

[3] C. N. Johns, Historical Introduction to map, *Palestine of the Crusades*, p. 3.

[4] IA, p. 490; WT, pp. 581, 638, 779, 797.

[5] Below, pp. 230–2.

[6] Rey, *Monuments*, p. 4; Grousset, II, pp. 154–8.

[7] WT (pp. 638–9) describes the Franks' intentions before they fortified Bait Gibrin: 'Nostri vero videntes praesumptionem eorum non cessare . . . post multa consilia, optimum judicant . . . municipia in circuitu per gyrum aedificari, unde collecta facilius militia, et de vicino commodius hostium discurrentium refrenari posset impetus, et civitas fre quentius impugnari.'

+Quljinsawa
Nablus
Arsuf ⊞
+Majdal Yaba
(Mirabel)
Jaffa ⊞
+ Khan el Burj
Et Tayibeh
●Ramla
MONT GISARD
+El Burj
(Castrum Arnaldi)
+Yibneh
(Ibelin)
Latrun
⊞ Jerusalem
Minet el Kala
Bethlehem
+ Tell es Safi
(Blanchegarde)
Ascalon ⊞
+Bait Jibrin
(Gibelin)
+ Hebron
⊞Gaza
+ Kurmul
+Darum
+Semoa

DEAD SEA

R. Jordan

⊞Karak

+ Castle
⊞ Walled town with castle
Jordan Depression
Land below sea-level

SOUTHERN PALESTINE

0   10   20
Scale of miles

MAP III

William, the objects of the castle at Gaza were first, to check raids from the city and to watch it from the south, as did the other three new castles from east and north; to make attacks upon the city and to maintain an unceasing and aggressive warfare.[1] The castles of southern Palestine were not, therefore, established for general purposes of frontier defence. During the period of their construction the political state of Egypt was such that there was no danger of the Fatimids renewing their earlier invasions. The castles were built for a particular purpose: to check sorties from Ascalon and to enable attacks to be made against it. Except that it was wider in space and time, the plan was identical with that adopted at Antioch by the leaders of the First Crusade.

The subsequent history of these castles in Philistia emphasizes once more that such places were more than a military weapon. The garrison at Tell es Safi brought such security to the country-side that families settled in its neighbourhood, and the land became more productive. The Hospitallers, into whose charge Bait Gibrin had been given at the time of its fortification, were attempting to attract Franks to settle in the district which it controlled, and the consequences of Amalric's foundation at Darum have already been noted.[2] These castles were instruments of colonization and the extension of Latin dominion.

When Saladin became master of Egypt and made that country once more a base for the invasion of the Latin kingdom, those same castles took on a military importance of a kind different from that which they had possessed at the time of their foundation. In the campaigns of 1170 and 1177 they may be seen fulfilling the functions special to border strongholds which have already been described. In 1170 Saladin chose to attack both Darum and Gaza. They held firm; Amalric hastened from Jerusalem to make contact with the invaders; his army was swelled by a contingent of Templars from Gaza; as a result Saladin was

---

See also first and last sentences of WT. lib. xv. cap. xxv, pp. 697–9; and Usamah, p. 41.

[1] WT, pp. 777–8: 'Gazam . . . reformare proponunt [sc. rex et principes], ut sicut a septentrione et ab oriente fundatis in gyrum municipiis eam quasi obsederant, ita eidem ab austro simul non deesset stimulus; et ex ea quoque parte continuis impugnaretur congressionibus, et frequentibus lacesseretur insidiis.'

[2] Above, p. 61.

compelled to retire without inflicting permanent loss on the kingdom.[1]

Seven years later Saladin again invaded southern Palestine, and some account has already been given of the ensuing campaign.[2] Baldwin IV took a force to meet him, but when he saw the Muslim's strength he used the fortified place of Ascalon as a shelter for himself and his army. Saladin ignored all the strong places which lay in his path and swept on towards Ramla and Jaffa; yet those strong places influenced the campaign in many ways. They did not halt the enemy at the frontier, nor prevent his temporary control of the open country-side. But intact they remained as the repositories of overlordship. Latin dominion shrank to within their walls until the danger was past. This preservation of the settlement was achieved not only by the places on the frontier, but by those also in the heart of the kingdom like Majdal Yaba (Mirabel).[3] In addition the walled city of Ascalon enabled the king to preserve his small force until he could employ it in more favourable circumstances, while the severity of Saladin's ultimate defeat and the disasters of his retreat were attributed to his lack of any friendly stronghold north of the Nile delta.[4]

In writing of the castle, as of many other medieval institutions, it is difficult to separate the public aspect from the private, the military from the civil. In Latin Syria a castle gave to its overlord power to control the district which surrounded it. He could derive from the land and its inhabitants an income in goods, money, and services which at once supported his personal needs and enabled him to discharge his feudal obligations in government and warfare. The control which he exercised was part of the whole Latin overlordship in Syria; the force on which it was based was part of the whole force available to meet Muslim invasion. The domination of the ruling class in feudal society, the domination of the Frank over Armenian, Syrian Christian, and Muslim, the resistance of the Frank to Muslim attack, all these rested on force which was embodied partly in the army and partly in the fortified places. This was the true importance of the castle and walled town in Latin Syria.

---

[1] Grousset, II, pp. 559–62.   [2] Above, p. 185.
[3] WT, p. 1040.   [4] BD, p. 64.

During the First Crusade and in the following years, therefore, rulers extending their states and individuals seeking their own fortunes eagerly occupied existing castles; they did so wherever such places could be found, and without reference to frontiers which did not yet exist. New castles were built in those areas into which it was desired to carry the Latin dominion and in those in which force was particularly required to support the work of administration or exploitation. It is easy to see that there was a military element in such use of fortified buildings, but it was fused with administrative, economic, and social considerations.

The walled town and castle are seen most clearly as military instruments during the crusaders' conquest and settlement in Syria, and during the great Muslim counter-attacks on the Latin states. When the Franks were the invaders, the castle was used as an offensive weapon. When they themselves were invaded, the castles were the final refuge of their authority. The frontier strongholds had a special importance, since by reason of their proximity to the enemy they were exposed to frequent and surprise attack; and when invaders were challenged on the frontier, friendly fortresses served as a base and a shelter for the forces operating there. Every strong place had, however, the same fundamental importance. Wherever it stood, it was the embodiment of force, and therefore the ultimate sanction of the Latin settlement.

II. FORMS OF THE CASTLE

The history of fortification in feudal Europe is usually presented as one of progress. The motte and bailey castle of the eleventh century, the stone keeps of the twelfth and early thirteenth, the successive enceintes of the concentric castle of the late thirteenth and fourteenth centuries, each is seen as a type of fortification more highly developed than the predecessor from which it had evolved. And because the men of the First Crusade and those of them who settled in Syria saw, attacked, and occupied Byzantine and Arab strongholds more skilfully fortified than those then known to western Europe, their experience has been accounted a decisive factor in that story of progress which most historians tell.[1] Here no more is attempted than a description of the types of

[1] See Oman, II, pp. 10–42; Enlart, *Manuel d'archéologie française*, II,

castle on which the Franks relied for maintaining their dominion in Syria. Something will be said in turn of those places which were strong in the natural strength of their site; of those which, like many contemporary castles in the West, had as their principal feature the great tower, now generally called the keep; of those which lacked both natural strength and keep, and which were defended by a curtain wall strengthened by many towers.

If medieval castles are discussed only in terms of the scientific principles of fortification which they are held to embody, the subject can be made to appear more difficult and complex than perhaps it is; yet, before the age of gunpowder, the problems of fortification and the means of solving them were comparatively simple. For many centuries the essential features of a fortress were the enclosure with its main defence of earth bank, wooden stockade, or stone wall, usually preceded by a fosse. Such works presented to the besieger more than a merely passive obstacle; from their shelter the garrison conducted an active defence. During the twelfth century the stone wall could be a well-equipped fighting platform. On its inner face were mural galleries, and at its summit a rampart walk; from such vantage points the defenders could, through archères or between merlons, discharge their missiles at the enemy. The wall was further reinforced by towers set in its length, and these works discharged a number of useful functions. They buttressed the wall; they provided accommodation; they enabled the defenders to fight at an elevation greater than that provided by the rampart walk of the wall, and at a correspondingly greater advantage; if they projected beyond the line of the wall, they enabled the archers of the garrison to shoot along its face, and so to take any storming party in the flank. Other features in the scheme of medieval fortification were the provision of successive lines of defence and the careful fortification of entrances.

It has been noted above that some historians have considered

---

pp. 494–545; Hamilton Thompson, *Military Architecture in England during the Middle Ages*; Toy, *Castles*; Braun, *The English Castle*.
For references to the effect in Europe of crusading experience, see Oman, II, pp. 24–33; Hamilton Thompson, *op. cit.* p. 65; Toy, *op. cit.* p. 90; Braun, *op. cit.* pp. 70–1; Viollet-le-Duc, *Essai sur l'architecture militaire au moyen âge*, p. 23.

that the science of fortification was a branch of knowledge in which Europeans advanced between the years 1000 and 1300. Certainly castles changed in size and appearance during that time, but this was partly due to the greater wealth and the changing needs of a society which became increasingly settled and civilized during the twelfth and thirteenth centuries. At first sight a Château Gaillard, a Crac, or a Caerphilly bear little resemblance to the motte and bailey castles of the early twelfth century or to the earthworks of primitive peoples; but the principles of defence which their respective architects sought to express were unchanged. An obstacle, or a succession of obstacles, was presented to the besieger; the garrison used the obstacle as a means of fighting back at the enemy; gateways were recognized as a vulnerable point and were fortified with special ingenuity.[1] In Latin Syria, too, despite the existence of great strongholds of the past, the achievements of the Franks are not to be considered merely as a product of the conscious application of progressively improving ideas of defence. Their work was to a far greater degree the result of native common sense, 'of instinctive skill in the face of constant danger',[2] and of the knowledge which they brought with them from western Europe.

If the castles occupied or built by the Syrian Franks are considered as a whole, the predominant feature of the majority is not the embodiment of a sophisticated theory of fortification, but the reinforcement of strength already provided by nature. The best defence was inaccessibility, and this was provided by cliff and ravine more effectively than by wall and fosse. Where approach was impossible or very difficult the construction of cunningly sited obstacles was unnecessary: the strength of man-made defences was often in inverse proportion to those of nature. Many places were effective fortresses simply by virtue of inaccessibility. That of the cave fortresses, for example, was so complete that, when besieging that at el Habis in 1182, the Franks literally dug out the Muslim garrison.[3] Beha ed-Din recorded the problems

---

[1] For these features in ancient earthworks, see Hamilton Thompson's excellent description in *Military Architecture in England during the Middle Ages*, pp. 1–10.

[2] Hamilton Thompson, *op. cit.* p. 7.

[3] WT, p. 1106; identification by Deschamps, *Revue Historique*, CLXXII (1933), pp. 51–5. See also Schumacher in *ZDPV*, XL (1917), pp. 164–8. See

which confronted Saladin in 1188 of mounting an attack against certain Antiochene castles.[1] In the Jabal Nusairi the strongholds of the Assassins owed their comparative impregnability to their remote situation rather than to strong construction.[2] The Franks, too, occupied many sites which were protected on all sides by difficult approaches, Qala'at al-Mudiq,[3] Araima, Subeibe and, possibly, al-Musailiha[4] among them.

The mountain ranges on either side of the Syrian rift valley are cut by many water-courses, of which the junction provides a defensible feature in the form of a spur. Already separated from neighbouring high ground on all sides but one, complete isolation could be achieved by the provision of a ditch and wall on that one side. To name only the greatest crusader strongholds, Sahyun, the two Cracs, Marqab, and Beaufort were all built on sites of this kind; among the smaller were Harim,[5] Bourzey[6] and Qala'at Mehelbe.[7] On the coast a similar use was made at Tripoli and Tyre, and later at 'Atlit, of a peninsula washed on three sides by the sea.

At any medieval fortress the buildings must be considered in relation to the natural strength of the site on which they stand. Failure to do so has led to false conclusions, and Professor Oman's generalizations on Karak in Moab provide a clear example of this. Karak is therefore discussed here in some detail, both for this reason, and because it was finally lost to the Franks in 1189, and is therefore one of the few great castles which was in Latin possession only during the twelfth century.[8]

Oman, working on the simplification of a plan by Rey, who had

---

especially the outstanding work by Deschamps on the cave-fortresses in *Défense*, pp. 111–16, 217–20. While in Syria I did not see any of the caves, but I was able to visit all of the other crusader castles mentioned in this chapter. At the largest of them, Karak, Sahyun, Marqab, Crac, Subeibe, I spent three or four days; at the remainder, usually one day, sometimes two.

[1] BD, pp. 113–15.   [2] Dussaud, *Topographie*, p. 139.

[3] Van Berchem, *Voyage en Syrie*, pt. 1, p. 188; Deschamps, *Le Crac*, Album, pl. x.

[4] Van Berchem, *Voyage en Syrie*, pt. 1, pp. 113–16.

[5] Van Berchem, *Voyage en Syrie*, 1, 229.

[6] Cahen, *Syrie du Nord*, p. 164.

[7] Van Berchem, *Voyage en Syrie*, 1, pp. 283–6.

[8] The best description of Karak in Moab is in Deschamps, *Défense*, pp. 80–93. It is illustrated by some excellent plans and photographs, and on p. 39, there is a full bibliography.

also never visited Karak,[1] discussed the place as one built by the
Franks, as one which embodied the principle, in his view 'new'
to Europeans, of successive lines of defence, and one in which the
most vulnerable sector was defended by a curtain wall, of which
the face could be swept by flanking fire from two mural towers.[2]
The most cursory inspection of the castle shows all these assumptions to be unjustified.[3]

In the first place, it is much ruined, and has never been cleared
nor excavated. It already had a long history as a fortress when
Paganus the Butler began to build there during Fulk's reign,[4]
and that history continued after its conquest by Saladin's forces
in 1189. Deschamps and Anus have been able to distinguish the
masonry of the crusaders from that of later Muslims, but the
extent to which Karak in its existing form may be ascribed to
Frankish ideas and activity must remain uncertain until it has
been even more thoroughly explored.

What is certain, however, is that the plan of the castle has at all
times been largely determined by the physical conformation of its
site. The junction of two wadis forms a spur on which the town
of Karak stands, and which is connected to neighbouring high
ground only by a narrow neck of land to the south. Here the castle
is placed, and its function was to cover the town in that sector
from which attack was most probable. It was itself isolated from
that avenue of enemy approach by a fosse dug across the whole
width of the spur, while a second and similar ditch north of the
castle divided it from the town. East and west of the castle the
ground fell away so steeply that no heavy assault was possible
from either direction. The only practicable lines of attack were
along the ridge from the south, or from within the town to the
north.

The emplacement of the castle is divided naturally into two
levels, an upper and a lower.[5] Each forms a bailey or 'ward', and
they are the 'upper' and 'lower' wards, in which Oman saw two
successive stages of defence, and the embodiment of a sophisti-

---

[1] Rey, *Monuments*, p. 132 and his pl. XIV.   [2] Oman, II, p. 31.
[3] See Plan I and Plates I and II.
[4] It is shown as a fortress on the sixth-century Byzantine mosaic map at
Madaba in Transjordan.
[5] The wall dividing upper and lower baileys partly covers and is partly
founded on a small cliff, which is clearly shown in Plate II (a).

cated principle of fortification which the Franks had learned as a result of their settlement in the Levant. The lower ward, however, lies to the west of the upper, and each extends the whole length of the castle site from north to south. An attack delivered from either direction (the only practicable) would engage simultaneously the curtain wall of the upper and lower wards. On north and south both were covered by the same ditch. On the south the wall of the lower court was slightly the more accessible, but the assaulting troops were commanded by the lofty defences of the upper. The besiegers were faced not by successive obstacles, but by a single line of wall at two levels.[1] They had the same problem at the north curtain, except that there the wall of the lower court was probably as serious an obstacle as that of the upper. Thus Paganus was not, as Oman saw him, the pupil of an older civilization who applied theoretical principles in advance of those known to contemporary feudal society in western Europe. The form of his work was dictated, possibly by the remains of an earlier fortress, and certainly by the accidents of the terrain.

The third point made by Oman was that the north curtain wall of the castle, which met any attack from the town, was 'flanked by two large towers, which gave a lateral fire into the ditch'.[2] In fact the two towers which stood one at either end of this wall did not project beyond the line of the curtain, and did not make possible the cross fire of which Oman speaks. The face of the wall could be commanded only from two shallow offsets, neither of which enabled the garrison to offer effective flanking fire, for their projection is slight, and they are more than a hundred yards apart. The purpose of one of them, moreover, was certainly to provide a means of entrance at right angles to the face of the wall.[3] When the close-set, deeply projecting towers of Constantinople or Ankara are recalled, then it must be said that the north curtain wall of Karak was virtually unflanked.[4] Oman could have made a somewhat better case for the eastern defences. Here there are

[1] See Plate I (*a*) where that part of the wall in shadow is the line of wall to which reference is made above.

[2] Oman, II, p. 31.

[3] They are numbered 1 and 2 in the plan. No. 2 is shown in Plate II (*b*).

[4] Van Millingen, *Byzantine Constantinople*, pp. 47–51; G. de Jerphanion. S.J., 'Mélanges d'archéologie anatolienne', in *Mélanges de l'Université St-Joseph, Beyrouth*, tom. XIII, fasc. I, pp. 144–222.

four square or rectangular towers of the twelfth century set in the curtain wall.[1] The distances which separate them vary from 25 to 55 yards, their projection from the face of the wall varies from 10 to 23 feet. Yet the fact that they do so mattered little in the scheme of defence; more important was the fact that this wall stands at the head of a steep slope which the Franks clothed in a glacis of masonry.[2] The main strength of the castle as a whole lay not in 'new' principles of scientific defence but in its comparative inaccessibility from heavy assault afforded by its rock-hewn ditches and by its elevation above its immediate surroundings. The lie of the ground determined the line of the curtain wall which reinforced the natural strength of the site. The mural towers provided accommodation and command, but little opportunity for lateral fire. Active defence was possible from the roof of each tower, from the rampart walk which crowned the wall, and through the arrow slits which lit the rooms in each tower and the vaulted galleries sometimes built in two or three storeys which backed against the inner face of the curtain. Karak, like most crusader castles, was not a miracle of scientific fortification; it was a naturally strong site reinforced by wall and ditch.

The defences of Beaufort (Shaqif Arnun) were in some ways similar to those of Karak.[3] The main part of the castle stands on an outcrop of rock which elevates it a few feet above the surrounding country but attack, although difficult, was possible from all sides but the north.[4] On the east, however, the natural site of the castle was separated, by a shelf at a lower level only some fifty yards wide, from the edge of a precipitous cliff which falls some 1000 feet into the valley of the Litani. By the inclusion of this shelf within the castle area, where it formed a lower bailey, complete protection was secured from the east. The castle could therefore be attacked only from west and south. An assault from the west was met by the ditch and by the curtain wall of the upper bailey; that from the south by the defences of both the upper and

---

[1] Deschamps, *Défense*, pp. 84–5 and his plans.   [2] See Plate I (*b*).
[3] Both Rey, *Monuments*, p. 132 and Deschamps, *Défense*, p. 197 emphasize this similarity, although for different reasons from those stated here. On Beaufort see Rey, *op. cit.* pp. 127–39; Guérin, *Galilée*, II, pp. 533–4; *Survey*, I, pp. 128–33; Deschamps, *Défense*, pp. 197–208, with photograph and plans.
[4] See Plan 2, and Plate III.

the lower bailey. Those of the lower were less forbidding, but could be attacked on a frontage of less than 20 yards, and were commanded by the powerful southern works of the upper. Thus a simplified plan of Beaufort would show two 'wards' and, by generalizations like those which Oman applied to Karak, might be thought to present successive lines of defence. In fact its form, like that of Karak, was determined by the ground; large scale attack on a broad front was possible only against the works of the upper bailey.

Nor could Beaufort be defended by a carefully flanked curtain wall. As the visitor approaches it today from the west, he sees at first little evidence of towers; and although this first impression is due to accidents in the process of ruin, Beaufort was in fact less well equipped with these works than were most castles of its size and importance. Its main defence was the curtain wall which faithfully followed the edge of the rocky outcrop on which it stands. There are offsets and angles in its trace, but these are imposed by the contours of the site and are not the result of engineering art. On the vulnerable west wall are the remains of only one Frankish tower, which was the great tower, or keep, of their castle.[1] Its outer wall is built flush in line with the curtain, so that its flanks are wholly within the bailey. On the equally vulnerable south there are, in the upper castle, two rounded towers, beautifully constructed and boldly projecting, but both are Muslim work of the thirteenth century.[2] These may have replaced similar and earlier crusader works; while the site remains in its present ruined and overgrown state this fact cannot be confirmed. The only identifiable Frankish towers of the twelfth century which enabled a garrison to take a storming party in the flank are two small rounded towers which stand on the southern wall of the lower castle. The main elements of defence at Beaufort were the same as those at Karak.

Similar arrangements exist at Subeibe.[3] This castle stands on a

[1] Denoted by A in plan.
[2] B and C in plan. The various periods of construction at Beaufort, as well as those at Subeibe and Crac des Chevaliers mentioned in the paragraphs which follow, were identified by Deschamps. It was a piece of field-work of outstanding skill and importance. Personal observations recorded in these paragraphs can be checked in Deschamps, *Défense*, Plates LIII–LXXV, and in his plans of the castle.
[3] For a description of Subeibe see Deschamps, *Défense*, pp. 167–74,

spur of the south-western slopes of Mount Hermon, within an hour's walk of the walled town of Banyas, identified both by twelfth-century and by modern scholarship as Caesarea Philippi. The site of the castle is unusually large, measuring some 480 yards from east to west, and from north to south distances which vary between 80 and 180 yards. At its eastern end the Franks, during one of the two periods of their occupation of the castle in the twelfth century, built a tower keep which they tightly enclosed in a small bailey.[1] They defended the remainder of the site by a single line of curtain wall of the usual irregular trace, since it follows the edge of the plateau.[2] The western curtain, 180 yards in length, was provided with four towers, one at each end and two in the intervening wall. These were square or rectangular in plan, and projected distances between 20 and 30 feet beyond the curtain. To the north the castle is sufficiently protected by the steepness of the hillside, and the curtain is scarcely reinforced. The south is more accessible, and six projecting works of irregular plan were set in the wall, but these did not make possible an effective defence from a flank. As at Beaufort, the rounded towers which provide such a defence were built by the Muslim successors of the Franks, who also increased the projection of the square towers from the east wall, as if they considered that the Franks had not sufficiently provided for this kind of defence. Subeibe was, in fact, a castle like many in the West, with a tower keep, inner and outer bailey. It was more imposing than contemporary European castles, because of its great size and because, since Syria lacked wood and commonly built in stone, its outer defences were of masonry. But there was no greater art in its means of defence.

Even the great Crac des Chevaliers can be included among the crusader castles of the twelfth century which were defended by

---

together with his photographs and plans; also Guérin, *Galilée*, II, pp. 324–7; *Survey*, I, pp. 125–8.

[1] The Franks held the castle from 1129 to 1132 and again from 1140 to 1164. Deschamps is inclined to believe that the main building operations took place during the first of these periods, but the shortness of the time available makes this doubtful. For the time factor in castle-building see J. G. Edwards, 'The Welsh castles of Edward I', in *Proceedings of the British Academy*, XXXII, pp. 15–81.

[2] See Plan 3.

the use of comparatively simple means to reinforce nature. In its present form it certainly illustrates to perfection those arts of fortification evolved in the ancient world and passed to the Christian and Muslim societies of the Middle Ages. It presents successive obstacles of fosse, outer and inner walls, and three great towers which serve as a redoubt. The inner defences are so much higher than the outer, and yet stand so close to them, that an enemy could be engaged simultaneously from both. Round towers, projecting at close and regular intervals from both lines of wall provided the means of defence from a flank; and the varied equipment of glacis, machicolation, casemates, archères, and rampart walks made these walls the most effective means known to the age of striking back at a besieger.[1]

The best of this work, which in strength and beauty surely yields nothing to any other military architecture in the world, was undertaken by the Hospitallers at the very end of the twelfth or at the beginning of the thirteenth century. The unforgettable aspect of the castle when seen from the south-west has long been a favourite with photographers, to whom the curtain to the north and east might almost count as the back premises. Yet it is only here that the castle of the twelfth century stands fully revealed.

More than fifty years ago Clermont-Ganneau showed that the buildings of the Syrian Franks could sometimes be identified by certain characteristic methods which they employed in dressing masonry.[2] The marks on the stone reveal the kind of tool with which the mason squared and smoothed the blocks and the manner of its use.[3] Intensive study of evidence of this kind available at Crac, considered in conjunction with historical and architectural data, enabled Deschamps to establish the main periods of construction at the castle.[4] Of this the oldest is distinguished by drafted masonry; the face of each block is smoothed at the edge, but the central portion is left raised and in a rougher state.

[1] See Deschamps, *Le Crac des Chevaliers*. His book, the product of thorough field-work and study of the documentary sources, is without doubt the best study yet made of any medieval castle.

[2] C. Clermont-Ganneau, *Archaeological Researches in Palestine during the year 1873–4*, I, pp. 1–41; R. Dussaud, 'Les travaux et les découvertes archéologiques de Charles Clermont-Ganneau (1846–1923)', in *Syria* (1923), pp. 140–73.

[3] Deschamps, *Le Crac*, pp. 229–39.   [4] *Le Crac*, pp. 275–305.

In other parts of the castle the Muslims used drafted masonry at a later date; but that on the northern and eastern inner curtain is Frankish because it includes, not as an addition, but as part of the original construction, the semi-polygonal apse of the chapel, which can be established by its architectural details as a romanesque building of the twelfth century.[1] This evidence, decisive enough in itself, is corroborated by other details. Masonry of the same kind was used in castles, like Sahyun and Karak in Moab, which were in their possession only in the twelfth century, and not at all in the thirteenth.[2] The same comparison, as well as the nature of the objects depicted, establishes that the marks made by the masons on the wall at Crac now being discussed are Western in character. Associated with the same masonry there is a window above which flat stones have been laid between the voussoirs of its arch and the wall above. This is a device found in France in buildings of the late eleventh and early twelfth centuries.[3]

There seems to be no doubt that this curtain wall which includes the chevet of the chapel, and which links that feature with the tower on either side, was built during the twelfth century,[4] either soon after 1110, in the early years of the Latin occupation, or after 1142, when the castle was given to the Knights of the Hospital. In 1927, however, Deschamps made the remarkable discovery that the greater part of this early curtain, together with its towers, was still in existence, although obscured from view. In clearing the debris deposited by the population of the village which used to stand on and within the walls, he found a narrow passage within the whole length of the glacis which defends the inner ward on the south and west.[5] It is lit by archères which look over the outer ward, and on that side the passage, like the glacis, is built of smooth blocks of stone. But its other, inner wall is of drafted masonry. Moreover, half-way along its western length the passage is cut short by a wall of the same drafted blocks.[6] In order to continue along the passage it is necessary to leave it and then to re-enter it on the other side of the obstacle. The inner wall of the passage is, in fact, the outer face of the earlier curtain

---

[1] *Le Crac*, pp. 197–8.
[2] For drafted masonry at Sahyun, see Plates VI (*a*), VII (*b*), VIII (*a*) and (*b*).
[3] *Le Crac*, p. 204.   [4] See Plate IV (*a*).   [5] See AAA in Plan 4.
[6] See BB in Plan 4.

226 CRUSADING WARFARE

wall as it existed before it was covered by the glacis and wall of smooth blocks and of a later period of construction. The obstacle is the flank of a rectangular tower of the twelfth century which now stands within the rounded tower of a later period. Deschamps was therefore able to reconstruct the plan of the castle as it stood until the end of the twelfth century.[1] It had then only a single line of curtain wall, which followed the edge of an outcrop of rock, and which was strengthened by square or rectangular towers. It is true that these were disposed at more regular intervals and projected more effectively than those at Beaufort or Subeibe, but the contribution of nature to its defence was equal to that of art.

The feature common to most crusader castles is their foundation on naturally strong sites reinforced by constructions of the kind already described. Others, however, can be considered as a group because they have in common as their principal building the great tower, called by modern, though not by medieval writers, the keep.

This type of castle was that most commonly constructed in western Europe throughout the twelfth century, and the most valuable and original contribution made by T. E. Lawrence to the subject of crusader castles was to emphasize that the Franks continued to erect such buildings in Syria.[2] Lawrence's predecessors, as well as scholars who have written since, had been concerned to show that the Syrian Franks, profiting by the lessons learned from Byzantine models, inspired the progress of military architecture in western Europe. They wrote at length on the Crac des Chevaliers, and other great castles; but the Syrian tower keeps they mentioned hardly at all. There are in Syria a number of well-preserved monuments of this kind. One of the best is at Safita (Chastel Blanc), where the first view of the tower which still dominates the village is a vivid reminder that the Latin settlement was based on feudal institutions.[3] Strongholds of the same kind still stand at Jubail (Giblet)[4] and Qala'at Yahmur (Chastel Ruge),[5] while the principal tower at Sahyun (Saone)[6] and at

<hr>

[1] *Le Crac*, pp. 205, 277. See Plan 4.
[2] Lawrence, *Crusader Castles*, I, pp. 33–8.   [3] See Plate IV (b).
[4] Rey, *Monuments*, pp. 115–21; van Berchem, *Voyage en Syrie*, pt. I, pp. 105–110; Lawrence, *Crusader Castles*, I, p. 37. See Plate V.
[5] Dussaud, *Topographie*, p. 120 and n. 3; Lawrence, *op. cit.* I, p. 34.
[6] See below pp. 236–43 and frontispiece.

Beaufort[1] are similar in dimensions and design. After allowance is made for differences which resulted from local methods of construction, these buildings have the same appearance and characteristics as those erected in western Europe in the twelfth and early thirteenth centuries. They are comparable in dimensions.[2] Their exterior, without the projections of a Conisborough or the decoration of a Castle Rising is even plainer than that of most European keeps. Their main strength was passive, and lay in their thick walls and excellent construction. The wall of the great tower at Sahyun which looks towards the most likely direction of attack is 17 feet thick; at Jubail and Safita it is a little more than 11 feet, and at Beaufort a little less. Additional strength was sometimes given by the use of single pieces of masonry of great dimensions; there are some impressive examples at Jubail.[3] The only openings in the wall were narrow archères, and these were normally few in number. At Safita, on the ground floor, there are three in each of the longer walls and, on the upper, four in the longer and two in the shorter walls. At Sahyun and Beaufort only two archères looked out towards the enemy. The European custom of placing the main entrance to the tower at first-floor level was uncommon in Syria. Such a doorway existed in the main tower at Akkar, and there seems to have been another in the castle of Sarc, built by Tancred as a vantage point from which a garrison could watch the Muslims of Shaizar;[4] but it was more general, as at Jubail, Safita, Sahyun, and Beaufort, for a single small doorway placed at ground level to open into the ground-floor apartment. Access to the first floor and thence to the flat roof is provided by a staircase built within the thickness of the walls.

In essentials these Syrian great towers were like contemporary buildings in the West. They shared the same plainness, the same

---

[1] Rey, *Monuments*, p. 130; *Survey*, I, p. 130; Deschamps, *Défense*, p. 205.

[2] The tower at Jubail is 80 × 60 ft.; Yahmur, 52 × 46 ft.; Safita ,100 × 58 ft.; Sahyun, 80 × 80 ft.; Beaufort, 75 × 75 ft.; Subeibe, 123 × 59 ft. I took these measurements when alone, either by pacing or with a steel tape, and they are therefore not exact. Wherever possible they have been checked against existing plans, although such plans can be misleading. Rey, for example, shows the great tower at Sahyun as 120 ft. sq. Compare the dimensions given above with Castle Rising, 75 × 64 ft.; Scarborough, 56 × 56 ft.; Middleham, 98 × 96 ft.; Portchester, 65 × 62 ft.

[3] See Plate v (*b*).

[4] Deschamps, 'Les entrées des châteaux des croisés' in *Syria* (1932), p. 380.

immense solidity, the same limited means for conducting an active defence. There were also certain differences, some of which were not without military importance. In Syria towers were built without the use of wood, and were vaulted throughout. Perhaps because of this they were generally only of two storeys instead of the three which were common in the west, and they were therefore not often as high as many of their European counterparts. Sometimes this inferiority was offset by the height of the vault. In the ground floor of Safita, a hall of rare and austere beauty used by the Templars as a chapel, the vault is some 55 feet above the floor. The total height of the tower exceeds 100 feet and is its greatest dimension; but in Syria this is exceptional. Among the military advantages of a vaulted stone building was an immunity from fire. In the west, wooden defences were often destroyed by this means, and in the east, where Greeks and Arabs were expert in the employment of combustibles in war, such immunity was highly important. Vaulting also made possible the provision of a flat roof, which provided a better means for active defence than did the pitched roof of many European towers. The Syrian keeps were sometimes tightly enclosed in a ring wall; such an arrangement is to be found at Qala'at Yahmur, Jubail, Subeibe,[1] and Safita. Against the inner face of that wall it was normal to construct a continuous range of vaulted buildings of such a height that the flat roof provided a spacious rampart walk which afforded easier movement around the circuit of the walls than the usual narrow ledge and must have facilitated the organization of defence in a threatened sector. The wall of these buildings nearest the great tower was separated from it by distances which were at some places as little as 6 feet.[2] These dispositions have been the occasion for little comment, yet they not only distinguished the Syrian keeps from the European in appearance, but they were an interesting variant on the usual defensive scheme. The ground floor of the great tower was entirely masked from the attacker; the garrison could defend both from the tower roof and from the spacious rampart walk of the enclosing wall. Some observers may wish to regard this arrangement as a marriage of *turris* and *castrum* and as yet another demonstration of the integration of East and

---

[1] See Plan 3.
[2] This distance is found at both Subeibe and Qala'at Yahmur.

West which is said to have been a principal result of the Crusades. It may equally well be regarded as Western in the sense that it embodies the defences both of tower keep and inner bailey. But it is distinctively Syrian in the very close association of the two.

Mention has been made of the best-preserved tower keeps built by the Syrian Franks. Remains less complete and references in the sources provide evidence of many more. There was a great tower at Subeibe[1] and Montfort,[2] while at Caesarea[3] and Tartous the citadel was built in this form.[4] It is known that there were towers of some importance at Batroun[5] and Maraqiya,[6] and possibly at Safad[7] also. There were besides smaller towers in plenty. That at Tokleh was described by Rey and discussed by Viollet-le-Duc;[8] in the neighbourhood of Crac des Chevaliers are Burj Mi'ar and Burj 'Arab,[9] which, although part of the Hospitallers' possessions, may originally have been independent of the greater castle. East of Tyre stand Burj al-Qibly and Burj esh-Shemaly,[10] both square towers of drafted masonry and apparently of crusader origin. In the county of Caesarea there were a number of small castles of which a tower was the principal feature. Like most of the lesser monuments these have never been carefully studied, but it has been said that the tower at Khirbet al-Muntar is 'perhaps of crusading times',[11] while that on the seashore at al-Helat 'has every appearance of Crusading origin'.[12] In the same way the evidence of existing masonry and of documentary records shows that the towers of al-Mesra'a, Burj al-'Atot, Qaqun, and Qulunsawa date from the twelfth century.[13] North of Jerusalem and overlooking the Nablus road was the Burj al-Lisaneh; not far distant from it were towers at Khan al-Burj and at Tayibeh.[14] In southern Palestine there were small tower keeps at Kurmul and

---

[1] *Survey of Western Palestine*, I, p. 126; Lawrence, *Crusader Castles*, I, p. 37; Deschamps, *Défense*, pp. 173–4.
[2] Rey, *Monuments*, p. 147; *Survey*, I, p. 186; Deschamps, *Défense*, p. 139.
[3] *Survey*, II, pp. 25–6.   [4] Rey, *Monuments*, p. 79.
[5] Lawrence, *op. cit.* I, p. 37.
[6] Dussaud, *Topographie*, p. 126 and references; Rey, *Monuments*, p. 161.
[7] *Survey*, I, pp. 248–50.
[8] Rey, *Monuments*, p. 102; Viollet-le-Duc, *Dictionnaire raisonné de l'architecture française*, art. Tour, IX, p. 163.
[9] Deschamps, *Le Crac*, p. 107.   [10] *Survey*, I, pp. 57–8.
[11] *Survey*, II, p. 61.   [12] *Survey*, II, p. 33.
[13] *Survey*, II, pp. 33, 178, 195, 199.   [14] *Survey*, II, pp. 307, 370.

Semoa.[1] Such places have been regarded by historians as part of the defensive system of the kingdom;[2] but many of them were in areas which were little exposed to enemy attack, and it is probable that they had an everyday importance as residences, police posts, centres of administration, or local refuges.[3]

Historians of the subject have generally paid little attention to crusader castles of this type, but have concentrated on those which appear to show Frankish architects as the pupils of their Byzantine and Arab predecessors. The disappearance of the keep from the castle plan is usually regarded as an important symptom of progress, and scholars have shown marked interest in a number of Latin fortresses from which this feature was omitted.

William of Tyre provides good evidence that a number of such places were built on the coastal plain of southern Palestine. King Amalric planned his new castle at Darum in the form of a curtain wall enclosing a square bailey, at each corner of which stood a tower.[4] Except that one of these 'was more massive and more strongly fortified than the rest', the plan was that of a Roman *castrum*, a form which had been freely used both by Byzantines and Arabs. In his description of the castles already built in the same region during the reign of King Fulk, William states that Yibneh was 'praesidium cum turribus quatuor';[5] Tell es-Safi, 'oppidum cum turribus quatuor congruae altitudinis';[6] Gaza, 'opus muro insigne et turribus';[7] Bait Gibrin, 'praesidium muro insuperabili turribus munitissimum'.[8] There is insufficient detail here to construct even a simple plan, but there is reason to believe that at these places, as at Darum, the defences consisted of curtain wall and mural towers; that none included a great tower;[9] that at Yibneh and Tell es-Safi there was a *castrum* with the same regular plan as that at Darum.

---

[1] *Survey*, III, pp. 372, 412; Rey, *Monuments*, pp. 102–4.

[2] Rey, *ibid.*; Deschamps, *Le Crac*, p. 76; *Défense*, p. 21.

[3] On the difficulty of assigning a function to these small towers, which were common in Roman and Byzantine, as well as in Latin Syria, see H. C. Butler, in *Publications of the Princeton University Archaeological Expeditions to Syria*, II, p. 235.

[4] WT, p. 975.   [5] WT, p. 697.   [6] WT, p. 698.   [7] WT, p. 778.

[8] WT, p. 639; *Survey*, III, p. 268.

[9] Rey, *Monuments*, p. 124 claims to have found traces of a great tower at Tell es-Safi. There are none now. See also Lawrence, *Crusader Castles*, I, p. 40.

Castles of this type may still be studied *in situ*, as well as in the literary sources. On the seashore ten miles north of Ascalon there is a small *castrum* at Minet al-Kala (180 × 144 ft.),[1] while at Kawkab al-Hawa, on the heights above the right bank of the Jordan and overlooking the course of that river between Lake Tiberias and Baisan, stands the larger Hospitaller castle of Belvoir (380 × 320 ft.).[2] Between the two in size is al-Qulei'at (220 ft. sq.), to be found fifteen miles from Tripoli on the main road to Hims.[3] Its appearance to the approaching traveller might be described in those same phrases with which William of Tyre depicted the similar castle at Darum: 'Castrum modicae quantitatis, vix tantum spatium intra se continens quantum est jactus lapidis, formae quadrae, quatuor turres habens angulares, quarum una grossior et munitior erat aliis.'[4] One of the towers at al-Qulei'at is better preserved than the rest, and at first sight appears to be the largest and best fortified, but closer inspection shows that all four angle towers were alike in size and defensive scheme.

None of these places, with the possible exception of Belvoir, appears to have included a great tower. All were fortified with a tower at each corner of the enclosure, and at certain other points on the curtain wall. Minet al-Kala has a gateway in both its eastern and western walls; as each gateway is flanked by two towers the castle has eight of these works in all. So has al-Qulei'at, where there is a projecting bastion at an intermediate point on each side of the enclosure. Belvoir has only seven, since its eastern wall is protected by the steep hillside of the Jordan valley, and needs no additional defence. The size of the towers varies with that of the castle. At Minet al-Kala they are round, solid at the base and some 17 feet in diameter. Those at the other two castles are square or rectangular in plan and project into the ditch beyond the line of the curtain. At Belvoir, all but one of the seven towers have sides more than 30 feet in length, and their usual projection is between 15 and 20 feet. The angle towers of al-Qulei'at are some 25 feet square and the longest side of the intermediate bastions is equal in length. Although the castle is equally accessible from all sides,

---

[1] *Survey*, II, pp. 426–7.

[2] See Plan 5; *Survey*, II, p. 117; Guérin, *Galilée*, I, pp. 129–32.

[3] Van Berchem, *Voyage en Syrie*, pt. I, pp. 131–5; Dussaud, *Topographie*, p. 90.

[4] WT, p. 975.

the projection of these works varies. On the north curtain it is no more than 2 feet; on the south, 6 feet. The only towers with deeper projection are those which flank the gateway on the southern half of the eastern curtain.

Historians have seen in these *castra* of the crusaders clear evidence that the Syrian Franks were learning from the Byzantines. Emphasis has been laid on the large number of enclosures fortified in this way at the instance of Justinian's government in the reconquered North African province;[1] however, if it is to be held that such places served as models to Latin architects, it is more relevant that they stood also in lands where the crusaders were likely to see them.[2] The extent to which the Franks were influenced by such examples is more doubtful than historians sometimes allow. It has been assumed that before they came to Syria the Franks built only castles which included a tower keep, and that they lacked the skill to fortify a curtain wall and to strengthen it with towers. In the light of such assumptions the *castrum*, because it lacked a keep and was defended by ring wall and towers, is regarded as a mark of progress and as part of the debt owed by western Europe to Byzantium.[3]

There are objections to this thesis. Even in the typical castle of the eleventh century the baileys were defended as well as the keep.[4] These defences were always of wood, and so have not survived, but early literary descriptions show that they might have

---

[1] See Lawrence, *op. cit.* I, p. 28; Deschamps, *Le Crac*, pp. 47–53; in *Syria* (1932), pp. 372–3; in *Gazette des beaux-arts* (Dec. 1930), p. 351; for the use made of Diehl, *L'Afrique byzantine.*

[2] For remains of Roman *castra* in the southern Hauran see H. C. Butler, 'Syria', in *Publications of Princeton University Archaeological Expeditions to Syria*, II (Architecture, sect. A, Southern Syria), e.g. pp. 70–6, 145. For those on the Damascus-Palmyra road or in the Euphrates valley, both of which areas were accessible to the Franks, see R. Père A. Poidebard, *La Trace de Rome dans le désert de Syrie*, especially pp. 43–9, 54 and Atlas, pls. XX, XL, XLII, XLV, LXXV. For Qasr al-Hair, see K. A. C. Cresswell, *Early Muslim Architecture*, I, pp. 330 *et seq.* For Salamiya, see van Berchem, *Voyage en Syrie*, pt. I, pp. 167–71. Deschamps, *Le Crac* draws attention to Byzantine buildings with this plan which the Franks either saw or occupied.

[3] E.g. Oman, II, p. 30.

[4] Because the keep was a typical feature, writers are prone to discuss it as if it were the whole castle. But equal regard must be given to the bailey and its defences. See F. M. Stenton, *The Development of the Castle in England and Wales*, p. 11.

been constructed with skill and care.[1] Before 1100, too, stone castles without a keep had been built, and the defences of Ludlow, for example, were a stone curtain wall and mural towers.[2] And if architects required the inspiration of the *castra* or flanked stone walls of an older world in order to produce similar works, these stood in western Europe as well as in the Levant. It is necessary to recall only Portchester or Pevensey,[3] and the walls of Rome[4] or Carcassonne.[5] That the Franks were to some extent influenced by examples of such works in the east is an irresistible conclusion, but the importance of this diffusion has been over-estimated because other factors which led the Franks to build *castra* have scarcely been considered.

Diehl, like other writers on Byzantine fortification, studied and discussed the North African forts in relation to the writings of military theorists known to the late Roman world, of authors like Vegetius, Vitruvius, Procopius of Caesarea, and Philo of Byzantium. These wrote on the science of fortification,[6] and discussed such matters as the ideal arrangement of main wall, forewall, and ditch,[7] the spacing, ground plan, and interior arrangement of towers,[8] the construction of gateways[9] and the provision of water. In their study of Byzantine fortresses historians have always been ready to identify architectural features which seemed to be in

[1] See description by John of Colmieu quoted in Enlart, *Manuel d'archéologie française*, II, p. 499.

[2] G. T. Clark, *Mediaeval Military Architecture*, II, pp. 273–90. Hamilton Thompson, *Military Architecture*, pp. 95–6.

[3] See Official Guides issued by H.M. Office of Works to Portchester and Pevensey.

[4] I. A. Richmond, *The City Wall of Imperial Rome*.

[5] Viollet-le-Duc, *La Cité de Carcassonne*; J. Poux, *La Cité de Carcassonne*. The point made in this paragraph is argued in greater detail by Lawrence, *op. cit.* pp. 16–24.

[6] Vegetius, *Epitoma rei militaris*, ed. C. Lang; Vitruvius, *De architectura*, ed. F. Krohn; Procopius, *De aedificiis*, translated A. Stewart. A translation of the treatise of Philo of Byzantium by Rochas d'Aiglun will be found in the *Mémoires de la Société d'Emulation du Doubs*, sér. 4, tom. VI (1870–1), pp. 183–441. The translator also adds extracts from the works of Aeneas Tacticus, the Anonymous of Byzantium and Hero of Constantinople.

[7] Vegetius, p. 129; Philo, pp. 237–8; Anon. of Byzantium, p. 341; Procopius, pp. 42–4 (the work of Justinian at Dara).

[8] Vegetius, p. 129; Vitruvius, p. 18; Philo, pp. 211–22, 236; Anon. of Byzantium, p. 340.

[9] Philo, p. 226.

accordance with the precepts of these theorists.[1] They have also found that theory and practice were often widely separated. For example, the authors mentioned were unanimous in recommending that towers should be round or polygonal in plan; but, in the words of Tafrali, 'malgré ces récommendations, souvent on construisait en Orient des tours carrées, soit par tradition, soit parcequ'elles étaient d'une construction plus facile'.[2] Jerphanion, too, has emphasized how many important fortresses there were with only one polygonal tower, or none at all.[3] Diehl, for his part, was also forced to conclude that the form of many buildings which he studied, including the *castra*, was determined less by abstract principles of fortification than by practical considerations of more immediate importance in North Africa during the sixth century.[4] The period of their construction followed immediately on the conquest of the province by Justinian's armies. Byzantine hold on this territory was insecure, and in order to strengthen it fortifications were needed without delay. As in Syria, the selection of sites already strong by nature often reduced the need for building;[5] but even in open country there was usually no time for elaborate and multiple defences. An area enclosed by wall and towers was enough, and the towers were often few and far between.[6] The materials of construction were not carefully quarried and squared but were usually those which already lay to hand in ruined or even in existing buildings.[7] Speed and simplicity in construction were additionally justified by the primitive nature of the enemy; the Berber tribesmen had neither the technique nor the material to conduct major siege operations. For all these reasons the Byzantine fortifications in North Africa were more often the product of circumstances than of precepts. 'Dans l'Afrique byzantine', writes Diehl, 'les nécessités particulières du terrain et l'obligation de faire vite ont, bien plus que les principes absolus, déterminé la forme et les dimensions des forteresses.'[8]

The same was true of many crusaders' castles. The building of

[1] Diehl, *L'Afrique byzantine*; Jerphanion, *Mélanges d'archéologie anatolienne*; Tafrali, *Topographie de Thessalonique, passim*.
[2] Tafrali, *op. cit.* p. 58.   [3] Jerphanion, *op. cit.* p. 157, n. 3.
[4] Diehl, *op. cit.* pp. 172–4.   [5] Diehl, *op. cit.* p. 217.
[6] Diehl, *op. cit.* p. 184.   [7] Diehl, *op. cit.* p. 174.
[8] Diehl, *op. cit.* p. 221.

the *castra* near Ascalon was a military operation carried out in the neighbourhood of the enemy and the preparation was the same as for a major campaign in the field. The king and his magnates were present and the armed strength of the kingdom was mustered.[1] Because such service was a burden and was never unduly prolonged, construction was presumably hurried and completed as quickly as possible. It is significant that the plan of Chastellet near the Jisr Banat Yakub, built by 'the king and the whole strength of the kingdom' in less than six months, was that of a *castrum*.[2] Another feature common to all the crusader *castra* so far discussed was the open country in which they stood. Most Syrian fortresses were protected by nature on all sides or on all but one. Of the *castra* some, like Kawkab, Hunin, or Tell es-Safi, were so protected on only one side; others, like al-Qulei'at, Chastellet, Bait Gibrin, Yibneh, Minet al-Kala, Gaza, Darum, not at all.

It is suggested that, even if the Latins had never seen a Byzantine or Arab fort, these factors of haste and ground would have gone far to impose frequent use of the *castrum* plan. The first requirement was a protected enclosure, so that had the architects of Chastellet or Bait Gibrin envisaged a conventional European castle of the period, the need for haste made the enclosing of the bailey of more urgent importance than the keep, which might be added later.[3] A ring wall was therefore constructed, and with it mural towers, which were required to fulfil a number of functions and to the existence and construction of which the Franks were accustomed by their experience in western Europe. Since the country was open, the plan of the defences was not dictated by the

---

[1] The phrases used by William of Tyre to describe the preparations for castle-building are comparable to those he employs to describe the muster for a campaign; e.g. p. 639 (Bait Gibrin), 'convocato universi regni populo'; p. 698 (Tell es Safi), 'dominus rex et principes ejus, una cum domino patriarcha et praelatis ecclesiarum . . . et vocatis artificibus, simul et populo universo necessaria ministrante'; p. 778 (Gaza), 'Convenit universus populus, quasi vir unus, ad praedictum locum'.

[2] WT, p. 1050; Guérin, *Galilée*, I, p. 341; *Survey*, I, pp. 250–1.

[3] Even in Europe the work was often carried out in this order; Stenton, *Development of the Castle in England and Wales*, p. 12. When work was begun on the castles built in Wales during the reign of Edward I, the first operation was normally the provision of temporary defences for the whole area on which the castle was to stand; J. G. Edwards, in *Proc. Brit. Acad.* XXXII, pp. 38–9, 44.

contours of the ground; it was necessary to provide against the possibility of attack from three or four sides. The need for haste demanded defences which could be easily and economically constructed; the need for all-round defence imposed a symmetrical ground plan. These specifications were best fulfilled by the *castrum*. Latin architects were possibly, even probably, influenced by Greek and Arab buildings which they had seen; they were certainly influenced by considerations of time and ground.

It is possible, however, to turn from the realm of conjecture and to study a crusader castle built on a site on which the remains of an earlier Byzantine fortress were still standing. By comparing these with the Latin work, it is possible to deduce with certainty the extent to which, on this particular site, the Franks were influenced by their predecessors. There are a number of additional reasons for discussing Sahyun in detail.[1] It was lost to Saladin in 1188 and never subsequently recovered. It is, therefore, like Karak, a castle which was in Latin hands only during the period of the twelfth-century kingdom, but its buildings are more characteristically crusader than those of the Transjordan fortress, and have not been altered or concealed by later Muslim rebuilding. Sahyun, too, embodies many of the features which have been discussed in this section. The work of the architect was complementary to the great natural strength of the site; the defences are in the form of curtain wall and mural towers; one of these towers is larger and finer than the rest and has all the attributes of a tower keep.[2]

The site of Sahyun is typically Syrian. It is formed by the junction of two water-courses which run in deep and precipitous ravines. The spur so formed was entirely isolated from the adjoining high ground by an enormous fosse cut some 700 yards east of its tip. The whole castle was naturally on two levels, with an upper court on the east and a lower on the west. The lower was secure from heavy attack, and was enclosed by a plain curtain wall of which the irregular trace is dictated by the edge of the

[1] See Plan 6, frontispiece and Plates VI–VIII.
[2] Rey, *Monuments*, pp. 105–13, and *Colonies*, pp. 15–18; van Berchem, *Voyage en Syrie*, pt. I, pp. 267–83; Lawrence, *op. cit.* I, pp. 32–4; Deschamps in *Gazette des beaux-arts* (Dec. 1930), pp. 329–64.

plateau. The most powerful defences were constructed on the east and south sides of the upper court, and it is these which will be discussed here.

The east wall was built of medium-sized blocks of drafted masonry typical of twelfth-century Frankish work. Set in this wall, near the north-east angle of the upper castle, is a gateway which could be reached by the bridge across the great fosse; this entrance is flanked by two rounded salients which project very slightly beyond the line of the wall. South of the gateway, set on the line of the east curtain wall and projecting only a few inches beyond it, is the great tower, a building which measures externally some eighty feet square.[1] South again are three small rounded towers, of which the third was at the south-east angle of the whole site. On the south curtain wall of the upper castle there were three more towers of rectangular plan; that farthest to the west was a gatehouse. All historians have agreed that the great tower, with its massive construction, its drafted masonry, its interior arrangements 'like any keep in Normandy',[2] was built by the crusaders, and there seems no good reason to doubt that the rest of this curtain wall and its mural towers were their work also. The masonry is not all of the same dimensions as that of the great tower, but most of it is only slightly smaller. It is drafted in the same way, and it carries masons' marks of an incontestably Latin character.[3] Nor does it seem necessary to follow Lawrence in treating the great tower as a work which is essentially different from the other rectangular towers on the curtain wall. In comparison with the majestic solidity of the main tower they appear smaller than their measurements show them to be; their dimensions in fact are equal to those of many European tower keeps.[4] They are vaulted rather differently from the great tower, but this is more reasonably explained by difference in size rather than by any difference in origin.

Lawrence did not seem to observe the significance of the fact that at Sahyun there were other walls of an entirely different character. A few yards to the west of the great tower a stretch of

---

[1] Numbered 1 in plan.   [2] Lawrence, *op. cit.* I, p. 33.

[3] Including those of the kite-shaped shield then carried by the Latin knights. See the mason's mark on Plate VIII (a) and (b).

[4] Tower 4 is 62 × 46 ft.; tower 5, 48 × 42 ft.

this wall still stands to a height of some 20 feet.[1] The masonry is of rubble faced with squared blocks much smaller than those used in the Latin work; some of them are laid to form a diamond pattern.[2] The ruins of a tower projecting from the wall show that it was hexagonal in plan and solid to the level of the rampart walk. Similar masonry with the same characteristics is to be found in parallel lengths of wall still further to the west which are the remains of successive lines of defence culminating in a citadel placed on the highest point of the whole site.[3] It is still encumbered with undergrowth and debris, but it appears to be in the form of a ring wall, bounding a square enclosure and strengthened by angle towers and a salient in its eastern face. As Rey supposed, and as van Berchem and Deschamps have shown,[4] there can be little doubt that this succession of walls and the citadel are the remains of a Byzantine fortress which stood at Sahyun before its occupation by the Franks. The polygonal tower with its solid base, the *opus reticulatum* in the masonry, the plan of the citadel, all are characteristic of Greek work. Sahyun, therefore, in its twelfth-century form, consisted of a crusader wall and towers added to the defences of a fairly large Byzantine fortress.

It is uncertain whether the cutting of the fosse was Greek or Latin work. It is usually credited to the Franks; Lawrence supposed that it was Byzantine. Certainly any defence of the Sahyun spur required the ditch to complete an isolation almost achieved by nature, and since it is known that the Greeks made similar cuttings elsewhere,[5] it is reasonable to suppose that they did so at Sahyun. On the other hand the rounded towers which project from the east curtain wall are based on rounded projections of rock cut exactly to fit them. If the Franks, as it is generally agreed, built the towers, then they also cut the rock in this way, and on

[1] See Plate VI (a).

[2] See Deschamps in *Gazette des beaux-arts* (1930), p. 350. He points out that this is the *opus reticulatum* described by Vitruvius. This stretch of wall and a corner of the Latin great tower are shown in Plate VI (a).

[3] See frontispiece.

[4] Rey, *Monuments*, p. 111; van Berchem, *Voyage en Syrie*, pt. I, especially pp. 269, 280–1; Deschamps, *Gazette des beaux-arts* (1930), p. 350.

[5] The Byzantines strengthened the citadels at Edessa and Gargar with a rock-hewn ditch, in which, as at Sahyun, a pinnacle of rock was left as the central pier for a wooden bridge; Lawrence, *op. cit.* I, p. 31; Rey, *Colonies*, p. 314.

this evidence they may have widened, as they may also have deepened, an existing ditch.

The same facts, however, allow an alternative hypothesis. The width of the ditch which presumably protected the Greek fortress can only have been equal to or less than its present, which is also its twelfth-century, width. Therefore the Byzantine wall which stands west of the great tower must always have been at least its present distance from the edge of the fosse. It is therefore natural to suppose that during the Greek occupation there was in front of that wall another overlooking the ditch itself, and which was replaced by the crusader wall. It is possible that the earlier Byzantine wall was set with rounded towers based on rounded rock projections left when the fosse was cut, and that the existence of these bases dictated the plan of the later Frankish towers.[1] The extent to which the fosse at Sahyun was Latin work therefore remains uncertain.

These questions have been discussed at some length because the relation between Byzantine and crusader work at Sahyun makes an important contribution to the problem of assessing the influences which determined the form of the crusaders' castles. Historians have laboured to solve the problems by searching three continents for evidence: at Sahyun Greek and Latin work are found quite literally side by side.

Professor Oman mentioned the castle as one which illustrates 'the earlier developments of Frankish architecture in the Holy Land' and goes on to say that 'an examination of such castles shows that in the twelfth century the two great principles of Byzantine military architecture—the defence of the curtain by towers and the combination of concentric lines of fortification— were thoroughly well understood and practised by the Frankish builders'.[2] Like Karak in the desert, Sahyun has neither been excavated nor studied in detail, and does not therefore provide a sound basis for confident generalizations, but those of Oman appear to be without foundation. The defence of a curtain wall by towers was known and practised in Europe before the time of the

---

[1] This is made more probable by the foundations of the Byzantine round tower beneath tower 4. See Deschamps in *Gazette des beaux-arts* (1930), p. 351.

[2] Oman, II, p. 29.

First Crusade.[1] Nor does Sahyun furnish evidence for any theory of the development of flanking defences, for nature and artifice had provided it with such inaccessibility that the provision of such a form of defence was largely unnecessary. The small rounded towers gave something of a lateral fire to the counterscarp of the fosse, but the rectangular towers project very little beyond the line of the curtain. Nor is it easy to see how Oman deduced that Sahyun shows the Franks advancing in their application of principles of concentric defence. They constructed on the outer edge of the plateau, which formed the upper castle, a massive curtain and mural towers which overshadowed the older walls. Even if the Franks kept the Byzantine defences in good repair, as Deschamps is inclined to believe, there could be no question of using them in combination with their own wall. This work, which enclosed the whole site, was so much more massive than the Greek that the enemy was not faced with a succession of obstacles of increasing difficulty. The strongest and most effective defences were to be found in the outer ring formed by the new wall built by the crusaders, which represents an emphatic rejection of the scheme of concentric defence embodied in the older fortress.

To conclude, however, that the evidence provided by Sahyun helps to prove that Latin architects in Syria learnt nothing from their new surroundings is an oversimplification. The Franks used local materials and, presumably, some local craftsmen; Syrian influence is therefore to be expected in details of construction, if not in the general plan and form of the castle.[2] At Sahyun there are other signs of local influence not only in the vaulting of the towers, but in the interrupted communications of the ramparts, in the two stages of defence there provided, in the planning of the gateways, in the form of the archères and in that of the relieving arches. Something will be said of each in turn.

The towers are cut off from the rampart walk of the curtain; thus they divide the walk into separate sections, with the single exception of tower 6, where it is possible to enter the first-floor room from the curtain. Elsewhere access to each section of the ramparts was possible only by exterior staircases which led up from the courtyard. In the same way, in towers 4, 5, and 6 there

---

[1] Above, p. 233.
[2] See the same conclusion in Lawrence, *op. cit.* I, p. 34.

is no direct access from the ground-floor room to that on the first floor. This interruption of communication was presumably a defensive device; it is described and recommended in the works of theorists known to the Byzantines, and was embodied in certain of their buildings.[1] If the enemy gained a foothold in a tower or in any particular section of the curtain it was easier to hold him there, and the danger to the garrison could be, as it were, isolated. But at all other times such arrangements must have been inconvenient, and even during an attack they had the disadvantage of making more difficult the quick reinforcement of a threatened sector of the defences. They never became typical of Frankish strongholds, and were not embodied in the great castles of the military Orders built at the end of the century. At Sahyun, therefore, although a form of defence typical of some Byzantine buildings was adopted, the process of diffusion seems to have been confined to the site.

The upper defences of the great tower and curtain wall were of a kind which the crusaders adopted in most of their castles. They include two superposed lines of defence. The lower was a chemin de ronde in the curtain wall or on the level of the terrace of a tower; it had a parapet wall to the field in the thickness of which were a number of vaulted casemates serving archères. From these casemates bowmen were thus able to shoot at the enemy without interrupting movement on the chemin de ronde or terrace which lay to their rear. The parapet wall was thick enough to contain the casemates, and to carry above an open rampart walk which was the upper stage of defence. This was covered from the field by a crenellated parapet. Such double defences at the top of the wall were nearly everywhere employed in crusader fortification.[2] It is significant that they had long been used in the East, but never became general in western Europe.

[1] Deschamps, in *Gazette des beaux-arts* (1930), p. 355; Diehl, *op. cit.* p. 156; Tafrali, p. 59; Lawrence, *op. cit.* I, p. 27; Philo of Byzantium (translated by Rochas d'Aiglun), in *Société-d'Émulation du Doubs, Mémoires*, sér. 4, tom. 6), p. 236; Vitruvius, *De architectura* (ed. F. Krohn), pp. 18–19; Procopius of Caesarea (translated by A. Stewart), p. 118.

[2] For those at Sahyun, see Plate VI (*b*), where those on the roof of the great tower are shown, and Plate VII (*a*), which shows those on inner face of east curtain south of the great tower. Only the casemates on chemin de ronde level remain; the crenellated rampart walk above them has disappeared. In defences built somewhat later these defences were sometimes in three stages.

Another possible result of Byzantine influence has already been carefully studied by Deschamps.[1] The southern gateway of the upper castle, and both southern and northern gateways of the lower, are carefully placed in the flank of a tower in order that if the enemy wished to rush the entrance, then his whole line of approach was exposed to lateral fire from the curtain wall.[2] At two of the entrances he found that if he did succeed in forcing the first gate, he must then change the direction of his attack, for the access to the second gateway, which led from gatehouse to bailey, was at right angles to that of the door by which he had just entered. This again is a late Roman and Byzantine arrangement seen in the buildings of North Africa, Asia Minor, and Syria.

There is also a suggestion of a Byzantine model in the archères constructed by the Franks at Sahyun. The type adopted in later crusaders' castles was carefully cut in the masonry itself. Its head was usually arched, while the foot was stirruped and splayed to permit a more effective plunging fire. Most of those at Sahyun had no need for such arrangements; they are most numerous on the east curtain wall and there they are practically on a level with the counterscarp of the fosse. But it may be noted that the actual openings were not arched nor were they cut in the outer masonry. As the blocks which faced the wall were laid, an aperture was left between them, and so there was formed a narrow rectangular opening exactly equal in height to two or three courses of the masonry.[3] There may be nothing especially significant about this method of construction, but it was certainly not that generally adopted in Western castles at any time during the Middle Ages. On the other hand, the archères at the Byzantine citadel of Angora were formed in this way, while at Dara it is known that the architects of Justinian blocked the battlements of the older Anastasian wall, but left archère openings between the old masonry and the new.[4]

Finally, some of the doorways in the crusaders' walls at Sahyun

---

[1] For the whole of this paragraph see Deschamps in *Syria*, XIII (1932), pp. 369–87.

[2] Plate VII (*b*) shows the southern gateway of the upper castle; marked B in Plan 6.

[3] See Plate VIII (*b*). It is interesting to note that the same method of construction was used at the other great twelfth-century castle of Karak in Moab.

[4] Jerphanion, *op. cit.* p. 168.

are covered by a lintel which is surmounted by a flat relieving arch of three or five heavy voussoirs.[1] It was used not only at Sahyun, but over the door of the great tower at Jubail,[2] while van Berchem noted it at Qala'at ez-Zau and Burj al-Mohash.[3] This feature is not characteristic of Western construction, but it is seen in Byzantine buildings,[4] including those at Sahyun.[5]

The most typical and best preserved castle built by the Franks before the collapse of the first Latin kingdom also provides the clearest evidence of Byzantine influence on Western architects. The form and style of their buildings at Sahyun were wholly western European, but, possibly as a result of employing local craftsmen and materials, and of arrangements found in the earlier Byzantine fortress, they adopted certain minor features peculiar to the Levant. Their debt to the East lay not in scientific principles but in details of fortification and construction.

An account of Sahyun fittingly concludes any discussion of fortification in twelfth-century Latin Syria. The great castles, Crac, Marqab, Tartous, 'Atlit, more properly belong, with the wealthy and powerful military Orders who gave them their present form, to the second Latin kingdom.

Those writers who have made a brief survey, of the kind attempted here, of the whole field of early crusader fortification have not emphasized the very limited value of their conclusions. It cannot be otherwise, for little but the surface of the subject has yet been explored. During the past century the castles have been visited by a succession of itinerant students for periods rarely exceeding a few days and often for only a few hours. These travellers have been handicapped, not only by the ruinous state of the monuments, but by the debris, vegetation, and modern buildings which encumber them; as a result their contribution to exact knowledge of the subject has been small compared to that made

---

[1] Plate VIII (a).   [2] Plate V (b).

[3] Van Berchem, *Voyage en Syrie*, I, pp. 104, 109, 243. Dussaud in *Revue archéologique*, 3 sér. tom. XXVIII (1896), p. 306.

[4] For example, in the church at Deir Sim'an. See van Berchem, *Voyage en Syrie*, I, p. 226, and II, pl. LV.

[5] No previous visitor has remarked that part of the Byzantine wall is included in the base of tower 4, and that it includes a doorway, which appears to be part of the original structure, surmounted by the same type of lintel and relieving arch.

by the detailed field-work of Deschamps at Crac and of C. N. Johns at 'Atlit.[1]

Confident generalizations on the crusaders' castles have sometimes been made as the result of discussing part of the subject as if it were the whole. Some scholars, for example, have written on the early castle in western Europe solely in terms of one of its features, the keep. Others have commented on Byzantine military architecture in terms of its greatest achievements; Lawrence, on the other hand, concentrated on its most indifferent. But if all known buildings are considered, good and bad, simple and complex, they defy any but the broadest and most general of classifications. Nor can it be said that any one factor predominated in the determination of their form. Byzantine and Arab example, western European experience and custom, the compulsions of ground, function, available time, available material, available wealth, all played their parts. The problems of the subject can be solved only by the patient and exhaustive exploration of individual sites.

[1] The confident assertions of Lawrence regarding 'Atlit (*op. cit.* p. 42) make strange reading in the light of the findings of Mr Johns. See *Quarterly of the Department of Antiquities in Palestine,* iii, pp. 152–64.

PLATE I

(a) KARAK FROM THE SOUTH-WEST

(b) KARAK FROM THE NORTH-EAST

PLATE II

(*a*) KARAK: THE LOWER BAILEY

(*b*) KARAK: THE NORTH CURTAIN

PLATE III

(*a*) BEAUFORT FROM THE WEST

(*b*) BEAUFORT FROM THE SOUTH

PLATE IV

(*a*) CRAC DES CHEVALIERS: THE INNER CURTAIN WALL
FROM THE NORTH-EAST

(*b*) SAFITA

PLATE V

(*a*) JUBAIL: THE GREAT TOWER

(*b*) JUBAIL: THE DOORWAY TO THE GREAT TOWER

PLATE VI

(*a*) SAHYUN: THE FRANKISH GREAT TOWER
AND THE BYZANTINE WALL

(*b*) SAHYUN: THE ROOF OF THE GREAT TOWER

PLATE VII

(*a*) SAHYUN: THE INNER FACE OF THE CURTAIN WALL

(*b*) SAHYUN: THE GATEWAY TO THE UPPER BAILEY

PLATE VIII

(*a*) SAHYUN: LINTEL AND RELIEVING ARCH

(*b*) SAHYUN: ARCHÈRE

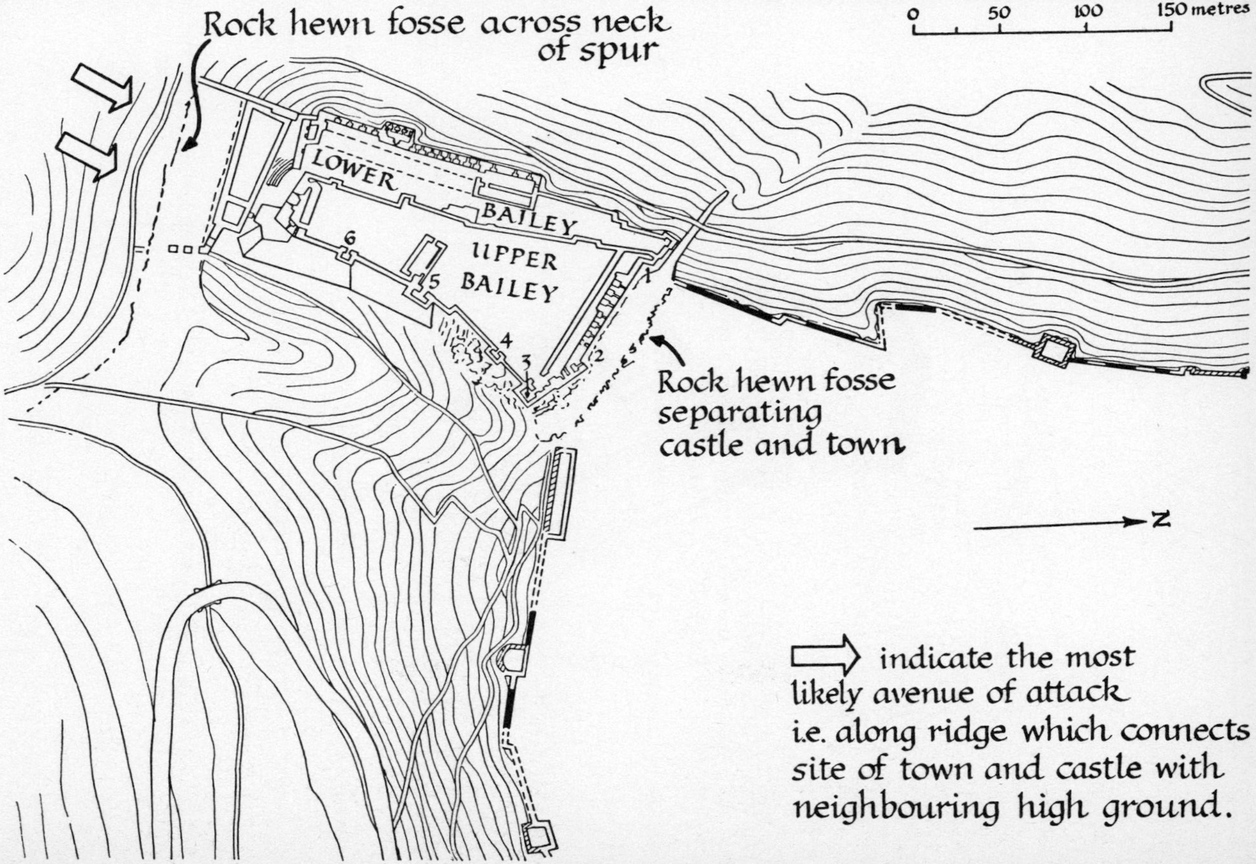

Rock hewn fosse across neck of spur

Rock hewn fosse separating castle and town

LOWER BAILEY

UPPER BAILEY

N

⇧ indicate the most likely avenue of attack i.e. along ridge which connects site of town and castle with neighbouring high ground.

150 metres

100

50

0

1. KARAK IN MOAB

[245]

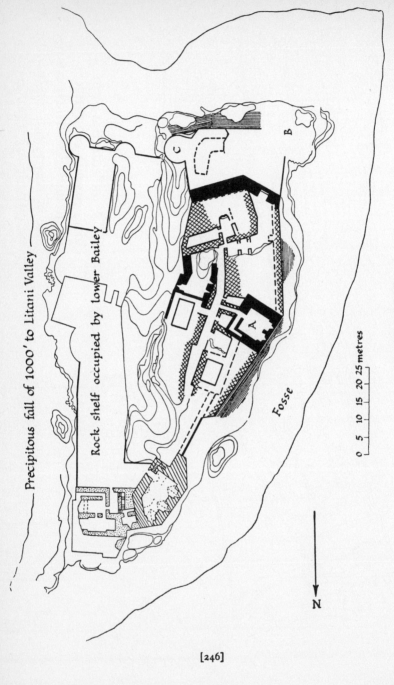

Precipitous fall of 1000' to Litani Valley

Rock shelf occupied by lower Bailey

Fosse

A

B

0 5 10 15 20 25 metres

2. BEAUFORT

N

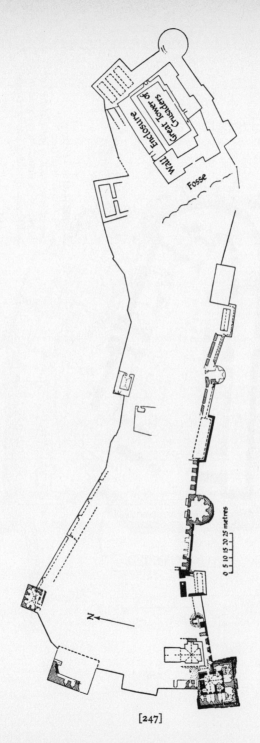

Great Tower of Crusaders

Wall Enclosure of

Fosse

3. SUBEIBE

0 5 10 15 20 25 metres

N

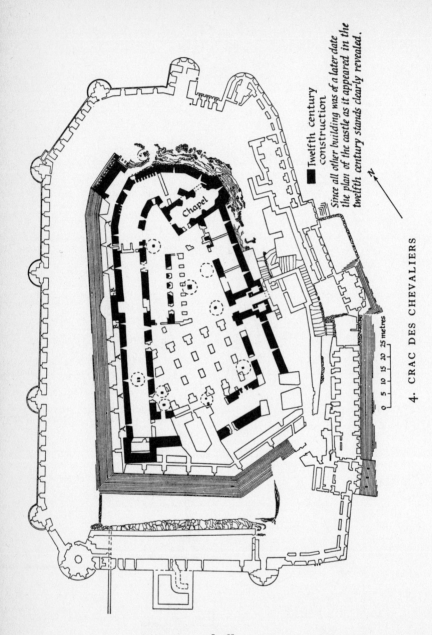

Chapel

■ Twelfth century construction

Since all other building was of a later date the plan of the castle as it appeared in the twelfth century stands clearly revealed.

N

0 5 10 15 20 25 metres

4. CRAC DES CHEVALIERS

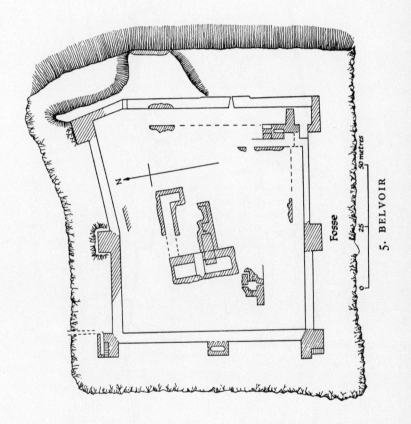

Fosse

N

50 metres

25

0

5. BELVOIR

N

Byzantine

Frankish

Rock hewn fosse

Upper citadel

Byzantine citadel

Upper Castle

Lower Castle

[250]

50 metres

25

0

⇨ indicate most likely direction of attack
along ridge which connects the castle
with the neighbouring high ground.

6. SAHYUN

BIBLIOGRAPHY

PART I. SOURCES

A. LATIN AND FRENCH

(a) *Chronicles*

Anonymous. *Gesta Francorum et aliorum Hierosolimitanorum*, ed. H. Hagenmeyer, Heidelberg, 1890; ed. L. Bréhier, Paris, 1924. All references are to Bréhier's edition.

Raimundus de Aguilers. *Historia Francorum qui ceperunt Iherusalem*, in *RHC, Hist. occ.* III, 235–309. Paris, 1866.

Fulcherius Carnotensis. *Historia iherosolymitana*, in *RHC, Hist. occ.* III, 319–485, and ed. H. Hagenmeyer, Heidelberg, 1913. All references are to *RHC* edition.

Radulfus Cadomensis. *Gesta Tancredi in expeditione hierosolymitana*, in *RHC, Hist. occ.* III, 603–716.

Albertus Aquensis, *Historia hierosolymitana*, in *RHC, Hist. occ.* IV, 271–713. Paris, 1879.

Ekkehardus, *Hierosolymita*, in *RHC, Hist. occ.* V, 1–40. Paris, 1895.

Cafarus. *De liberatione civitatum orientis*, in *Annali Genovesi di Caffaro e de' suoi continuatori*, I, ed. L. T. Belgrano. Rome, 1890.

Galterius Cancellarius. *Bella antiochena*, ed. H. Hagenmeyer. Innsbruck, 1896.

Willermus archiepiscopus Tyrensis. *Historia rerum in partibus transmarinis gestarum*, in *RHC, Hist. occ.* I. Paris, 1844.

Odo de Diogilo. *La Croisade de Louis VII, roi de France*, ed. H. Waquet. Paris, 1949. Ed. and trans. V. G. Berry. New York, 1948. All references are to Waquet's edition.

Anonymous. *Die lateinische Fortsetzung Wilhelms von Tyrus*, ed. M. Salloch. Leipzig, 1934.

Chronique d'Ernoul et de Bernard le Trésorier, ed. M. L. de Mas Latrie. Paris, 1871.

L'Estoire de Eracles empereur et la conqueste de la terre d'outremer; la continuation de l'estoire de Guillaume arcevesque de Sur, in *RHC, Hist. occ.* II. Paris, 1859.

De expugnatione Terrae Sanctae per Saladinum libellus, in Radulphus de Coggeshall, *Chronicon anglicanum*, ed. J. Stevenson. London, 1875. (Rolls Series.) *Libellus* also ed. H. Prutz in *Quellenbeiträge zur Geschichte der Kreuzzüge*. Danzig, 1876.

Itinerarium peregrinorum et gesta regis Ricardi, in *Chronicles and Memorials of the reign of Richard I*, ed. W. Stubbs. London, 1864. (Rolls Series.)

Ambroise. *L'Estoire de la Guerre Sainte*, ed. G. Paris. Paris, 1897.

Historia de expeditione Friderici imperatoris, in *Quellen zur Geschichte des Kreuzzuges Kaiser Friedrichs I*, ed. A. Chroust. Berlin, 1928. This work is part of the *Monumenta germaniae historica, scriptores rerum germanicarum*, n.s., tom. v.

Historia peregrinorum, ed. A. Chroust in *Quellen zur Geschichte des Kreuzzuges Kaiser Friedrichs I*, 116–72.

Jacobus de Vitriaco, *Historia orientalis seu hierosolymitana*, in *Gesta Dei per Francos*, i, ed. J. Bongars. Hanau, 1611.

(b) *Letters, law books, and other documents*

Epistulae et chartae ad historiam primi belli sacri spectantes, ed. H. Hagenmeyer. Innsbruck, 1901.

Epistola de morte Friderici imperatoris, ed. A. Chroust in *Quellen zur Geschichte des Kreuzzuges Kaiser Friedrichs I*, 173–8.

'Epistola regis Angliae ad abbatem de Claravalle', in *Rogerus de Houeden, Chronica*, iii, 130–2, ed. J. Stubbs. London, 1870. (Rolls Series.)

Regesta regni hierosolymitani, MXCVII–MCCXCI, ed. R. Röhricht. Innsbruck, 1893. *Additamentum*, 1904. In order not to overburden this bibliography the various chronicles, collections, and cartularies, which contain the complete texts of the documents summarized in the *Regesta* and used in this work, are, with two exceptions, not included here. The necessary references to these works are given both in the *Regesta* and in my footnotes.

Cartulaire général de l'ordre des Hospitaliers de St Jean de Jérusalem, 4 vols., ed. J. Delaville le Roulx. Paris, 1894–1906.

Cartulaire général de l'ordre du Temple, 1119?–1150, ed. Marquis d'Albon. Paris, 1913.

La Règle du Temple, ed. H. de Curzon. Paris, 1886.

Le Livre au roi, in *RHC, Lois, les assises de Jérusalem*, i, 601–44. Paris, 1841.

Le Livre du Jean d'Ibelin, in *RHC, Lois, les assises de Jérusalem*, i, 7–432.

B. Arabic

The Damascus Chronicle of the Crusades, extracted and translated from the Chronicle of Ibn al-Qalanisi, by H. A. R. Gibb. London, 1932.

Usamah ibn Munqidh. Memoirs, ed. and trans. by P. K. Hitti as *An Arab-Syrian Gentleman and Warrior in the period of the Crusades*. New York, 1929.

Ibn al-Athir. *Kamel-Altevarykh* (extrait), in *RHC*, *Hist. or.* I, 189–744 and II, 1ère partie, 3–180. Paris 1872–87.

Ibn al-Athir. *Histoire des Atabecs de Mosul*, in *RHC*, *Hist. or.* II, 2ème partie, 5–375. Paris, 1876.

Ibn Jubair. *Extrait du voyage d'Ibn Djobeir*, in *RHC*, *Hist. or.* III, 445–56. Paris, 1884. Translated in full by R. J. C. Broadhurst. London, 1953.

Kemal ed-Din. *Extraits de la Chronique d'Alep*, in *RHC*, *Hist. or.* III, 577–690; trad. Blochet, in *Revue de l'Orient latin*, III–VI, 1895–8.

Abu Shamah. *Le Livre des deux jardins*, in *RHC*, *Hist. or.* IV, V. Paris 1898–1906.

Beha ed-Din. *Anecdotes et beaux traits de la vie du Sultan Youssof (Salah ed-Din)*, in *RHC*, *Hist. or.* III, 3–370. Also English trans. by C. W. Wilson, London, 1897.

C. Armenian and Syrian

Matthew of Edessa. *Chronique*, in *RHC*, *Doc. arm.* I, 4–150. Paris, 1869.

Gregory the Priest. *Chronique*, in *RHC*, *Doc. arm.* I, 152–201.

Basil. *Oraison funèbre de Baudouin, comte de Mar'asch et de K'eçoun*, in *RHC*, *Doc. arm.* I, 204–22.

Chronique de Michel le Syrien, patriarche jacobite d'Antioche (1166–99), ed. J. B. Chabot. 4 vols. Paris, 1899–1910.

'The First and Second Crusades from an anonymous Syriac chronicle', trans. by A. S. Tritton, notes by H. A. R. Gibb, in the *Journal of the Royal Asiatic Society* (1933), 69–101 and 273–305.

D. Greek

Anna Comnena. *The Alexiad*, trans. E. A. S. Dawes. London, 1928.

PART II. SECONDARY WORKS

A. Historiography and Criticism of the Sources[1]

Boase, T. S. R. 'Recent developments in crusading historiography', in *History* (n. s.), XXII (1937), 110–25.

Buckler, G. *Anna Comnena*. Oxford, 1929.

Chroust, A. *Tageno, Ansbert und die Historia Peregrinorum*. Graz, 1892.

Edwards, J. G. 'The Itinerarium regis Ricardi and the Estoire de la Guerre Sainte', in *Historical Essays in honour of James Tait*, 59–79. Manchester, 1933.

Funk, P. *Jacob von Vitry, Leben und Werke*. Leipzig, 1909.

Glaesener, H. 'Raoul de Caen, historien et écrivain', in *Revue d'histoire ecclésiastique*, XLVI (1951), 5–21.

Gibb, H. A. R. 'The Arabic sources for the life of Saladin', in *Speculum*, XXV (1950), 58–72.

Grandeclaude, M. *Étude critique sur les livres des assises de Jérusalem*. Paris, 1923.

Krey, A. C. 'William of Tyre: the making of an historian in the Middle Ages', in *Speculum*, XVI (1941), 149–66.

Kugler, B. *Albert von Aachen*. Stuttgart, 1885.

La Monte, J. L. Introduction to *The Crusade of Richard Lion-Heart*, by Ambroise (trans. by M. J. Hubert, notes by J. L. La Monte). New York, 1941.

—— 'Some problems in crusading historiography', in *Speculum*, XV (1940), 57–75.

Norgate, K. 'The Itinerarium Peregrinorum and the Song of Ambroise', in *EHR*, XXV (1910), 523–47.

Prutz, H. 'Studien über Wilhelm von Tyrus', in *Neues Archiv der Gesellschaft für ältere deutsche Geschichtskunde*, VIII (1882), 93–132.

Sybel, H. von. *Geschichte des ersten Kreuzzugs*. 2 Auflage. Leipzig, 1881.

B. General Works on the Crusades and the Latin States

Archer, T. A. and Kingsford, C. L. *The Crusades*. London, 1894.

Baldwin, M. W. *Raymond III of Tripolis and the Fall of Jerusalem (1140–1187)*. Princeton, 1936.

---

[1] See also the editors' introductions to the printed texts mentioned in Part I above.

BARKER, SIR ERNEST. *The Crusades*. London, 1925.
—— 'The Crusades', in *Legacy of Islam*, ed. T. Arnold and A. Guillaume. Oxford, 1931.

BELLOC, H. *The Crusade*. London, 1937.

BRÉHIER, L. *L'Église et l'Orient au moyen âge: les croisades*. 6th ed. Paris, 1928.

CAHEN, C. *La Syrie du nord à l'époque des croisades*. Paris, 1940.

CARTELLIERI, A. *Philipp II August*, Bd. II. *Der Kreuzzug (1187–1191)*. Leipzig, 1906.
—— 'Richard Löwenherz im heiligen Lande', in *Historische Zeitschrift*, CI (1908), 1–27.

CHALANDON, F. *Essai sur le règne d'Alexis Ier Comnène (1081–1118)*. Paris, 1900.
—— *Jean II Comnène (1118–1143) et Manuel I Comnène (1143–1180)*. Paris, 1912.
—— *Histoire de la Première Croisade*. Paris, 1925.

CONDER, C. R. *The Latin Kingdom of Jerusalem*. London, 1897.

FISCHER, K. *Geschichte des Kreuzzugs Kaiser Friedrichs I*. Leipzig, 1870.

GROH, F. *Der Zusammenbruch des Reiches Jerusalem, 1187–1189*. Jena, 1909.

GROUSSET, R. *Histoire des croisades et du royaume franc de Jérusalem*. Paris, 1934–6.
—— *L'Empire du Levant*. Paris, 1946.

KUGLER, B. *Studien zur Geschichte des zweiten Kreuzzuges*. Stuttgart, 1866.

LANE-POOLE, S. *Saladin*. London, 1898.

NORGATE, K. *Richard the Lion Heart*. London, 1924.

PAETOW, L. J. (Ed.) *The Crusades and other historical essays presented to Dana C. Munro*. New York, 1928.

RICHARD, J. *Le Comté de Tripoli sous la dynastie toulousaine (1102–1187)*. Paris, 1945.

RÖHRICHT, R. *Geschichte des Königreichs Jerusalem (1100–1291)*. Innsbruck, 1898.

RUNCIMAN, S. *A History of the Crusades*. 3 vols. Cambridge, 1951–4.

SCHLUMBERGER, G. *Renaud de Châtillon, prince d'Antioche*. Paris, 1898.

STEVENSON, W. B. *The Crusaders in the East*. Cambridge, 1907.

C. THE INSTITUTIONS, LAWS, AND CONDITIONS OF SETTLEMENT IN MEDIEVAL SYRIA

BECKER, C. H. 'Steuerpacht und Lehnswesen', in *Der Islam*, v (1914).

BEUGNOT, 'Mémoire sur le régime des terres dans les principautés fondées en Syrie par les Francs à la suite des croisades', in *Bibliothèque de l'École des chartes*, sér. 3, IV (1853), 529–45; V (1854), 31–57, 236–62, 409–29.

CAHEN, C. 'Indigènes et croisés', in *Syria*, XV (1934), 351–60.

—— 'Notes sur l'histoire des croisades et de l'Orient latin', in *Bulletin de la Faculté des lettres de Strasbourg*, Nov. 1950; April 1951; October 1951.

DELAVILLE LE ROULX, J. *Les Hospitaliers en Terre Sainte et à Chypre, 1100–1310*. Paris, 1904.

DERENBOURG, H. *Ousâma ibn Mounkidh*, 1ère partie, *Vie d'Ousâma*. Paris, 1889.

DODU, G. *Histoire des institutions monarchiques dans le royaume latin de Jérusalem (1099–1291)*. Paris, 1894.

Encyclopaedia of Islam. Ed. M. T. Houtsma and others. London, 1913.

FARIS, N. A. (Ed.) *The Arab Heritage*. Princeton, 1944.

HAYEK, D. *Le Droit franc en Syrie pendant les croisades*. Paris, 1925.

HEYD, W. *Histoire du commerce du Levant au moyen âge*, éd. française refondue (publ. par F. Raynaud). 2 vols. Leipzig, 1936.

JOHNS, C. N. 'The attempt to colonise Palestine in the twelfth and thirteenth centuries', in *Journal of the Royal Central Asian Society*, XXI (1934), 288–300.

LAMBTON, A. K. S. 'Contributions to the study of Seljuq institutions.' (Dissertation accepted for Ph.D. at University of London, 1939; available in the London University Library.)

LA MONTE, J. L. *Feudal Monarchy in the Latin Kingdom of Jerusalem, 1100 to 1291*. Cambridge, Mass. 1932.

LANE-POOLE, S. *A History of Egypt in the Middle Ages*. London, 1901.

MADELIN, L. *L'Expansion française; de la Syrie au Rhin*. Paris, 1918.

—— 'La Syrie franque', in *Revue des deux mondes*, 6ème sér. XXXVIII (1917), 314–58.

MUNRO, D. C. *The Kingdom of the Crusaders*. New York, 1935.

PRAWER, J. 'Colonization activities in the Latin Kingdom of Jerusalem', in *Revue belge de philologie et d'histoire*, XXIX (1951), 1063–118.

—— 'The settlement of the Latins in Jerusalem' in *Speculum*, XXVII (1952), 490–503.

PRUTZ, H. *Kulturgeschichte der Kreuzzüge*. Berlin, 1883.

—— *Die geistlichen Ritterorden*. Berlin, 1908.

REY, E. G. *Les Colonies franques de Syrie au XIIème et XIIIème siècles.* Paris, 1883.

RISTELHUEBER, R. *Traditions françaises au Liban.* Paris, 1918.

SCHLUMBERGER, G. *Numismatique de l'Orient latin.* Paris, 1878.

WIET, G. *L'Égypte arabe.* Paris, 1937.

WÜSTENFELD, H. F. 'Geschichte der Fatimiden Chalifen nach der arabischen Quellen', in *Abhandlungen der königlichen Gesellschaft der Wissenschaften zu Göttingen,* XXVII (1880) and XXVIII (1881).

D. GEOGRAPHY, TOPOGRAPHY, AND ARCHAEOLOGY OF LATIN SYRIA

ABEL, F. M. *Géographie de la Palestine.* 2 vols. Paris, 1933–8.

ALLCROFT, A. H. *Earthwork of England.* London, 1908.

BERCHEM, M. VAN and FATIO, E. *Voyage en Syrie.* Mémoires de l'Institut français d'archéologie orientale du Caire, XXXVII, XXXVIII. Cairo, 1914–15.

BEYER, G. 'Das Gebiet der Kreuzfahrerherrschaft Caesarea', in *Zeitschrift des deutschen Palästina Vereins,* LIX (1936), 1–91.

—— 'Neapolis und sein Gebiet in der Kreuzfahrerzeit', in *ZDPV,* LXIII (1940), 155–209.

—— 'Die Kreuzfahrergebiete von Jerusalem und S. Abraham (Hebron)', in *ZDPV,* LXV (1942), 165–211.

—— 'Die Kreuzfahrergebiete Akko und Galilaea', in *ZDPV,* LXVII (1944–5), 183–260.

—— 'Die Kreuzfahrergebiete Sudwestpalästinas', in *Beiträge zur biblischen Landes- und Altertumskunde* (herausgegangen aus der *ZDPV*), LXVIII (1946–51), 148–92, 249–81.

BRAUN, H. *The English Castle.* London, 1936.

BUTLER, H. C. Publications of the Princeton University archaeological expeditions to Syria in 1904–5 and 1909. Division II. *Architecture.* Leyden, 1919.

CLARK, G. T. *Mediaeval Military Architecture in England.* 2 vols. London, 1884.

CLERMONT-GANNEAU, C. *Archaeological Researches in Palestine during the year 1873–4.* 2 vols. London, 1890–6.

CONDER, C. R. and KITCHENER, H. H. *Survey of Western Palestine. Memoirs of the Topography, Orography, Hydrography and Archaeology.* 3 vols. London, 1881–3.

DESCHAMPS, P. *Les Châteaux des croisés en Terre Sainte.* I. *Le Crac des Chevaliers.* Paris, 1934. II. *La Défense du royaume de Jérusalem.* Paris, 1939.

DESCHAMPS, P. 'Le Château de Saone dans le principauté d'Antioche', in *Gazette des beaux-arts* (Dec. 1930), 329–64.

—— 'Les entrées des châteaux des croisés en Syrie et leurs défenses', in *Syria*, XIII (1932), 369–87.

—— 'Deux positions stratégiques des croisés à l'est du Jourdain: Ahamant et el Habis', in *Revue historique*, CLXXII (1933), 42–57.

DIEHL, C. *L'Afrique byzantine*. Paris, 1896.

DUSSAUD, R. 'Voyage en Syrie', in *Revue archéologique* (1896), 3ème sér., tom. XXVIII, 299–336 and (1897) tom. XXX, 305–57.

—— *Topographie historique de la Syrie antique et médiévale*. Paris, 1927.

DUSSAUD, R., DESCHAMPS, P. and SEYRIG, H. *La Syrie antique et médiévale illustrée*. Paris, 1931.

ENLART, C. *Manuel d'archéologie française depuis les temps mérovingiens jusqu'à la renaissance*. 3 vols. Paris, 1902–16.

—— *Les Monuments des croisés dans le royaume de Jérusalem*. Paris, 1926–7.

GRANT, C. P. *The Syrian Desert*. London, 1937.

GUÉRIN, M. V. *Déscription géographique, historique et archéologique de la Palestine*, 3ème partie, *Description de la Galilée*. 2 vols. Paris, 1880.

Guides Bleus. *Syrie-Palestine*. Paris, 1932.

JERPHANION, G. DE. 'Mélanges d'archéologie anatolienne', in *Mélanges de l'Université St Joseph, Beyrouth*, tom. XIII, fasc. I. Beyrouth, 1928.

JOHNS, C. N. 'Excavations at Pilgrims' Castle,'Atlit (1932)', in *Quarterly of the Department of Antiquities in Palestine*, III (1933–4), 145–64.

—— *Guide to 'Atlit*. Jerusalem, 1947.

LAWRENCE, T. E. *Crusader Castles*. 2 vols. London, 1936.

LE STRANGE, G. *Palestine under the Moslems*. London, 1890.

—— *Translation of Mukaddasi's Description of Syria, including Palestine*. London, 1892.

MACKENZIE, W. MACKAY. *The Medieval Castle in Scotland*. London, 1927.

MILLINGEN, A. VAN. *Byzantine Constantinople*. London, 1899.

PAINTER, S. 'English Castles in the Middle Ages', in *Speculum*, X (1935), 321–2.

POIDEBARD, A. *La Trace de Rome dans le désert de Syrie*. Paris, 1934.

POUX, J. *La Cité de Carcassonne*. 3 vols. Paris, 1927–38.

REY, E. G. *Étude sur les monuments de l'architecture militaire des croisés en Syrie et dans l'île de Chypre*. Paris, 1871.

RICHMOND, I. A. *The City Wall of Imperial Rome*. Oxford, 1930.

RÖHRICHT, R. 'Studien zur mittelalterlichen Geographie und Topographie Syriens', in *ZDPV*, x (1887).

SMAIL, R. C. 'Crusaders' Castles of the twelfth century', in *Cambridge Historical Journal*, x (1951), 133–49.

SMITH, G. A. *The Historical Geography of the Holy Land.* 26th ed. London, 1935.

STENTON, F. M. *The Development of the Castle in England and Wales.* Historical Association Leaflet, no. 22. London, 1933.

TAFRALI, O. *Topographie de Thessalonique.* Paris, 1913.

THOMPSON, A. HAMILTON. *Military Architecture in England during the Middle Ages.* London, 1912.

TOY, S. *Castles.* London, 1939.

VIOLLET-LE-DUC, E. E. *Dictionnaire raisonné de l'architecture française de XIème au XVIème siècle.* 10 vols. Paris, 1854–68.

—— *Essai sur l'architecture militaire au moyen âge.* Paris, 1854.

—— *La Cité de Carcassonne.* Paris, 1888.

E. HISTORIES OF MEDIEVAL WARFARE

ALTEN, G. VON (Ed.). *Handbuch für Heer und Flotte. Enzyklopädie der Kriegswissenschaften und verwandter Gebiete.* Berlin, 1909–14.

BALTZER, M. *Zur Geschichte des deutschen Kriegswesens in der Zeit von den letzten Karolingern bis auf Kaiser Friedrich II.* Leipzig, 1877.

DELBRÜCK, H. *Geschichte der Kriegskunst im Rahmen der politischen Geschichte.* 7 vols. Berlin, 1900–36.

DELPECH, H. *La Tactique au XIIIème siècle.* 2 vols. Paris, 1886.

DRUMMOND, J. D. *Studien zur Kriegsgeschichte Englands im 12 Jahrhundert.* Berlin, 1905.

ERBEN, W. *Kriegsgeschichte des Mittelalters.* Munich, 1929. Beiheft 16 der Historischen Zeitschrift.

FRAUENHOLZ, E. VON. *Das Heerwesen der germanischen Frühzeit, des Frankenreiches und des ritterlichen Zeitalters.* Munich, 1935.

GLOVER, R. 'English warfare in 1066', in *EHR*, LXVII (1952), 1–18.

HEERMANN, O. *Die Gefechtsführung abendländischer Heere im Orient in der Epoche des ersten Kreuzzugs.* Marburg, 1888.

JÄHNS, M. *Handbuch einer Geschichte des Kriegswesens von der Urzeit bis zur Renaissance.* 2 vols. Leipzig, 1880.

KÖHLER, G. *Die Entwickelung des Kriegswesens und der Kriegführung in der Ritterzeit von Mitte des 11 Jahrhunderts bis zu den Hussitenkriegen.* 3 vols. Vol. III is published in three separate parts. Breslau, 1886–90.

LOT, F. *L'Art militaire et les armées au moyen âge.* 2 vols. Paris, 1946.
MORRIS, J. E. *The Welsh Wars of Edward I.* Oxford, 1901.
OMAN, SIR CHARLES. *A History of the Art of War in the Middle Ages.*
2nd edition. 2 vols. London, 1924.
—— *A History of the Art of War in the Sixteenth Century.* London,
1937.
POWICKE, F. M. *The Loss of Normandy.* Manchester, 1913.
SCHLUMBERGER, G. *Campagnes du roi Amaury Ier de Jérusalem en
Égypte.* Paris, 1906.
SPATZ, W. *Die Schlacht von Hastings.* Berlin, 1896.
SPAULDING, O. L., NICKERSON, H. and WRIGHT, J. W. *Warfare.*
London, 1925.

F. MILITARY ORGANIZATION AND EQUIPMENT
DURING THE TWELFTH CENTURY

AUDOUIN, E. *Essai sur l'armée royale au temps de Philippe-Auguste.*
Paris, 1913.
BALDWIN, J. F. *The Scutage and Knight Service in England.* Chicago,
1897.
BLOCH, M. *La Société féodale. La formation des liens de dépendance.*
Paris, 1939.
—— *La Société féodale. Les classes et le gouvernement des hommes.*
Paris, 1949.
BOUSSARD, J. 'Les mercénaires au XIIème siècle. Henri II Plantegenet
et les origines de l'armée de métier', in *BEC*, CVI (1945–6),
189–224.
BOUTARIC, E. *Institutions militaires de la France avant les armées
permanentes.* Paris, 1863.
CHEW, H. M. *The English Ecclesiastical Tenants-in-chief and Knight
Service.* Oxford, 1932.
DEMAY, G. *Le Costume au moyen âge d'après les sceaux.* Paris, 1880.
GERAUD, H. 'Les routiers au XIIème siècle', in *BEC*, III (1841–2),
125–47.
—— 'Mercadier. Les routiers au XIIIème siècle', in *BEC*, III (1841–2),
417–43.
GIBB, H. A. R. 'The armies of Saladin', in *Cahiers d'histoire égyptienne*,
série III, fasc. 4 (May 1951), 304–20.
GUILHIERMOZ, P. *Essai sur l'origine de la noblesse en France au moyen
âge.* Paris, 1902.
HASKINS, C. H. *Norman Institutions.* Cambridge, Mass. 1918.

LAKING, G. F. *A Record of European Armour and Arms through Seven Centuries.* 5 vols. London, 1920–2.

LOT, F. and FAWTIER, R. *Le Premier Budget de la monarchie française.* Paris, 1932.

LYON, B. D. 'The money fief under the English kings', in *EHR,* LXVI (1951), 161–93.

MITTEIS, H. *Lehnrecht und Staatsgewalt.* Weimar, 1933.

STENTON, SIR FRANK. *The First Century of English Feudalism.* Oxford, 1932.

SCHMITTHENNER, P. *Das freie Söldnertum im abendländischen Imperium des Mittelalters.* Munich, 1934.

G. MAPS

SPRUNER-MENKE, L. *Hand-Atlas für die Geschichte des Mittelalters and der neueren Zeit.* 3 Auflage. Pl. 85, 'Syrien zur Zeit der Kreuzzüge', von Th. Menke. Gotha, 1880.

LANE-POOLE, R. *Historical Atlas of Modern Europe.* v, pl. 76, 'Syria during the period of the crusades, 1096–1291', ed. T. A. Archer. Oxford, 1902.

Carte dressée et publiée par le Bureau topographique des troupes françaises du Levant. Syrie et Liban. 1:1,000,000. Beyrouth, 1936.

Survey of Palestine. Map of Palestine in 14 sheets. 1:100,000. Jerusalem, 1935–7.

JOHNS, C. N. *Palestine of the Crusades.* A map of the country on scale 1:350,000 with historical introduction and gazetteer. Jerusalem, 1938.

See also maps in Grousset, *Histoire des croisades*; Lawrence, *Crusader Castles;* G. A. Smith, *Historical Geog. of the Holy Land*; Deschamps, *Le Crac*; Dussaud, *Topographie*; Conder and Kitchener, *Survey of Western Palestine*, sheets ʏ–XXVI.

INDEX

(Clarendon figures in the entries under 'battle' mark the principal references.)